Effective Communication for Lawyers

ELGAR GUIDES TO PROFESSIONAL SKILLS FOR LAWYERS

The Elgar Guides to Professional Skills for Lawyers is a suite of books by leading experts designed for practitioners and students on professional legal courses. Combining practical insight with fundamental concepts, each volume provides guidance on a key skill essential for modern legal practice, from effective client communication to negotiation skills, and from drafting legal documents to understanding technology in a legal context. This insight is complemented by a range of tools including checklists, glossaries, sample documentation and recommended actions. The guides are indispensable resources for the busy practitioner or professional student seeking to support their professional development.

Titles in the series include:

Negotiation and Dispute Resolution for Lawyers
Barney Jordaan

Effective Communication for Lawyers
A Practical Guide
David Cowan

Effective Communication for Lawyers

A Practical Guide

DAVID COWAN

Assistant Professor, School of Law and Criminology, National University of Ireland Maynooth, Ireland and Associate Lecturer, Faculté de droit, Université Catholique de Lyon, France

Elgar Guides to Professional Skills for Lawyers

EE Edward Elgar PUBLISHING

Cheltenham, UK • Northampton, MA, USA

Published by
Edward Elgar Publishing Limited
The Lypiatts
15 Lansdown Road
Cheltenham
Glos GL50 2JA
UK

Edward Elgar Publishing, Inc.
William Pratt House
9 Dewey Court
Northampton
Massachusetts 01060
USA

Paperback edition 2023

A catalogue record for this book
is available from the British Library

Library of Congress Control Number: 2022941081

This book is available electronically in the **Elgar**online
Law subject collection
http://dx.doi.org/10.4337/9781839106910

ISBN 978 1 83910 690 3 (cased)
ISBN 978 1 83910 691 0 (eBook)
ISBN 978 1 0353 2031 8 (paperback)

Printed and bound by CPI Group (UK) Ltd, Croydon, CR0 4YY

To Professor Michael Doherty and all my colleagues at Maynooth with great thanks

Contents

Preface

The writing of this book was finished at the height of the Covid-19 pandemic. To what extent this turns out to be a radical change in society and attitudes remains unclear at this point. That said, there are some specific points to make in this respect. A little like film and television shows, which have not done all their shows with characters wearing masks, this book is not going to have a heavy dose of Covid points applied. This is partly because I am optimistic that some sense of normality will return in due course. Writing at this point, I do not expect to see revolutionary change in how the world of law operates dues to Covid-19. I do, however, see some radical changes that will be like pulling up potatoes, where we will one day pull up the field and find a wonderful crop.

I say this because in so many ways the new approaches we have taken to communicating, such as Zoom and other virtual gatherings, are not new. They are being deployed more extensively, that is for sure, but we have talked about these changes for a long time. We have talked about remote working and virtual courts in the sense they are always in the future, but Covid has forced us into experimentation that we were too busy, too entrenched in old ways or unconvinced of the value of specific changes to undertake a transformation. What all organizations and individuals need to do now is to sift through the evidence and see what works and what doesn't, and strike a new balance in how we communicate and what tools to use. The problem we face is not an either/or situation, it is a both/and solution. We can use both new tools and old methods. We can use them together and separately, depending on our needs and objectives.

There are two key parts to *Effective Communication for Lawyers*. The first offers foundational material with practical and theoretical insights into communication and its place within the legal profession and the law. The second is the practical tool of the Dialogue Box. In Part I, I invite you to take a deep dive into understanding communication as behaviour. In Part II, I invite you to explore the Dialogue Box, which is an immensely practical tool that I have taught to practising lawyers and law students, as well as leaders in organizations on five continents. They have found the tool to be helpful irrespective of their culture and activity. The book as a whole is intended for practitioners to reflect on their communication needs and to make use of the tool.

The writing of a book always incurs debts of gratitude. My first thanks go to Professor Michael Doherty, head of the Law Department at Maynooth University. When we first discussed teaching communication and technology as part of the LLB, his approach was very much 'let's do it!', which is a rarer approach in academia than it should be. I also want to thank my colleagues at Maynooth, which is such a wonderful place to be – and a more collegiate environment would be hard to find. Thanks to my students at Maynooth, as well as the Faculté de droit Université Catholique de Lyon, who have been pioneering law and technology with me and put up with my sense of humour. To the many legal practitioners and executive leaders who have undertaken training in the Dialogue Box, I give them my thanks. My thanks also go to Professor Richard Susskind, Tara Doyle and Christina Blacklaws for previewing the book. My appreciation goes to Mary Heaney, who has been a constant support in my work with Global Legal Post and as a longtime friend. I would also like to thank my research assistant Yashas, who is a law student at Jindal Global Law School, India. As always, my personal thanks go to my wife Hanny, who so often exposes my own communication failures, and also to my two children David and Yasmin, who have now grown up pursuing their own careers and have found excellent partners in their lives.

1 Dialogue and law – new horizons

Throughout a long history, lawyers have relied on twin pillars of legal communication: priesthood and fear. The first pillar of priesthood is the notion that the lawyer, once trained, has been admitted into the secrets and mysteries of the law; or if you prefer Kafka, has passed through the door of the law.[1] The second pillar is the use of fear to ensure a genuflecting response from those outside of the mysteries, a constituency perhaps somewhat disparagingly called the 'non-lawyers' – as if the 'law' is only truly understood by 'lawyers' for use by 'lawyers'. The mystery of legal language, and the opaque nature of the legal system, seemingly impenetrable to those outside of the priesthood, meant non-lawyers would respond in fear. These twin pillars are being undermined in ways that can be seen as analogous to the impact of secularism on religious faith in the West.[2] Like academic theologians, Roberto Unger has suggested that the 'professoriate' of legal studies is 'a priesthood that had lost its faith and kept their jobs'.[3] This may seem a provocative opening for a book intended for lawyers and law students, but it is defensible and a necessary

---

[1] Franz Kafka, *The Trial* (New York: Schocken Books, 1998), the chapter entitled *In the Cathedral* has a priest telling the Parable 'Before the Law' to Josef K, pp. 215–17; see later discussion. Also, Katharina Pistor, in *The Code of Capital*, seems to have in mind the same 'hidden' motif in her intriguing argument that the law selectively 'codes' certain assets, endowing them with the capacity to protect and produce private wealth. With the right legal coding, any object, claim, or idea can be turned into capital and lawyers are the keepers of the code. She argues that capital is created behind closed doors in the offices of private attorneys – a little-known fact, she says, which is one of the biggest reasons for the widening wealth gap between the holders of capital and everybody else.

[2] The ideas of 'declinism' and secularism may suggest in the western tradition the end of religion, but this is not reflected in the rest of the world where religion continues to flourish, with the vast majority of the planet adhering to the Abrahamic faiths. A useful religious map has been formulated by the World Economic Forum, https://www.weforum.org/agenda/2019/03/this-is-the-best-and-simplest-world-map-of-religions

[3] Roberto Unger, *The Critical Legal Studies Movement* (1983) Harvard Law Review, Vol. 96, No. 561, pp. 674–5. Unger restates the point in the last paragraph of his book *The Critical Legal Studies Movement: Another Time, A Greater Task* (Harvard University Press, Cambridge, MA, 1983).

starting point for reasons that will soon become clear. Whatever the mysteries, legal knowledge and language have been used, and abused, to put fear into, or mystify, non-legal audiences. Lawyers and courtrooms have long had a reputation for being intimidating, right down to the physical language of the courtroom itself and the choreography of court actors. Law has also been traditionally confrontational, exhibited in a variety of ways: describing cases as A v B, 'I'll set my lawyer on you,' 'legal demands', 'legal letters', interrogation at a police station, cross-examination in the courtroom, and the list goes on. Legal language has been used to create distance, and with distance comes power. Legal language has traditionally been part of the language of power and authority, with Latin still stubbornly part of law, albeit increasingly in decline. However, Latin was not the only language used in English law. In the 16th and turn of the 17th century, the Archbishop of Canterbury Thomas Cranmer, who wrote the first English liturgy, and James I, who sponsored the translation of the Bible into English, were critics of a legal language known as 'law French', being used in the courts of England and Wales, and Ireland.[4] They were joined by secular critics, the radicals of that latter century John Liliburne and John Warr.[5] Such use of language was seen as ways of the ruling classes to control society and the law. Whether it is Latin, French or English, the effect is often seen as one of distancing the law from the people and reinforcing the mystical power of the lawyer and the legal system. Legal jargon, phraseology and style have been packaged to code, precise and obfuscate, often all in the same communication.[6]

This is changing, and today the legal profession is on the verge of even more change. It is a change very much tied to innovation, both technological and social, which is disrupting the legal space. It is also tied to the quest for increased access to justice in the context of a legal system

---

[4]   Peter Burke, *The Art of Conversation* (Cornell University Press, Ithaca NY, 1993), offers a potted social history of language, including a discussion of Law French. Frederick Pollock and Frederic William Maitland, *The History of English Law* (2 vols) (Cambridge University Press, 1895), J.H. Baker, *Manual of Law French* (Routledge, London, 2016), Peter M. Tiersma, *Legal Language* (2nd edn, University of Chicago Press, 2000), see also discussion of *Dialogue with a Lawyer* below.

[5]   Burke (n 4).

[6]   A deep appreciation of the range of issues involved is offered in the volume Michael Freeman & Fiona Smith (eds), *Law and Language: Current Legal Issues Volume 15* (Oxford University Press, Oxford and New York, 2013).

that many organizations and critics[7] suggest is groaning under its own weight and coming under pressure from societal change and increased understanding of rights, particularly minority rights. Underpinning these changes is a more highly educated and diverse citizenry that is more legally self-aware and insistent on knowing the 'why' of law and not just the 'what' of law, along with increased demands for inclusion and coverage. These changes, and what is the central theme of this book – that the legal world needs to change the way it communicates – run in parallel to the technological disruption of the profession of law and the legal system. This is mirroring changes in other professions and elsewhere in society. The direction is toward the creation of a legal space that ought to be an increasingly participatory one, from inclusive language through to changes in access to courts. This, in turn, means there is an increasing demand for a new kind of lawyer, what I call the 'communicating lawyer'. The challenges are manifold. Changing notions of authority, increased transparency, technology and a smarter audience means fear is no longer an effective, let alone an acceptable, strategy. Paradoxically, some of the mysteries are being commoditized as they are now being captured in an automated box of mysteries,[8] whilst also being made less mysterious by machines making the mysteries more accessible. Thus, the mysteries are more accessible in use, but their content may remain a mystery! Beyond this technological change, it is also the reality today that no matter how brilliant your qualification and experience, you are not doing your job 100% if you are not communicating your expertise. To communicate effectively requires contextually understanding your dialogue partners and stakeholders and finding a neutral space in which you can converse and respect others' story or narrative and how they use language to

---

[7] The Law Society of England and Wales ran a campaign under the rubric 'Fix the broken system – back our criminal justice campaign'. Fabian Society, *The crisis in the justice system in England & Wales: The Bach Commission on Access to Justice*, Interim report, November 2016. Lord Wily Bach succinctly summarized the problem in the report:

> Courts and legal advice centres are closing down, while fees for courts and tribunals continue to rise. The scope of legal aid has suffered deep cutbacks. Exceptional case funding, which was meant to be a safety net for those in most need, has failed to deliver. The desultory result is that now only 17 per cent believe it is easy for people on low incomes to access justice.

See also: Simon Jenkins, *The UK justice system is in meltdown. When will the government act?* The Guardian, 2 April 2018, and the editorial board of the *Financial Times* stated *British criminal justice needs an urgent repair*, 27 November 2019.

[8] So-called 'black boxes' where rules of technological code, as well as legal code, can be enclosed that are difficult to interrogate. The interests of transparency may not be well served by such black boxes, and if we are to have 'judge-bots', it may be difficult to interrogate their decision-making.

communicate their story – all of which may be quite different from your own story and language. Simply put, the communicating lawyer needs to locate the sweet spot of the law and its application to the individual in context, which means connecting the objective use of the law with the subjective experience of the law. Making this connection is advisable as a routine practice, and essential in conflict and crisis; indeed, failing in daily communication can often lead to conflict and crisis. What is needed is a communicative approach to innovation and change that makes effective use of technological tools as we move increasingly towards an augmented reality and augmented intelligence.[9]

In this emerging augmented world what is called for is a new balancing of our understanding of the human and machine. To recognize and manage these changing dynamics is to realize that communication has to be a core competency for lawyers today, and lawyers need to manage the direct correlation between communication change and the rapid advance of technology. With areas of legal practice being commoditized, this increasingly places a premium on human skills. Technology is good at handling rules and big data. This makes it an obvious area for the law, which is based on rules and uses a lot of data in many areas such as conveyancing and contracts, for instance. Using technology effectively and imaginatively can help lawyers to be more responsive to clients while respecting the formal boundaries of the relationship. Irish barrister Patrick O'Callaghan succinctly described the essential features of this relationship:

> The universal touchstone of the existence of a fiduciary duty is a relationship of confidence and reliance. The relationship is one which requires the utmost good faith on the part of the solicitor and a full and frank disclosure of all facts in the solicitor's dealings with his client. An obligation is cast on the solicitor

---

[9]   Readers are likely familiar with the terms 'artificial intelligence' and 'virtual reality' but less so 'augmented intelligence' and 'augmented reality'. The latter terms look at the balance between humans and technology. The IEEE defines augmented intelligence as 'a subsection of AI machine learning developed to enhance human intelligence rather than operate independently of or outright replace it. It's designed to do so by improving human decision-making and, by extension, actions taken in response to improved decisions.' https://digitalreality.ieee.org/publications/what-is-augmented -intelligence. It is this relationship that I advance here and put into an even wider perspective than technologists might be used to doing, and thus I perhaps elevate it above the idea of it being a subsection of machine learning.

to act in the best interests of the client and to avoid any other duty or interest which conflicts with those owed to the client.[10]

This sense of relationship should not be lost in technology; rather, it should be enhanced by technology through effective communication. Technology and formal boundaries aside, the issue does not stop there, because clients are sentient beings. They have emotion, and predicting behaviour and choices in the specific circumstances of a client is not quite so easy. When we talk about predictive analytics (PA), say, we should understand that whilst there is a narrow technological deployment of PA tools to do this, we ought equally to understand that prediction is also about people and behaviours. To select the former without fully understanding the latter is to end up with a technocratic conclusion rather than a holistic understanding of the situation we face. The difference between human 'relationship' and a social and commercial 'transaction' is becoming starker by the day, and this is the lens through which we can perhaps best understand the human versus machine dynamic: it is about relationship versus transaction.

To push this idea of the increasing relational and participatory nature of legal practice and the legal system, we can analyse it as a change being driven in part by technology, and the legal space is in the early stages of this new evolution. This is tied to the notion of the commoditization of law noted above, whereby lawyers are not only working with technology to do their work and serve their clients, but they are finding aspects of their legal work are being automated to the point where in some areas they are not directly needed. The use of machine learning, robotics and artificial intelligence is on the verge of revolutionizing legal practice and is already impacting other aspects of law and society. I will explore further this theme of augmented intelligence a little later, but for now keep in mind it refers to the working relationship between intelligent automation and the human lawyer. We should not overestimate where we are technologically speaking in the legal profession, but neither should we be short-sighted as to where this is leading.

---

[10] Patrick O'Callaghan, *The Law on Solicitors in Ireland* (Butterworths, London, 2000) para 5.01. Each nation has codes of conduct which are common across jurisdictions but with some differences, and these are an important part of effecting change in the attitudes of the profession. In the Irish context in respect to clients, for solicitors see Law Society of Ireland, *A Guide to Professional Conduct of Solicitors in Ireland* (2nd edn, 2002), and for barristers see *Code of Conduct of the Bar of Ireland* (2010) chapter 3.

1.1   Legal thinking in context

Nurturing the communicating lawyer includes how we think about and use legal reasoning in context. I am not here simply talking about the professional lawyer in practice. I am talking about anyone undergoing or using legal training to do their chosen profession or other work – given that part of this disruption to the legal profession will arguably change what it means to practise law.[11] By legal reasoning, with all due respect to some brilliant legal thinkers past and present, I do not mean the siloed exercise of legal thinking, but using law in a more holistic way to communicate legal ideas and solutions and thus explore new horizons.[12] Having a legally trained mind can be both powerful and necessary in many settings, which can be applied to many situations. Legal reasoning – as a logical and methodical way of assessing practical situations – can be powerful in a whole range of activities in society. Using legal learning and skills combined with other disciplinary knowledge, or in relationship with individuals from other disciplines, lies at the heart of developing a successful collaboration of lawyers and law-educated individuals in modern society. The organization of society is often too siloed, or too greatly structured around disciplines and specific identities, meaning that we lose this collaborative edge, which can create and improve new ways of working and being together in the world. The days – certainly by reputation if often not in reality – of a supercilious and high-handed legal profession are numbered, if not already over. This is one of the ways in which we can see a move from the transactional lawyer to the relationship lawyer; though it should be made clear here that there are always going to be transactional elements to legal work. This is not to say we need to reject specialized or highly developed disciplines, but rather to stress how these specialisms need to work collaboratively in the real world. I stress this is not an either/or situation. The world of humanity is interdisciplinary by nature, and thinking as persons or lawyers we can all find many ways to connect, communicate and collaborate.

---

[11] Richard Susskind, *Tomorrow's Lawyers: An Introduction to Your Future* (2nd edn, Oxford University Press, Oxford and New York, 2017).

[12] Philip M. Langbroek, Kees van den Bos, Marc Simon Thomas, J. Michael Milo and Wibo M. van Rossum, *Methodology of Legal Research: Challenges and Opportunities* (13 December, 2017), Utrecht Law Review, Vol. 13, No. 3, pp. 1–8.

While automation is certainly driving much of the change in the legal profession, it is not a serial activity; the relationship is much more dynamic. In the workplace, this is what I mean in saying that we will increasingly witness a higher premium placed on the human lawyer, which requires the human lawyer to be more agile and adaptive to change. This is a change that needs to be built into legal education from the beginning, instead of the serial education of 'hard' or 'black letter' law followed by 'professional training' and subsequently by 'work experience'.[13] These need to be integrated if today's young lawyer is to work with the law for the next few decades of their life, and if they are to explore successfully the many and various avenues that their legal knowledge and training can take them as they progress their careers and life experience. Over one hundred years ago in the US, the medical profession started to enhance the integration of medical education between classroom and clinical work,[14] and while there has been much development in clinical legal education (principally moots and legal skills courses), there is still some way to go; and technological change is expediting the need to integrate theory and practice more holistically. Hence, I am not simply addressing my remarks to 'lawyers' in the sense of professionally qualified lawyers. This is why these remarks are addressed to anyone who has become academically trained in law, so they can find the best outlet for the knowledge and skills they have developed from the undergraduate level onwards. Even those who have been professionally qualified need to respond to change through fostering transferability of skills. They may find that continuing in practice is not something they want to do, and they go on to use this training as a basis for developing their careers elsewhere – so they need to redeploy their skills in a new context. This approach is also about simply staying relevant enough not to be replaced by someone younger or some-

---

[13] In 2020 at Maynooth University, I introduced Law and Technology modules into the undergraduate LLB for years one to three of a four-year degree – the first such extensive programming I can find in Europe or globally. This will become the norm in due course as all law schools will need to integrate technology better into the curriculum to prepare law students, which is not to devalue the traditional aspects of a law degree but perhaps to support the transformation of legal education in the digital world. More can be read in the Law Society of Gazette coverage: https://www.lawsociety.ie/gazette/top-stories/maynooth-rolls-out-tech-module-for-all-law-students

[14] A. Flexner, *Medical Education in the United States and Canada* (Carnegie Foundation for the Advancement of Teaching Bulletin No. 4, 1910). This report advocated the merger of clinical and classroom approaches and association of medical schools and the university. See also, Michal Kielb, *Legal Education from the Perspective of Legal Practice* (13 December, 2017), Oñati Socio-Legal Series, Vol. 7, No. 8, pp. 1–11.

thing automated. This transferability of skills is a communication issue at heart, not a legal issue. New legal knowledge can be learned, and old legal knowledge revisited, but how this works towards developing one's career is about being able to communicate in a new context. It is about participating in new areas with new people, using a new legal and sector language[15] and handling different dynamics.

1.2   Law and society

This participatory understanding of law is also societal and covers improving communication with a variety of stakeholders in society, working in the more interdisciplinary way noted above, enhancing more collaborative ways of working with people as suggested, and thereby increasing access to justice in innovative ways – all with a view to working with legal knowledge and skills to produce better outcomes for all. This is achieved more effectively by dialogue. Societies globally today are under immense pressure, and nuance is a frequent casualty of modern communications warfare. There are also increasing concerns about technology and its impact on people, particularly in areas like employment, data privacy and surveillance. There are concerns about the environment and how we sustain our world. There are economic concerns about increasing inequality and power. There are concerns about how we best manage our societies politically. All of these concerns are made obvious by the world of social media, increased transparency, changing notions of authority and meaning, and diversity. We are changing through communication, and we need (but are currently struggling) to be better at communicating through change. This difficulty has been well illustrated by the Covid-19 pandemic and how governments and society dealt with all these issues from the outset, exposing many of the fault lines in our societies. These are big societal changes and dynamics, but there is not the space or the need here to analyse and answer these in detail. What I will do is address these issues as best I can in terms of their impact on the legal profession and the law – but even here I will need to draw boundaries and direct the reader elsewhere.

---

[15]   By sectors I mean distinct working environments such as business, academic government, and so on, all of which have their own language and discourse.

1.3   Practising law

The way in which law is practised is one of form and style. Both dimensions are changing the landscape of future legal employment. It is not simply a case that technology will create new kinds of jobs, some of which are usefully indicated by Richard Susskind, who has done much to educate the profession on technology over the past four decades.[16] There is also the question of redefining the legal profession, and how legal skills are deployed in society and by whom. This is going in both directions. The emergence of alternative business models and licences is bringing other disciplines, and consultancy roles, into the law firm, while legal skills are being taken into other roles, with increasing numbers of legal counsel taking up 'C-suite' positions in businesses, for instance. The nature of practising law is undergoing radical transformation, and this is leading to an increased need to have collaborative ways of working. There is a limit to the amount of confrontation societies can take before they break down, and we are seeing such tears in the fabric of classical liberal democracy because of confrontation and non-engagement with the nuances of difference in society. Law has played its part in this confrontation and has traditionally been adversarial. However, court statistics are useful here. Less than 5% of cases go to court, and even within that statistic there are a number of cases which are more procedural than anything else.[17] We are also seeing the rise of negotiation, mediation and arbitration.[18] Yet the pinnacle of 'effective' legal training in our universities is moots. We are preparing lawyers through moots training – and don't get me wrong, it is

---

[16] Susskind (n 11). Susskind often says and writes, in self-deprecating Glasgow University humour, that he has been writing the same book over and again, and this book is the best introduction to his body of work.

[17] There are many ways to look at such figures, and across various jurisdictions, between civil and criminal cases, and in other ways – my statement is to give an indication rather than an exact analysis, which can be found more usefully elsewhere. Georgina Sturge, *Court statistics for England and Wales*, House of Commons Library, Number CBP 8372, 16 December 2019, provides a good view. US statistics can be found at www.uscourts.gov and in research from Pew by John Gramlich, *Only 2% of federal criminal defendants go to trial, and most who do are found guilty*, 11 June 2019, https://www.pewresearch.org/fact-tank/2019/06/11/only-2-of-federal-criminal-defendants-go-to-trial-and-most-who-do-are-found-guilty/

[18] There is much evidence for this, but the International Chamber of Commerce (ICC) has published a full statistical report, which breaks down the drivers in the growth of ICC Arbitration and ICC Mediation for 2019 and provides an overview of the cases administered by the International Court of Arbitration and the International Centre for ADR: https://iccwbo.org/publication/icc-dispute-resolution-statistics/

invaluable training – but how many law graduates will ever argue a case in court? It's like training the jobbing actor how to take a bow on Broadway, when they will only ever work on daytime soaps, television advertising or wait at tables in the theatre district.

Traditionalists may cite black letter law or hard law as the job of teaching at the university undergraduate level, and it is certainly the solid foundation for the practice of law.[19] I do not contend that we should 'dumb down' this law. In fact, we need to fight to maintain its centrality in the legal profession and education, and effective communication plays a key role in ensuring that this happens. Yet, the relationship between this law teaching and the use of so-called 'soft skills' needs to be closely re-examined, which brings us again to big questions like, 'What is law?' and 'What happens to law when it is communicated by legal experts and received by the communities they serve?' I'm not convinced that the 'hard' and 'soft' bisection really advances the cause. Apart from concluding that communication is in fact hard to do well, it doesn't really capture the dynamic relationship between the law and communication. How law is communicated is part of how legal change happens, and law can be communicated either effectively or poorly. And because society evolves, so does the interpretation of laws communicated in one time or context and deployed in another time or context. This point can be usefully explored through the lens of the legal maxim that 'hard cases make bad law'. Oliver Wendell Holmes stated, 'Great cases like hard cases make bad law,' citing 'immediate overwhelming interest, which appeals to the feelings and distorts the judgment' as a main reason.[20] Glanville Williams, discussing the law and morality of abortion, stated on the maxim:

> It used to be said that 'hard cases make bad law' – a proposition that our less pedantic age regards as doubtful. What is certain is that cases in which the moral indignation of the judge is aroused frequently make bad law.[21]

---

[19]   Indeed, this was the reaction I got when initially speaking to some of the older universities about introducing communication and technology into the undergraduate curriculum, and I am grateful to Professor Michael Doherty at Maynooth University for his foresight and for giving me the backing to progress my teaching.

[20]   Northern Securities Co v United States, 193 US 197,400 (1904) (Holmes dissenting); see also interesting discussion in Ronald Dworkin, *Hard Cases* (April 1975), Harvard Law Review, Vol. 88, No. 6, pp. 1057–1109.

[21]   Glanville Williams, *The Sanctity of Life and the Criminal Law* (Knopf, New York, 1968), p. 105.

In our media age, everyone has become a judge, and moral indignation has gone beyond the confines of the court more than ever. Televised court cases, 24/7 news coverage of major cases like the OJ Simpson case, the Brexit legal wrangling and multiple cases of fatalities amongst arrested black men in America at the hands of the police means law and moral indignation often go hand in hand in the media coverage. Though one should note before the advent of television there was big media coverage of court cases, so it is not entirely new. For instance, the famous 1925 Scopes Monkey trial, and the showmanship of its respective legal leads, well illustrates this point. The difference now is the speed, quantity, participation and reach of the coverage.

The context of legal cases, including the social agenda and mores at the time – or as Cicero stated it, 'O tempora! O mores!' – will impact decision-making and affect the various actors in a case, which in turn causes them to behave in a particular way, from playing to the gallery to being biased towards – and by – what they see and hear. Whether we are talking about the law made in courts or set down in legislation, the law evolves in context, and this can be done more effectively and in a participatory sense through communication. As Frederick Schauer helpfully explains, 'Common law method is not simply the discovery of immanent law, but rather an approach in which the decision of live disputes in concrete contexts guides the lawmaking function.'[22] This I suggest is an important dynamic, a looking toward new horizons, relevant to understanding the role of communication in the law. The intricacies of these issues require, in turn, more effective communication to help non-lawyers understand the issues, legal reasoning and decision-making more clearly. The judge is dealing with uncertainty and other interpretative issues in a specific context, and is the medium through which any lack of clarity is translated and applied to the case in front of them. This is then put into the sphere of the general public for whom – it should not be forgotten – laws are written. This line of inquiry is helpful in looking at legislative communication, because legal drafters also need to connect the issues and reasoning of legislation with both near sight and foresight. Drafters also seek to create a text that is as clear, free of doubt and unambiguous as possible, and thus 'legislation speaks in a monotone and its language

---

[22]   https://chicagounbound.uchicago.edu/cgi/viewcontent.cgi?article=5372&context=uclrev

is compressed'.[23] In this work primary legislation, as a key source of law, goes out of its way to be less than entertaining or instructive as it simply seeks to state the law. Yet, even then there still arises ambiguity and interpretative issues. The act of interpretation is a communicative issue, which covers not just what the regulator is trying to achieve but how it is received and adopted by the regulatee. It is essential to look towards an expanded horizon if we are to understand how we approach the communication of law, and how lawyers in practice use law when communicating in a variety of contexts.

1.4   Diversity

It is fair to say that lawyers have traditionally been informed by a narrow range of culture, with class and educational background being rather more rarefied than in many other areas of work; though this again is changing.[24] We are finding greater diversity within the legal profession now, and this is to be welcomed and encouraged further. Aside from being a matter of equality before the law, different perspectives and experiences can inform our understanding of the law, and our interactions between different cultures and ideas. Within a culture we get used to a range of language that is informed by our social background, and when not used to dealing with people from other backgrounds we can be less than sensitive in responding to their concerns or interpreting their meaning, because it does not mesh with our frames of meaning. It also leads to problems of bias. People who have moved around geographically, socially and in other ways are often more attuned to cultural difference or diversity – if they engage in those changes. Living in an expatriate enclave on the Costa del Sol doesn't really cut it, but working and living amongst diverse people does change our horizons and even our deepest values. This happens because of encounter. When we truly encounter the other, that which is

[23]   David Loew & Charlie Potter, *Understanding Legislation: A Practical Guide to Statutory Interpretation* (Hart Publishing, Oxford 2016), p. 5.

[24]   This is a complex but lively debate, as access to justice calls for greater access to the legal profession. By way of examples: a report from *The Times, Working-class lawyers 'being held back by City culture'*, highlights the dynamics in England and Wales, 2 October 2018: https://www.thetimes.co.uk/article/working-class-lawyers-being-held-back-by-city-culture-8c977dlbx. Contrast this, for instance, with experiences in Zimbabwe: George H. Karekwaivanane, *'Through The Narrow Door': Narratives of the First Generation of African Lawyers in Zimbabwe* (February 2016), Africa, Vol. 86, No. 1, pp. 59–77.

different from us, then we adjust, adapt or at least become aware of the differences. Sometimes we embrace these changes, and sometimes we reject them, or even ignore them. In such encounters we don't necessarily need to change our self radically, only our self-awareness and how we relate to, and engage with, the other. When we encounter difference, we develop strategies to either engage or repudiate. Engagement comes when people are either receptive to difference and change, or realize they have to engage for mutually beneficial reasons or simply out of human respect. We don't need to like people or their culture to work with them. The repudiation of differences leads to oppositional strategies, or simple rejection. People will ignore someone because they are new, different or they don't understand them. The social dynamics can be challenged or changed by newcomers, for better or worse. In conflict situations it is thus easy to dig trenches and refuse to encounter. We can see the other as a stereotype or something conforming to our view or case. In negotiation and mediation we are brought into encounter, which is why they are forms of dispute resolution that can work very well where parties are prepared to undertake such an encounter. We do, however, need to accept that encounter can be a double-edged sword, which can lead to either positive engagement or reinforcing separation.

Social dynamics today are an inherent part of the changing technological world, because technology has impacted society, driving greater individualism at the same time as globally connecting us all, which puts diversity into an interesting social fulcrum. Diversity is an important area where we can explore how the law applies to behaviour. After all, law regulates behaviour by providing rules on how to behave and delineating boundaries, or by chastising and punishing wrongdoing. The law communicates cultural and other values, which evolve in time. The law reflects our values and codes or reinforces dominant values, but it can also lead to new ideas and social groups challenging entrenched values, which in turn lead to legal principles, societal attitudes and specific situations coming together in catalytic change. It is this change, which we can take as dynamic and challenging, that brings the deployment of a legal education into a new paradigm: the collaborative interdisciplinary lawyer – who may not even be practising law bound by the professional legal bodies – using the discipline as part of how they think and work. In other words, the lawyer of the future is an individual who is socially and technologically attuned in a new way. The future lawyer may still have the heart of Atticus Finch[25] or the cynicism of Rumpole of the Bailey, but there are a great many ways in which the lawyer of the future will be very different.

1.5   Lawyers in Wonderland

The legal books that tackle communication skills specifically tend to focus on the written word and advocacy, and there are some classic books on the topic. Richard du Cann's *The Art of the Advocate* springs to mind on advocacy, while in written communication there are books and chapters reaching back to the 1845 classic *On Legislative Expression: Or, The Language of the Written Law* by George Coode.[26] General books on legal skills usually include a chapter or two on communication, which can serve as a useful introduction. Books on legal theory deal with matters of interpretation, understanding the law and an array of issues that touch on communication. However, the latter – while fascinating – are often not read by practitioners or students with a mind turned to 'doing' law. They are read as part of reading jurisprudence and legal theory. However, this is to miss a trick. It is worth reading a concern raised back in 1930 by University of Pennsylvania law professor John Dickinson, which still resonates in today's law school environment:

> [It] is interesting to hark back to an age which may not have been quite so practical as our own, but whose constructive achievements challenge comparison with ours, and to invoke the examples of Blackstone and Kent. Blackstone devoted more than 25 per cent of his Commentaries to theoretical and public law subjects and Kent devoted almost 30 per cent to the same topics. One of the valuable results still to be obtained from reading these classic treatises

---

25   This is a case in point on changing cultures. Atticus Finch was seen as an archetype for the idealistic liberal lawyer, yet more recent scholarship has pointed out his flaws. See Katie Rose Guest Pryal, *Walking in Another's Skin: Failure of Empathy in To Kill a Mockingbird* (21 November 2010) in *Harper Lee's To Kill A Mockingbird: New Essays*, pp. 174–89 (Michael J. Meyer, ed., Scarecrow Press, 2010), UNC Legal Studies Research Paper No. 1713002. This was confirmed by Harper Lee's subsequent book *Go Set A Watchman*, which explains Finch was a racist, see https://newrepublic.com/article/122295/these-scholars-have-been-pointing-out-atticus-finchs-racism-years

26   Coode observed, 'It is beyond a doubt that many of the more positive errors and gross defects of legislation are to be prevented by observing a very few intelligible and simple rules, which any person capable of dividing grammatically a sentence of his native language would be competent to apply.' George Coode, *On Legislative Expression: Or, The Language of the Written Law* (W. Benning, London, 1845), p. 9.

which helped to form so many great lawyers is the feeling that one brings away from them that property law and commercial law are not the whole of law, but are only parts of a system which embraces within its scope all the fundamental problems of human and social relations and of human organization and society. Insofar as we close the shutter to the prospective lawyer on all but the technical, commercial aspects of law we not merely degrade law from a profession into a mere means of livelihood, but we also impair the vocational fitness of coming generations of lawyers to deal with the largest and most important problems which under our system of government devolve upon the bar.[27]

The ambition of this book is the desire to refashion this intellectual pursuit of law, balancing the black letter law and the practice of law, to form the new communicating lawyer for the digital age. I introduce this thinking not as a sustained academic argument, but to highlight that theory and practice inform, and are informed by, the communication of law. The communicating lawyer has to go beyond the range delineated in the written texts and take the lessons of communication to heart and into practice. What these texts all share is a concern for the word, and this is a good place to start, and words are the target point of the Dialogue Box which follows in Part II of this book.

Words become stories, and so do cases. Every legal case tells a story, featuring characters and having a narrative flow. However, it would be too fanciful to leave the point there. Every case looks to facts, attempts to look at causes and applies specific principles developed by legal analysis. The story of a case features both fiction and non-fiction. Words are certainly important. They lie at the heart of a lawyer's education in the search for precision and exactitude. Words are carried through channels of communication, and we use them to achieve a communication objective, but they are not used alone or unchanging. They are buffeted, and thereby changed or distorted, by a variety of forces as they pass through the channels we use. The handling of legal issues, principles and cases is impacted by a number of factors of communication, chief of which I contend is emotion as integral to the process of interpretation. The more emotional a situation, the broader and more numerous the range of interpretations. Take, for instance, witnesses to a crime. They will describe a perpetrator who apparently is 6 feet tall but a small man, who is actually

---

[27] An address delivered at the Chicago meeting of the Association of American Law Schools, December 1930, published as John Dickinson, *Legal Education and the Law-School Curriculum* (1931), U. Pa. L. Rev., Vol. 79, No. 4, p. 435.

a young woman, who is wearing green pants but actually jeans – you get the picture. The emotional state is the lens through which the witness is processing the event, and emotion also confuses the recall of memory, driving the witness to emphasize particular aspects of what they see, or have seen, often to the detriment of a more accurate or holistic picture, and description in words, of events and their actors.

The process of communication changes our understanding, and the language we use in communication has to encompass more than the legal assessment or advice, which is true of other activities or disciplines. As English novelist Anthony Burgess observed:

> Language has, in fact, many of the qualities possessed by human beings themselves: it tends to be emotional when pure reason is required, it is sometimes unsure of what it means, it changes form, meaning, sound. It is slippery, elusive, hard to fix, define, delimit.[28]

Words matter in law and help us to find precision. The lawyer's job is to locate the legal issue, gather the relevant principles and cases, and deliver a set of legal opinions and options. The challenge for the lawyer with legal language is that the overarching objective of the lawyer is the pursuit of precision and exactitude, while using definition to hone the core legal matter. The legal task is to pin down actions and ideas in precise legal definition and protect the integrity of the legal content through a range of processes, from client meetings through to courtroom engagement. In these processes this content is impacted by other legally trained persons and a variety of non-legal persons, and open to the effects that Burgess noted. In the drive towards exactitude, there is a challenge in most common situations because people, clients or audiences use words differently, loosely, incorrectly, ironically, humorously … and emotionally. In fact, every which way, as Alice discovers in Wonderland:

> 'Must a name mean something?' Alice asks Humpty Dumpty, only to get this answer: 'When I use a word … it means just what I choose it to mean – neither more nor less.'[29]

---

[28] Anthony Burgess, *A Mouthful of Air* (Vintage, 1993), p. 287.

[29] Lewis Carroll, *Alice's Adventures in Wonderland and Through the Looking Glass* (Signet, New York), p. 862.

The question is, as Alice says to Humpty Dumpty, 'whether you can make words mean so many different things',[30] to which the lawyer might say 'probably'.

Words in communication may be used to renounce aspects of meaning and to mould our words into what we want them to mean, and to rein-terpret our experience. The power of words is thus much more than simply descriptive. We can take words and fill them with meaning or change their meaning. When we look at privacy laws in relation to, say, the Apple Corporation, we know the word Apple referred to is not a fruit but a company, a brand and a product. The founders of Apple had long taken the word denoting a fruit and creatively filled it with a whole new set of meanings. In this instance, the word Apple can have a legal meaning, a creative meaning, a commercial meaning, a reputational meaning, and so on. Apple is all of these things. Likewise, we can take a word like 'selfie' or 'Google', which did not exist before. When I was growing up the idea of taking a picture of yourself was not just suggestive of vanity; it would lead to people wondering about your sanity. Today, we call them 'selfies' and they are taken by various users, from world leaders at summits through to tourists celebrating their travels instantaneously rather than by boring people with photo albums after the holiday. The word 'selfie' being created is part of how taking pictures of yourself became socially acceptable, even normative. Likewise, Google is a word invested for a company, but it is also a verb. I google, you google, he/she/it googles, etc. Language is constantly changing and is buffeted in time and through multiple channels.

Thus, to find precision and hone the legal meaning is bedevilled for today's lawyer by words being seemingly much livelier, or slipperier, than perhaps they once seemed. Words have emotional resonance that make them effective for us to use in one generation that does not translate so emotionally in other generations. Fashion creates and transforms the words we use, and there are a variety of reasons why words differ across generations buffeted by time and use. If a youth today says in evidence at court someone is 'sick', they may well be flattering the person rather than registering information on their state of health (and, on the hope this volume has longevity, at some point the good reader of this book may find the usage has fallen out of favour). Of course, over the ages, words have

---

30   Ibid, p. 862.

always changed, but today they appear to be changing faster than ever. To discuss this issue is not to pass judgement on the change, as passing generations are often wont to do. Older people worry that language is suffering because of social media and texting. We ought not to worry. The linguist David Crystal[31] has written quite persuasively on the topic of judging standards of language, and also flags the *etymological fallacy*[32] that words have an original meaning that is the correct or true one. As Crystal notes, the fallacy is a common ploy used in arguments to justify one's position and seek to undermine an opponent's argument.

1.6   Our communications age

We have been living in a revolutionary communication age for some decades now, driven by television and successive changes in the media of communication as social media evolved. It is useful for the lawyer to have an overview of the landscape of this changing communication in society today. However, we are arguably in a particularly concerning phase of this revolutionary age, and a lot of it seems to be making us very uncomfortable. How, then, is communication changing? There are many ways to answer this question, and this is not the focus of this book, but what is helpful here is to focus on the point at which the disruption of law and communication meet, and that is, I suggest, the issue of authority. The reason the twin pillars of communication noted at the beginning of the chapter could use fear is because of the belief in the authority of law and the lawyer. Today, disruption, like Toto in the *Wizard of Oz*, has pulled away the curtain to reveal a rather more prosaic activity and person at work.

If we are indeed living through a troubling phase of the communication age, one of its hallmarks is 'fake news'. What lies behind much of what we hear and read about 'fake news' is a set of deep questions: what is authority? What is authoritative? What is credible? Who can I trust? If we go back to the 1970s and earlier times, television news was greatly intermediated and edited, and most of us in mature economies believed it to be authoritative. The limited number of channels, and the distance between

---

[31]   David Crystal, *How Language Works* (Penguin, London, 2007).
[32]   Ibid, p. 229.

the individual and media channels, were part of the process of conveying this authority. Today the power to publicize or access information is literally in our hands, and the choice of what we watch and when we watch it mean that we all have the means, via the smartphone and apps, to become writers, editors and publishers of news. We can select what we want to watch, and who we want to listen to. Hence, we find concerns raised that people are living in echo chambers, because they exclude contrary and unfamiliar voices. Again, there is a lot to be studied in these questions that is beyond the scope here, but I raise them briefly to illustrate that the notion of authority has been questioned in new ways, and this raises questions in our communication as to who and what should be believed. Law faces a particular difficulty with this set of problems, because it still relies on notions of authority. If these are being undermined, we have to understand that communication, and the proliferation of data and channels, are part of this macro problem, which creates for us in our day-to-day legal communication some very real issues.

There is another dimension to this social media environment to consider – again, briefly. Social media is a means by which anyone can also insinuate themselves into the story and make themselves part of the narrative. Our relationship with events is changing, as we go beyond external events that we can observe to ones where we can become insinuated. Sharing pictures of events, offering comment through social media, are ways people can build bridges of meaning from themselves to an event in which they otherwise would have little involvement. They can curate their life on social media, portray themselves as something different from what they are in reality, and edit people out of their online existence (up to a point). This is the drive towards individualism of which I write. There is much about social media that is narcissistic. On the other hand, individuals appear to have more access to the public audience, suggesting greater public power and access to authority. Recently heads of states have used social media to appeal directly to the public, rather than through the gatekeepers of policy advisors, PR functionaries and political hacks. Yet, despite this libertarian aspect of social media, there is a flip side, where communication and shared values are under increasing pressure through communication and its 24/7 channels of operation. As Pink Floyd expressed it in *Nobody Home*, 'I got thirteen channels of shit on the T.V. to choose from,' but while we have many more channels of speech there is rising concern over this speech.

According to the watchdog Freedom House, the world has witnessed a decline in free speech, an important corollary to the rule of law. Some repressive regimes classified as 'not free' by Freedom House, have increased their control, with 28% tightening control in the past five years compared with 14% that have loosened restrictions. 'Partly free' countries are described as being as likely to improve as to get worse. However, 'free' countries have regressed, with 19% (16 countries) becoming more hostile to free speech in the past five years, while only 14% have improved. *The Economist* notes:

> The notion that certain views should be silenced is popular on the left, too. In Britain and America students shout down speakers they deem racist or transphobic, and Twitter mobs demand the sacking of anyone who violates an expanding list of taboos. Many western radicals contend that if they think something is offensive, no one should be allowed to say it. Authoritarians elsewhere agree. What counts as offensive is subjective, so 'hate speech' laws can be elastic tools for criminalising dissent.[33]

This is the global context in which we all communicate. Social media has connected each one of us to these dynamics by the little box, the smartphone, we hold in our hand. It affects and influences the way we communicate. Any one of us could fall victim to a 'Twitter mob', or find what happens in social media spills over into our direct physical communication with people. Any holistic understanding of communication has to take these dynamics into account. It used to be that the 'man from the BBC' was remote, but now we are the social media reporter, and the BBC, like other outlets, is soliciting our tweets and film to do the reporting in a more dynamic relationship between platform and event. We could take heed of Noam Chomsky's warning in respect to the role of the media in contemporary politics:

> The compelling moral principle is that the mass of the public are just too stupid to understand things. If they try to participate in managing their own affairs, they're just going to cause trouble. Therefore it would be immoral and improper to permit them to do this … So we need something to tame the bewildered herd, and that something in this new revolution is the art of democracy: the manufacture of consent. The political class and decision

---

[33]   *The Economist, The new censors*, 17 Aug 2019, https://www.economist.com/international/2019/08/17/the-global-gag-on-free-speech-is-tightening?cid1=cust/dailypicks1/n/bl/n/20190815n/owned/n/n/dailypicks1/n/n/uk/294306/n1

makers have to provide some tolerable sense of reality, although they also have to instill the proper beliefs.[34]

This necessarily brief sortie into the communications landscape is important, as the individual lawyer and the legal profession is part of this communication environment. It frames and impacts our legal communication, and in turn affects our ability to be effective as a communicating lawyer. The profession has to be aware of the noise of communication, and how this distorts everyday legal work, the bigger picture of law in society and the rule of law. These dynamics are demanding change in how we communicate the law in terms of style of communication and also the channels we use. Courts are changing, formalities are changing, and the legal profession is changing. However, while there may be talk about robo-lawyers and disruption, there is also an exciting opportunity for lawyers to be engaged in a more holistic way as communicating lawyers working with expanded horizons.

---

[34]   Noam Chomsky, *Media Control: The Spectacular Achievements of Propaganda* (Seven Stories Press, 1997), p. 270.

2   Law as communication, communication as law

US Supreme Court Justice Oliver Wendell Holmes Jr stated, 'It is one of the misfortunes of the law that ideas become encysted in phrases and thereafter for a long time cease to provoke further analysis.'[1] In the language of new horizons, the evolving nature of law in context is made clear and we should strive always to understand what is universal and timeless, and what is contextual and passing. However, taking up Holmes' point, there is a tendency to have a high doctrine of the former at the cost of the latter. Language is fundamental to law, hence naturally the focus in the legal profession is on precision, with its 'side effects' of caution and risk aversion. Law is also seen as a normative activity, and the norms of legal research and reasoning distinctly differ from other disciplines, but they still operate in a social and cultural context. It is important to recognize such norms, and to understand that in using the Dialogue Box tool, which this book offers, I am not proposing we should necessarily change these norms, nor am I offering the Dialogue Box methodology as the output of empirical legal studies. The Dialogue Box is a methodology that helps the practitioner in the contingency of their day-to-day problem-solving to understand how the interdisciplinary nature of problems can be best engaged by one taking a legal approach and using legal norms aided by communication insights. Unfortunately, paying attention to communication in the work context is often seen as a form of dumbing down, or a way of just dressing things up and manipulation. While communication can be used in these ways, the Dialogue Box is based on a deeper approach of communication as law and behaviour. Just as we have behavioural economics and behavioural law and economics,[2] we can see there is

---

[1]   *Hyde v. United States*, 225 U.S. 347, 391 (1912) (Holmes, J., dissenting).

[2]   An interesting nexus of behavioural law, economics and communication is the 'nudge theory' developed in R. Thaler and C. Sunstein, *Nudge* (Yale UP, New Haven, 2008; revised as Penguin, 2009). See also: Christine Jolls, Cass R. Sunstein and Richard H. Thaler, *A Behavioral Approach to Law and Economics* (1 January, 1998), Stanford Law Review, Vol. 50, No. 1471; Eyal Zamir and Doron Teichman, *Behavioral Law and Economics* (OUP, Oxford, 2018); R.B. Korobkin and T.S. Ulen, *Law*

a behavioural communicative approach to practising law.[3] Law and communication have always been connected but tend to be split off into very specific parts of the formal legal communication process, with the emphasis on advocacy, legal drafting and the law as written text.[4] This book bridges the formal needs of law with the many and diverse stakeholders and situations that the lawyer has to engage with on a daily basis. I will focus on a more holistic and verbal approach to effective communication rooted in creating a foundation for communicating the law in context.

To develop a more holistic understanding of legal communication, we need to take a journey through the world of communication itself. It is a discipline not always well served by its practitioners. As noted, it is often seen as superficial and as 'PR' or 'spin', and ultimately as the pursuit of triumph of style over substance. These concerns are certainly worthy of discussion and often warranted, and in practice are precisely all of these things at one time or another. One of the worse examples of how low this approach can go occurred on 9/11 in the UK, when an aide advised the government to use the attack on the World Trade Center in New York to distract attention from any 'bad' news stories.[5] Jo Moore, who worked for Stephen Byers, the then Secretary of State for Transport, Local Government and the Regions, wrote a memo, written at 2.55pm on 11 September 2001, as millions of people were watching horrific television images of the terrorist attack, which said: 'It is now a very good day to get out anything we want to bury. Councillors' expenses?' Communication, as an evolving discipline, has been distorted by this spin approach, which has been a key factor contributing to a lack of trust in the public arena,

---

and *Behavioral Science: Removing the Rationality Assumption from Law and Economics* (2000), Calif. L. Rev., Vol. 88, No. 1051; Thomas S. Ulen, *The Importance of Behavioral Law*, in Eyal Zamir and Doron Teichman (eds), *The Oxford Handbook of Behavioral Economics and the Law* (OUP, Oxford, 2014); Klaus Mathis (ed.), *European Perspectives on Behavioural Law and Economics* (Springer, 2015); O. Lobel, *A Behavioural Law and Economics Perspective*, in R. Van Gestel, H. Micklitz and E. Rubin (eds), *Rethinking Legal Scholarship: A Transatlantic Dialogue* (Cambridge UP, Cambridge, 2017), pp. 476–98. In respect to regulation, Robert Baldwin, *From Regulation to Behaviour Change: Giving Nudge the Third Degree* (2014), The Modern Law Review, Vol. 77, No. 6, pp. 831–57.

3   Mark Van Hoecke, *Law as Communication* (Hart, London, 2002).

4   Jennifer Murphy Romig and Mark Edwin Burge, *Legal Literacy and Communication Skills Working with Law and Lawyers* (Carolina Academic Press, Durham, NC, 2020) offers a useful step-by-step through communication skills required for lawyers in terms of the written text. An earlier text that covers some of the same territory is Jacqueline Visconti (ed.) with Monika Rathert, *Handbook of Communication in the Legal Sphere* (De Gruyter Mouton, 2018).

5   https://www.telegraph.co.uk/news/uknews/1358985/Sept-11-a-good-day-to-bury-bad-news.html

whether it is government or the rise of 'fake news' we are talking about. We need to recover a better understanding of the crucial and constructive role of communication.

One way to start is with a definition of what we mean by communication, though the destination I have in mind is to understand communication as behaviour. In one sense, communication is an activity of communicating, which taps into the origin of the word. The origin traces through Late Middle English via Old French *comunicacion*, to the Latin *communica-tio(-n)*, from the verb *communicare* 'to share'. Hence, a more insightful way to understand communication is that it is the activity of sharing. This certainly chimes with the increasingly essential need for collaborative approaches to both communications and technology. In a second sense, it is the means or channel (physical and digital) through which we share. As we will explore later, the means of communication – aside from being what we communicate – can shape what is shared because different channels achieve different ends. We can have very effective channels of communication, but this does not mean we are communicating a particular message very well. If our content is garbage, we will only be effectively dumping garbage – and, indeed, a considerable amount of communication every minute, every second, for some is just distraction, garbage, nonsense or seemingly inconsequential, while for others it is meaningful. As we will see later, for the lawyer, garbage and nonsense can become very consequential.

As one would expect, a dictionary definition does not adequately convey the ubiquity, change and energy of communication. The drastic change in the means and role of communication in recent decades is part of the way law is changing and being disrupted, thereby influencing how we communicate law and operate in the legal world. The why, what, when and how we communicate is rapidly changing, and technology is playing a key role. We have very powerful tools, or channels, of communication in the palm of our hand. From a mobile phone we can send emails, texts, tweets, WhatsApps, IGs, and so on, to convey a message or a thought. We can select certain channels for specific needs. In business, emails may be used for certain business needs, while a tool like WhatsApp is used for team communication, for instance; people and organizations will have their different preferences. We can telephone, Zoom or Skype, thus choosing between hearing and seeing as ways we wish to communicate. We have the tools to communicate to a single person or theoretically to the whole world. Technology and innovation impact our choices and decisions about how we best communicate, while for some they can be excluded because they lack the technology or do not have access to our channels. These communication channels have also impacted our sense of time, with the instantaneous nature of information push and at times an addiction to checking our phone. In a consumer society, we want things and we want them now, and attention spans, acts of patience and reflection are increasingly in short supply. The Covid-19 pandemic has perhaps highlighted some of these dynamics, causing many people to look more at their work–life balance, while organizations are looking at the tools and practices they have to explore innovations hitherto seen as optional or for some time in the future, such as homeworking. In the legal space, virtual courts are a very good example of the latter case as well.

Embracing communication goes hand in hand with the embrace of technology, which in combination drives innovation and is reflected in how the practice of law today is changing. The results of a *2019 Business of Law and Legal Technology Survey*[6] focused on respondents holding allied professional titles or positions related to the business of law and legal technology in law firms – roles other than that of a practising lawyer. Chief among the results was that most law firms believed 2019 was at least as good as the previous year. However, those firms that find it easier to obtain partner buy-in for projects central to law firm innovation were more likely to say they were having a better year. The survey surfaced a connection among intangibles like leadership and management of change, to the downstream effects on the business of law. The researchers concluded there appears to be a link between law firms that are open to the possibilities of doing things differently and the efficiency that can be gained across law firm business processes. These new dynamics in communication are also impacting the law and society more broadly.

---

6   https://www.aderant.com/research/2019-business-of-law-legal-technology-survey/. ABA TECHREPORT 2019 is a report from the American Bar Association that gives a number of insights into technology use more broadly, and has been doing so for over 20 years: https://www.americanbar.org/news/abanews/aba -news-archives/2019/10/aba-releases-2019-techreport-and-legal-technology-survey-report-/

2.1   Contextual change

Law does not operate, nor communicate, in a vacuum. It is important, at this stage, to put some context around how communication has changed, given how communication has impacted the legal space as well. It explains some of why the law, and its operation, has changed. Communication is part of the disruption being experienced in the profession, and there are a number of specific changes we can touch upon here that can help us to understand communication better. To which it might be added that the communications profession and industry also have undergone a similar disruption that started much sooner. To understand communication change, it is useful to take a brief look back at the 20th century and how the communications environment was typified by the following factors, which are still in a process of transformation in the 21st century.

There are some core dynamics in the changing communication landscape, which are outlined in Box 2.1. The dynamic I want to emphasize here is the audience, because it is central to how we will approach understanding effective communication. These changing dynamics demonstrate how communication, and new channels created by constantly evolving technology, have impacted society. The 'Diana moment' discussed in Box 2.1 suggests a watershed moment of when this changed in British society, and similar dynamics can be traced in other countries – though it was an event that also made an impression globally. It highlights the way meaning is problematized in this new communication environment. We hear more about what happens outside of our own bubble, yet this new media and data landscape has allowed us to curate our own personal globalized bubble or echo chamber. This world of distorted meaning cannot be divorced from how the law and practitioners operate in this changing data world. The world of legal communication itself is changing due to this same matrix of factors.

BOX 2.1   CONTEXTUAL CHANGE: 20TH TO 21ST CENTURY

Hierarchy: Information in the 20th century was about power because it referenced the position you had in the hierarchy. To know something was a way to show you had power, and whom you shared it with demonstrated your power relations. To let someone in on the secret was a way of showing you had greater power. This is all very much a top–down approach to communicating. In the legal context, there has historically been a hierarchy of courts and practitioners. The profession has a hierarchy that – though it has long been relaxing in style – impacts how professionals communicate. It also impacts how we think about the law. Like the notion of Moses coming down from the mount with the Ten Commandments, the motif of law has for centuries been the idea of law being handed down from high. This is now deeply contested in theory and complicated in practice.

Information: Linked to hierarchy, the currency of communication is information, and this was traded on a need-to-know basis. The beloved maxim of this era was 'information is power', and so power was held rather than spread. The exercise of communication was akin to a command-and-control approach, as organizations sought to control the message and the spread of information to maintain command over events. Towards the end of the 20th century there was a shift as a focus was put on the notion that information cascades. This idea still persists today, but in truth it is still old-style communications thinking. Information is being radically transformed into data, which in turn is the currency of connectivity in society and raises a plethora of novel societal, legal and ethical issues. Though often used interchangeably, data and information are quite distinct but interrelated. Information contains data and data provides us with information.

New technologies: Related to the previous point, with rapid change in new technologies we see how they are taken up in a craze of fashion, rather than thought through. As Confucius observed, when a wise person points their finger to the moon, the fool looks at the finger. Often, in implementing new technologies, there has been a lot of foolishness. Lawyers are using these new technologies, called LawTech or LegalTech. However, they are also in the business of connecting law to technology, or TechLaw. For lawyers, it is becoming more and more critical to be involved in the TechLaw conversation earlier. It is frequently said that the law is always catching up with technology. In fact, it is not quite that straightforward. If we look at data privacy – with General Data Protection Regulation (GDPR) in Europe and the California Consumer Privacy Act (CCPA) in the United States – in some respects the technology has had to start catching up with the law's response to technology, while at the same time the law is catching up with the technology.

In the area of autonomous vehicles and artificial intelligence, there is a great need to have the legal and ethical implications considered long before products hit the market. Today, conferences and platforms on these technologies are now much more interdisciplinary and are forging new interdisciplinary ways of studying and doing law.

Obsolescence: The flipside of new technologies is the rapid obsolescence of these tools, as new tools come into being and themselves rapidly became obsolete. Words, phrases and information – all of these were made obsolescent by new technology and changes in fashion. This process of transformation, and in some cases destruction, has led to new debates about the economic system we have, the environmental impact of our technological and consumer society, and how we collaborate in society. In the age of Enlightenment and the Industrial Revolution, there was much discussion about a social contract, and arguably in today's digital economy we should perhaps be having discussions about a new digital social contract.

Broadcast: In a hierarchical society, communication replicated the hierarchy and was treated as a broadcast function. There was a notion of authority – a central truth. There was also the sense that communication came at the end of a process, announcing the completion of a project or the outcome of a series of actions, hence the broadcast/loudspeaker function. As a result, communication was process-driven and part of an end-to-end process, whereby communication was an outcome of different elements of the process, always following in the wake of actions taken, rather than driving actions. In business, communication was product-based, describing a product and what it can do, rather than being an integral part of a solution. Today, communication is more emotionally based and about experience. We have things like 'the Starbucks experience' and we are invited to experience the 'brand'. There is more focus on how we feel, rather than perhaps how we think. I recall a conversation with an academic colleague who said she was 'fed up hearing students tell me what they feel; I want to know what they think'. The whole controversy over culture wars or whether we are in a period of radical change, with dismissive terms like 'snowflakes' and 'wokeness' being bandied about, is an aspect of this changing landscape. The underlying issues should not be dismissed out of hand. They are factors of a new communication and digital age, and they are impacting the law and the legal profession.

Organizational communications: Traditionally, the business function of organizational communications was broadly split between external and internal, or what is public and what is private. This created an interesting dynamic, whereby in the external/internal divide the former takes priority over the latter, while in the public/private divide the latter takes priority over the former. As a business function, communication has tended to be servile rather than serving, with the head of communications doing as they were told rather than recommending or being a key strategic partner. In short, it was not taken seriously, and the communications people were just the 'PR' people, eager to please and brought in at the end of the process. The communications agenda was dominated by the media and was about enhancing the image and fame of the leadership. The role of communications as functional was not considered part of the organizational DNA. Finally, it was a cost centre. Today, the division of public and private is a demarcation dispute beyond the scope of this work, but one well worthy of further reflection. It is safe to say on this point that there is greater transparency today driven by twin factors of global standards and norms, and technology. Companies, for instance, have to disclose much more on social and environmental standards, while on the other hand, as Wikileaks and the proliferation of cybersecurity threats suggest, it is much harder to harbour secrets.

Audience: The interest of audiences still follows the pebble in a pool effect, where the interest is greatest the closer it is to the geographical source. For instance, news in the UK resonates more than news in the Indian Ocean, and vice versa, or where the event is of a specific scale that may generate similar newsworthiness. The same dynamics apply with so-called 'celebrities', who are insinuated into our lives and frames of reference, and so audiences may care more about celebrity woes than that of so-called 'ordinary' people. Let's take an example of how this works. The 1997 death of Princess Diana in the UK led to a public outpouring of grief, yet if you look at the newspaper reports just a week before her death, there were very critical articles about her behaviour. She was transformed from spoiled princess to sainthood in one swift change of headlines. More significant than the fickleness of public sentiment is the fact that on the same night of her accident and death, the news carried reports about a village of over 90 women and children in Algeria who had had their throats slit, but this was no longer 'news' as grief for the freshly minted motif of 'People's Princess' swept the media and people filled the Mall in London. Globalization now makes the pool a bigger pool, but the human dynamic of the relationship between the person and events has changed little. Historically, audiences were also passive, and needed editors and mediators to access and understand information and events. Today, with social media, there is more participation, greater interaction, and everyone is a journalist producing and curating their own content. Just as people filled the Mall before social media, they can now turn their attending such events into their own personal news feed. They insinuate themselves into the story as much as celebrities are insinuated into their lives.

2.2   Changing legal communication

One new and interesting innovation in communication that has arisen out of social media is the emoji. Social media is an arena of public discourse fraught with misunderstanding, vitriol and poor behaviours, but also powerful and often productive and of public benefit. Emojis help to clarify meaning where words might be taken in different ways, as the emoji can basically highlight whether the message was intended negatively or positively. The emoji has also made its appearance in the law courts.[7] An English High Court judge used an emoji when making a judgment in a family court case. He wanted to make the ruling 'comprehensible even for the children it affects – by replacing dry terminology with a battery of down-to-earth phrases and even a smiley face symbol'.[8] The ruling was handed down by Mr Justice Peter Jackson and published online, and it is thought to be the first in English legal history to incorporate an emoji, or web symbol, to explain a point of evidence. It was also hailed as a good piece of plain English. The judge said he hoped the children would read the judgment for themselves. The children in the case were aged 10 and 12, and the judge wanted to explain why they should have only limited contact with their father, a white British Muslim convert who, he explained, wanted 'to spirit them off to Syria under the guise of a trip to Disneyland Paris'. A note left by the mother had a smiling emoji next to the date, and the judge explained: 'The police … say that the J is winking, meaning that the mother knew they wouldn't be coming back,'

---

[7]   https://www.telegraph.co.uk/news/2016/09/14/smile-high-court-judge-uses-emoji-in-official-ruling/
[8]   Ibid.

he explained, saying, 'I don't agree that the J is winking. It is just a J,' and concluded, 'The police are wrong about that.' The judge's approach demonstrates that communication is more than words and language, but it is in one sense not entirely new. The use of images is commonplace, and as the saying goes, a picture can paint a thousand words. The emoji is a very effective use of image that is possible because of new technology, and because in social media there is a shared understanding of what emojis broadly mean, though the discussion over 'J' suggests even then it is still not always clear cut.

Emojis are engaging because they address one of the difficulties that lies in online and written communication, which on one level is simply the dispassionate transfer of data done by quite impersonal means. Such communication often lacks context and can be subject to a careless handling of words and sentiments, which leads to further communication problems. People think when they exchange information via data transfer that they have communicated, but this is often not the case because there is context or explanation lacking. We often communicate visually through other signs, including body language, which can be very difficult to interpret. Communication is also behaviour, which is studied in semiotics, the language of signs, actions and bodies. On a basic level such signalling can appear to be simply understood. I can give a 'thumbs up' to signal agreement or approval in most cultures, but in Iraq, Turkey and elsewhere, this has traditionally been deemed offensive, akin to the two-finger or middle-finger sign. Many seemingly well-understood signs in one culture can be understood differently in other cultures. The same can be said of the behaviour our bodies represent, because our bodies are constantly being interpreted. Before a word is said, we make assumptions or appraisals about a person, and their bodies may be very different from what we may have imagined before we meet them. Our bodies may be used to communicate to confirm what we are thinking, doing and saying. Alternatively, our bodies may contradict us or appear to others to contradict us. Our actions are a physical communication as well. I can say I care about you, but my action in refusing to help when you ask me to give assistance might suggest otherwise. Actions speak louder than words, as the saying goes. I can say I agree with what you say but have my arms crossed and appear uncooperative, though of course I may just be feeling the cold. The references to the clichés I have given suggest these are all well-known points, but it is remarkable how little observed these points are when it comes to an individual's communications approach, especially in circumstances of high emotion.

When we communicate, we are doing so in a multidimensional sense, and we are using the five senses as means of communication. We make judgements according to what we hear, what we see, what we smell, what we touch and what we taste. These senses are manipulated in our communication. We spray *eau de cologne* to smell, that is to appear, exotic or attractive. We touch someone's arm, much beloved by politicians, to solicit their attention or make a point about the balance in power of a relationship. We dine, or taste, together to promote socialization, and one can note in passing that food is an essential ingredient in all religious practices to promote relationships. We look at people to size them up and hold our gaze to show attention or avert our eyes to tell a lie. We make noises to show joy or disgust, tut with dismissal or whistle in awe. These senses all have their own language. All of these senses are interpretative. Touch can be a private gesture, a public one or inappropriately crossing an ill-defined boundary which has shifted over generations. As noted, within a culture the rules may be fairly clear, but across cultures and generations there may be less clarity and much scope for embarrassment or disapproval. This leads on to the point that communication is also contingent.

The nature of contingency in culture today is of paramount importance to understanding communication. Ethics have become highly contingent, and ruling principles or overarching narratives are becoming harder to discern in our postmodern environment. Notions of authority, of 'laying down the law', have changed dramatically. It is harder to order people to do things and expect them to obey; and in some respects, this is a very good thing too. However, it means communication has to be more nuanced or distinctive in order to be effective. We can be more successful if we encourage or inspire people to respond to our ideas or wishes. I have already discussed this question of authority in communication, as is well illustrated by reflecting on how 'the Media' has changed, from the authoritative reporter looking into the TV camera and earnestly reporting 'the truth' to today's plethora of media and individual voices influencing on social media to the point of propagating 'fake news'. Marshall McLuhan, the Canadian philosopher and media theorist, famously said television is the medium, to which one wit responded that this is because it is neither rare nor well done. Communication channels have proliferated. The radio signal may have started modern communication, but it was television that propelled us into a communications age. Whatever your view about the quality of television content today, it revolutionized the way we see the world, and indeed it has allowed us to see more of the world than our ancestors ever did. People could see and not just read or hear. This is significant, because the focus on words in communication can lead us away from understanding the visual impact of communication. Today's channels of social media have exponentially impacted communication. Social media has transformed reporting from an accepted rational, filtered and editorialized activity into a contested emotional, instantaneous and unexpurgated stream.

The communicating lawyer has to deal with all these issues and go beyond the text, the word and the law itself. A holistic communication is one that captures all of these aspects. Social media and digital communication make the process of communicating law more fraught today. Former US President Donald Trump is famous for his habit, perhaps even political art, of tweeting and bypassing traditional diplomatic and other filtering channels to communicate directly to the public. The communication and proliferation of often unfiltered, unedited and unadulterated content is made possible by the technology. The tools of the lawyer, such as legal words, statutes and instruments formed by words, legal reasoning and advocacy, are increasingly being assessed as contextualized, which is a nice word for what Alice was inquiring about. Your audience wants your words and your lawyerly activities to be meaningful to them. There are entire books on these communication topics I have discussed, and my task is not to elaborate on them all, but to emphasize that the act of communication for the lawyer needs to take into consideration all of these points. A holistic understanding of communication will need to take on board these points, and involves you in taking account of how you are communicating and how you are perceived to be communicating – the two are not identical points. Let us now turn to the issues you face in your day-to-day communication.

2.3   Your communication issues

When I teach lawyers and law students, in common with other professionals and executives, I find a good place to start is to ask this question: 'What is the biggest communication issue you face in your day-to-day work?'

The answers are many and varied, but they are not uncommon. Whatever part of the world – or profession – I ask the question, the same range of answers always arise and the top ten issues are captured in Box 2.2. They all boil down to one essential dynamic: how do I match my message to my audience? However, thinking this way requires a reversing of polarities. All too often, communication is about 'how do I get my message to my audience?' or 'why aren't people doing as I ask?' Instead, it should be this: how do I draw my audience towards my message? The point is you know the law – remember, you've been inducted into the mysteries! Seriously, though, you know the law, you know what advice or answer should work or the steps that need to be taken. If we tell, or sell, that answer to our audience, it can invoke a negative emotional response. Our audience can get frustrated, angered or fearful as a result of the advice. Therefore, we need to reverse polarities and find a way to communicate this advice in a way that draws the person from where they are to where you, and the law as you understand it, need them to be. Easier said than done, but it can be done, and the Dialogue Box was created in part to achieve this. To be a communicating lawyer means being able to reverse these polarities and tackle the range of communication issues you face. These issues are also the issues of others – and remember, you could perhaps be one of the causes of someone else's problems!

BOX 2.2 TOP TEN COMMUNICATION CHALLENGES

1. volume of email communications;
2. how to make my technical language understandable to a non-technical audience;
3. communicating upwards;
4. handling cultural difference;
5. communicating within teams, departments or units;
6. communicating across teams, departments or units;
7. communicating geographically and to remote workers;
8. getting an audience to respond or act upon the communication;
9. keeping an audience updated and interested;
10. getting communication at the right time and place.

The core communication issue in Box 2.2 is the second item: how to make technical language understandable to a non-technical audience. Emails are certainly the most common complaint, and we will come to that, but as you will discover later, it is partly answered by dealing with the second item on the list. This gets to the heart of reversing the polarities. The essential problem is not that it is difficult to get your audience to understand legal language. Rather, the problem is how do you, as a lawyer, draw your audience into an understanding of what the law can do for them, which can be understood in their terms and framework of reference? This requires a bit more than simply translating legal language into plain language. It also means connecting legal reasoning to everyday reasoning, and connecting the person's point of view, emotional state and context to the legal solutions and remedies available to them. The Dialogue Box will help you achieve this.

2.4   Communication as access to justice

On one level, access to justice is about the places, rules and procedures offered to people to get legal help and ensuring there are as few barriers to entry as possible. Money is certainly one way of ensuring access to justice where there are barriers, and money might even buy the best lawyers. However, there are many barriers that are in place due to communication. The language used by the legal profession – including the form of dress and the layout of the court – may scare people from seeking access to justice. As Lord Neuberger explained:

> I suspect that the most difficult message for judges and litigation lawyers to get is how artificial and intimidating the trial process seems to most nonlawyers. In particular to lay people who get involved with trials, the parties, their families, the victims, the witnesses and the jurors. Judges and litigation lawyers are so familiar with the court procedures and practices that we implicitly assume that there is nothing strange, unfamiliar or frightening about them. This is of course, perfectly natural: we all take for granted the world we have become used to and familiar with, and it requires a constant and conscious effort to remind ourselves how very different our world must appear to visitors and strangers.[9]

The reality is that it is frightening, with the result that 'visitors and strangers' may not feel confident going through the legal system or

---

[9]   *Fairness in the courts: the best we can do*, Address to the Criminal Justice Alliance, Lord Neuberger, 10 April 2015 https://www.supremecourt.uk/docs/speech-150410.pdf

in seeking advice, even from free legal aid centres. Speaking at the Chairman's Conference of the Law Library in Ireland, a women's health campaigner, Vicky Phelan,[10] told the assembly of barristers and judges her experience of going through her case. She suggested it would have been helpful to have been walked through the court building before, to be told she would be sitting and looking at the back of the head of her solicitor, and all these little discomforts that impacted her experience of going through the case, and ultimately the increasing fear she felt in giving her evidence. She is not alone in this, and more can be done to communicate with participants in the case. She also noted, however, that it seems to be in the interest of opposing barristers to manipulate the situation to their advantage, and wonders if this is really a level playing field.

Access to justice can also be difficult for people coming originally from other countries, who may feel they do not have the language skills to get help, or they may not trust that the law is for them as much as it is for anyone else. This is a scalable problem when one looks across jurisdictions, as some systems are more hostile or opaque for immigrants and visitors than others. There is much that members of the legal profession can do – and many do so – to encourage people into using legal services and to support them in accessing the right kind of legal services for their problems or needs. People want access to legal services for a variety of reasons and use it as a means of problem-solving in different ways, though not always successfully. Access to justice is a widely used phrase, and it can mean different things to different people. Aside from the many reasons to need justice, people may access the law as a stick to beat people with, to get revenge, ensure an opponent gets their comeuppance or as a matter of principle because they want to have their 'day in court'. People may use law because they feel they have run out of options, while enforcers of laws may use it because it is what a piece of legislation calls for. The law may be used manipulatively to avoid legal sanctions, evade or avoid tax, keep money safe from grasping spouses. These are all reasons to access justice. The question is, though, is there a right way to use the law?

---

[10]   Vicky Phelan campaigned to unmask a medical scandal and tragedy over cervical cancer results in Ireland, eventually winning her case in the High Court, which involved more than 220 women with cervical cancer who had initially been given the all-clear based on smear tests carried out by the CervicalCheck screening programme. She wrote her memoirs in Vicky Phelan, *Overcoming* (Hachette, Dublin, 2019). See also https://www.irishtimes.com/culture/books/overcoming-vicky -phelan-s-story-of-truth-and-bravery-1.4008935

Added to this are questions about what legal recourse is optimal. What alternatives or strategy can work best? Who can afford to do what within the legal system? Some people cannot afford to access justice, or they get priced out by a stronger opponent with deeper pockets. It is perhaps trite to add that what people want may not be what is best for them, legally or otherwise. The solution is to explore the most productive ways to get what the client wants, and perhaps one way to achieve this is to ensure they exhaust the complete range of legal options before ending up with the most expensive solutions. These questions are not new to lawyers, but what might be illuminating here is how effective communication can play an instrumental role in working our way through all these questions and aspects of access to justice.

Access to justice is partly an issue of transparency, and there are varying degrees and levels of transparency to communication that can play a part in the process. People use communication to obfuscate or hide as much as they might use it to help or clarify. Lawyers are not the only ones to use language and communication to mystify and mollify – many individuals, professions and organizations do the same to maintain their position. Transparency has become a key theme in government and commerce in recent times, partly driven by changes in legislation and global standards towards greater disclosure and security. However, it is also a by-product of technological change, as it becomes harder to hide information; the example of Wikileaks has already been noted. Like a live microphone, we have to assume our communications are open. Transparency places demands on accuracy and care in how we communicate. Simply forwarding an email can lead us into trouble if we have not expunged the email trail that may one day come back to haunt us. However, open communication is a good thing on the whole in this new communications environment, and we should be steering away from past notions such as 'information is power' and 'need to know'. It is also worth remembering that public communication is a cornerstone of access to justice, as legal and social reformer Jeremy Bentham (1748–1832) noted:

> Publicity is the very soul of justice. It is the keenest spur to exertion, and the surest of all guards against improbity. It keeps the judge himself, while trying, under trial.[11]

---

[11]   Lord Shaw quoted Bentham in *Scott v Scott* [1913] AC 417 (HL).

The communicating lawyer is not just one who upholds the ideals of the law; the communicating lawyer communicates the laws and thereby opens the door of access for all to the law. There are ways to be good in legal communication and interpersonal communication, but some people are happier playing a role, like that of a barrister, say, than themselves. However, even that role can be questioned, as John Cooper QC, a barrister at 25 Bedford Row, wrote:

> I recall my conversation in a previous chambers in the 1980s when I revolutionarily suggested that the Bar should adopt business cards, like most business people. A senior barrister told me in no uncertain terms: 'They are business people; we are gentlemen.'[12]

Such attitudes may represent a bygone age, but also highlight how behaviours are barriers to access. The barrister of which Cooper speaks, being the gentleman he believed himself to be, fits the model that set himself above others and belonged, in his mind, to a certain constellation within national, professional and family social spheres. Barristers are being called to the Bar now that are more like the people they represent and come from more diverse and non-traditional backgrounds.

The expectation of access to justice includes a range of issues, as discussed above, and fascinating as these issues are, we need to move on, and the legal profession has moved on from the 1980s in many and various ways. The impact of competition, growth of legislation, changing attitudes, the loss of mystery, changing nature of the profession, data growth, the digital office – these are all changes we can link to communication as articulated by this chapter title: changing through communication, communicating through change. Legal change also means that as we communicate, we also change, and central to this is the dynamic of encounter. In understanding encounter, we can explore here the main spaces in which lawyers find themselves in dialogue: client conferences, in chambers, the courts, corporation and board rooms, government bodies, academia, arbitration and ADR. Some are confrontational, others collegiate, but all are political in the broadest sense of that term. Each theatre has its own language, tone of voice and body language. Each space is also a place of encounter. A communicating lawyer is able to connect, through encounter, the law to their clients and other stakeholders in ways that can

---

[12]   https://www.newlawjournal.co.uk/content/archbold-v-blackstone-s

resonate with their audience while meeting the legal challenges they face. The distant and impersonal nature of traditional legal communication is increasingly unhelpful and unproductive. The idea of the communicating lawyer is intended to connect legal reasoning to how such reasoning can be communicated effectively, whilst ensuring the integrity of precision and quality of the legal advice. This leads into understanding the legal narrative inherent in the law and how it might contrast with the narrative inherent in the situation the law is being applied to. However, while communication has in some ways eased doing law and doing business, we cannot underestimate the extent to which this new communication environment has also generated new problems. Encounter has been problematized by the ubiquity of technology in our lives.

2.5   Technology and the law

For legal practitioners there are many challenges from technology, creating new threats and opportunities, but also new ways of communicating that are impacting their work. A good example of this is the workflow between law firms and their legal department clients. Cost-conscious clients are introducing higher levels of standardization to in-house legal work by creating template-based solutions to routine matters, creating self-service tools and implementing standard decision rules when appropriate. Research by Gartner[13] found that, on average, 63% of in-house legal work is routine or can be standardized. Companies are also hiring dedicated legal operations specialists, and those who do not hire such expertise spend 30% more on services than those who do not. The research also found that law firm expenses make up 93.5% of a legal department's outside spend. Lower-cost legal departments focus on consolidating outside counsel spend by limiting their work to critical matters, while investing in alternative legal providers and enabling non-lawyer staff to work on lower-risk activities when appropriate. Gartner found that after controlling for variables such as industry, revenue and legal work volume, lower-cost legal departments work with 55% fewer firms than the median legal department. By working with fewer firms, legal departments can negotiate better hourly rates in exchange for volume

---

[13]   https://www.gartner.com/en/legal-compliance/trends/cost-effective-legal-departments?utm
_medium=press-release&utm_campaign=RM_GB_2019_LCL_NPP_PR1_LEGAL-OPS-COST

or explore alternative fee arrangements with preferred outside counsel providers. Lower-cost legal departments also spend significantly more on alternative legal service providers. Cost-effective legal departments spend more than 6% of their outside spend on alternative legal service providers, compared with higher-cost legal departments, who spend less than 2%. Alternative legal service providers can be used for tasks that are high volume and less complex, such as e-discovery, contract management and document review. This is part of a technological revolution that is going on hand-in-hand with the communication changes, and is changing the relationship between firms and clients, as well as individuals and other aspects of society. Such change emphasizes the need for effective communication as it places the relationship at the forefront of maintaining an effective practice or legal department.

If we pull back our lens from the legal practitioner, we can see that technology and new media platforms have reduced the filters, and notions of authority, that previously stood between an individual and a public. It is cheap and instantaneous, and speed has made time more about urgency than patience. This is in stark contrast to the law, which has traditionally been more ponderous, controlling and expensive. Technology is challenging the way we do law, as well as creating new areas of legal work. In shorthand, I mean LegalTech, LawTech and TechLaw. Technology is not just a technocratic challenge; it has also played a part in making the human communication space a more emotional one. It is important to understand the relationship between the proliferation of technology in society and the new emotional landscape that has come to the fore. It is of little surprise to me that as the means and volume of communication have proliferated, the expression of content should become more emotional. For lawyers, this means you having a better understanding of how your audience is emotional, as well as an understanding that being drawn into the legal space is itself an emotional experience. And lawyers have feelings too! Lawyers are under increasing stress, with wellness and mental health becoming key challenges in legal practice. This is important for lawyers, where the focus has tended to be on the letter of the law but is increasingly recognizing personal and interpersonal dynamics.

Emotions are also visually driven, which means lawyers today need to be more visually aware – by which I do not mean you have to go all Hollywood on your audience. Learning to interpret visually, and using visual grammar, is important to the work of interpretation. The images we use to present our message involve editing and can have an impact. The famous 1970s picture of a naked young Vietnamese girl running in tears was an image that hugely impacted, indeed summarized, the feelings many Americans had about the war in Vietnam. Going back further, the Nazi regime understood very well the visual impact of their ideology, which in some ways could screen out the irrational nature of their policies. More recently, and commonly, is the use in social media of memes and movie clips edited or framed in such a way as to enhance the poster's interpretation and produce the desired response. There is the example of Donald Trump, which got a 'celebrity' boost from J.K. Rowling jumping on the bandwagon. A piece of film was tweeted showing President Trump shaking hands with two rows of people – one row standing and the front row sitting, which included a young boy in a wheelchair. As Trump shook hands along the two rows, he appeared to ignore the boy as he made his way past the boy without shaking hands. This was used to play into the narrative that Trump is arrogant, mean and so on. However, film later emerged that showed this edited narrative version distorted what was going on, as in the full film footage we see Trump first of all shaking hands with the boy and then everyone else. If we walk across the aisle, as they say in US politics, the same was done there. In a viral video of Rep. Ilhan Omar, she says, 'Our country should be more fearful of white men.' The footage quickly racked up 2.7 million views on Twitter alone as she said, 'We should be profiling, monitoring, and creating policies to fight the radicalization of white men.' It caused Republican opponents to condemn her statements. Again, the film was taken out of context. The full interview, which was aired some months previous, was one done with Al Jazeera in which Ms Omar was being somewhat sarcastic about how Muslims like her have been unfairly treated as terrorism risks by American politicians and law enforcement. Clumsy it may be, but all fodder for the social media trolls.

Technology has given individuals and organizations a means to edit and play with the interpretive quality of communication, and it drives emotion. We saw this with the repetitive smartphone viral footage of black men being arrested in America, and sometimes killed, which gave a global boost to the Black Lives Matter movement. This process is key to how the Dialogue Box works in helping us to get the full picture in emotional situations, where people feel their access to justice is frustrated or systematically blocked. Social media involves a great deal of manipulation, which may not be entirely new in communication, but is more prevalent and is more problematized in terms of how we have public discourse. The propaganda of Orwellian government has become the propaganda of the individual, who with some imagination and persistence can rise from obscurity to influencer fame. Emotional connections are at the heart of how this process works. Hence, the emotional (feeling) and sharing aspects stated at the beginning of this chapter in the dictionary definitions are the aspects that have come to the forefront in our communication revolution. It is insufficient to consider simply the idea of imparting information or transmission. This is how data processing works in today's terms, meaning all communication has to be assessed in terms of how it is impacting the audience. Effective data processing, passing of information or stating of facts, is not the same as effective communication, though they can successfully go hand-in-hand.

PART I

The communicating lawyer

3   Emotional lawyering

Every lawyer I have trained using the Dialogue Box has responded to the training by noting that emotion is something they never learned at law school and they have had to learn by trial and error. This seems to be leaving rather a lot to chance I would suggest. Recognizing this omission is your first step to being an 'emotional lawyer', which is the very reverse of the traditional image going back centuries of the 'rational lawyer'. This is not to say the lawyer has to gush with excitement or break down into tears of empathy, nor does it mean emotion trumps rationality – rather it enhances it by restoring emotions back into human thought and action. I mean something much deeper when I discuss emotion. It is more about mood, or what the writers of the Irish Scottish Enlightenment called the sentiments.[1] I will discuss emotion in more depth in Chapter 9. For our current purposes, at this point what I mean by emotion is to do with our mood and spirit, and our ability to connect with others. I want to look at communication challenges through the lens of the individual lawyer as an 'emotional' lawyer, which is pivotal when we come later to the Dialogue Box. I stress – this discussion does not mean that the lawyer has to forsake reason or cease being rational. Indeed, the reasoning and facts remain central to the business of law and are the starting points of the Dialogue Box. However, how you relate the facts and manage the aspects of law require grasping where the emotion comes into the picture, which plays a pivotal role in how law is received by clients and other participants in any legal process. To manage emotions requires the lawyer to develop their emotional intelligence (EI),[2] or emotional quotient (EQ), in rela-

---

[1]   I am principally here thinking of Francis Hutcheson (1694–1746), but also David Hume, Adam Smith, and not forgetting on the English side Lord Shaftesbury.

[2]   Emotional intelligence (EI) as a term was coined by Mayer and Salovey in 1990, who described it as 'the subset of social intelligence that involves the ability to monitor one's own and others' feelings and emotions, to discriminate among them and to use this information to guide one's thinking and actions,' and they provide 'a framework for *emotional intelligence*, a set of skills hypothesized to contribute to the accurate appraisal and expression of emotion in oneself and in others, the effective regulation of emotion in self and others, and the use of feelings to motivate, plan, and achieve in one's life.' P. Salovey and J.D. Mayer, *Emotional Intelligence* (1990), Imagination, Cognition and

tionship to their rational pursuit of the law and their intelligence quotient (IQ).

As noted in the previous chapter, how we communicate the law influences legal change, and legal change impacts how we communicate the law. This is a dynamic relationship. Effective communication by the legal profession can make the law more responsive, but to do this requires taking greater account of the emotions involved than lawyers have traditionally been used to. Take the language of the courtroom, an example raised in the previous chapter. Taking a client through the courtrooms, explaining to them what their experience of the courtroom will be like, will make clients feel less vulnerable and more effective in communicating their perspective. This has the potential to alter the dynamics of the case. Barristers in court being more aware of the vulnerability of a 'victim' may help to elicit evidence in a way that makes the experience less traumatic, without necessarily damaging the defendant's case. These are ways in which we might look at the legal system being more participatory and less confrontational, which in turn may save time, court resources and create a healthier society. Taking a step back, more emphasis on negotiation, mediation and arbitration may also lead to less confrontation and fewer demands on court resources. Taking a further step back, having legislation drafted that is clearer can make law plainer for people. Communication around the desired behaviours that might prevent legal problems occurring, and better dialogue around legal activities by clients and legal professionals alike, may also take us along more participatory avenues than taking the high road to the court. This may seem idealistic, and I am not the first to advocate such, but with the Dialogue Box there is a tool that can support lawyers to develop more effective communication in the specific instances of a case or client. Using the Dialogue Box, as well as other effective communication tools allied to legal skills, may take us further along the road of alleviating pressure on the courts in practical, realistic and productive ways.

The emphasis traditionally on the rational argument in legal training stops short of giving a holistic or experiential legal argument, though moots achieves this in part. Practising law means taking an argument

---

Personality, Vol. 9, No. 3, pp. 185–211. In the 1990s Daniel Goleman built on Salovey and Mayer's work and wrote *Emotional Intelligence: Why It Can Matter More Than IQ* (Bantam, New York, 1995) and subsequent works.

beyond the narrow confines of the law court. Traditionalists may argue this is exactly what legal argument means – arguing in court – but there are many points on the way to court where legal argument has failed to prevent an escalation to the courts, and subsequently has failed to stop appeals and miscarriages of justice thereafter. This is not an entirely novel point to make. In 1958, for instance, Walter Probert argued:

> If I had to choose, I think I would rather have a legal discourse which was informative than one which was merely 'logical'. By 'logical' I mean what usually passes for 'good reasoning' in legal circles, a matter of verbal consistency. If you are not familiar with general semantics, or at least the various notions that form its bases, then you may be inclined to think that verbal consistency is the epitome of any discourse. I must agree that verbal consistency is important, but my quarrel comes with those who would stop there. There are too many legal professionals – judges, lawyers, teachers, etc. – who stop right there.[3]

This chapter counsels a communications manifesto for change in the legal profession, offering encouragement and insight into how lawyers and the legal system can change through the communicative aspects of legal operations, and support more effectively and productively all those who participate in the legal system, which means the whole of society. From statutory drafting through to the courtroom, there is an arc of legal communication that can change for the better through more effective communication. This chapter explores ways in which communications can be done better by the emotional lawyer, who can be an agent for this change. The reader is also invited to reflect on their own current communication ideas and practices, in order to learn how to reframe their communications more effectively using the framework in Box 3.1.

BOX 3.1 THE COMMUNICATION PROCESS

Why communicate? This is a question that rarely gets asked, yet it is the starting point of discovering effective communication. Often it is just assumed we ought to communicate or (less often done than it should) desist from communicating. Getting to the heart of why is central to the Dialogue Box. We can discover the why when we understand our audience better and have determined the emotional issues we need to

---

[3]   Walter Probert, *Law, Logic and Communication* (1958), W. Res. L. Rev., Vol. 9, No. 129, p. 129.

acknowledge. There are many verbal and pictorial ways of presenting the communication process, but they all distil down to the same thing: the sender sending a message to the receiver. On one level this is quite correct, but it harbours a real danger of thinking that communication is a one-way process. Communication is all too often, in practice, the telling or selling of a viewpoint or argument, rather than an invitation to dialogue and exploration of the other's position. When we simply tell or sell, our audience isn't always listening or buying, and we can see this in their body language, for instance. Your 'listener' will sit swinging their leg because they want you to stop so they can put their viewpoint across, without listening or truly engaging. They too have something to tell or sell. In this case, the onus is on the sender to frame or encode the message effectively to reach the listener so they can – and will – listen and take this as their starting point. If their listener is not listening, the sender would do well to stop talking and investigate through dialogue how they might better engage. The starting point to effective communication is always the audience, and listening is key to understanding your audience and what dialogue will meet their needs and yours.

Listening for the why

Why are you communicating? Your audience may have legitimate concerns or questions about the information you are giving them, and you need to be sensing these concerns, which may not be obvious or well articulated. Listening and responding to the points in ways that make sense to your audience will help move your dialogue forward, or at least locate the area of concern for more exploratory dialogue. Asking questions that help to clarify or giving responses that reflect back the concerns raised by your audience are effective techniques to handle feedback and demonstrate that you are listening and understanding. If you are unable to answer a question immediately, make sure you make a note to find out the correct response and go back to your audience at the earliest opportunity. There may be no harm in parking an issue, so long as you are transparent about why and how you are doing so. The process of achieving this is more complex, and dynamic, than the simple representation of sender to receiver, and we need a tool and methodology to help us tackle this complexity. The Dialogue Box is such a tool, which takes us from the 'why' of having dialogue to effecting the dialogue we need to have. Before we get to this, we should also explore the questions that follow from the why. Listening is perhaps the hardest communication skill, and even if you have mastered it, your audience may struggle with listening and you need ways to deal with their impatience, for that is what typifies the lack of listening. Someone is not listening because they are thinking through what they want to say next and are impatient in listening to what you are saying. The lack of listening is evident from both verbal and non-verbal cues, as noted in the point about the swinging leg. People will interrupt you, in a rush to get to what they want to say. They will fidget while you are talking, which is a way of entertaining or distracting themselves until they can get their chance to talk. In these instances, the best plan is to stop talking, because you are not being listened to anyway. It is better to invite your dialogue partner or client to respond, explain or ask questions. At the heart of this is understanding what emotional space your dialogue partner or client is in, and to find ways to address that state.

Knowing the what

Knowing why we are communicating is the basis for discovering what it is we need to communicate, but we need to edit and present our message, and edit our responses to the specific audience to whom we are communicating. At this point we can then engage in effective dialogue. We can select words and images, as well as tone of voice, to texture our message that will be attractive or meaningful to our audience. Getting to the 'what' is facilitated by understanding the emotional state of our audience. Until we know this, and can find out what can be said that will acknowledge this state, the audience will not be listening to what you want to communicate. The starting point is to acknowledge the specific emotional state or states, and then you can lead your audience into a greater and deeper understanding of what it is you are communicating. Your 'what' may need to be attuned to their 'what' before you can get to your 'what', and thus you are looking to bridge from their situation to your objective. This may be a step process, rather than something achieved in a single exchange or session. Much depends on the emotional depth and force of the audience's state. We don't need to communicate everything, nor do we need to communicate everything at once, which brings us to the next related question of when to communicate.

Knowing the when

Timing is everything, as the saying goes. Choosing our moment is in part an emotional judgement. As children we learn that when we want something, it is often best to wait until our parents are in a good mood. This can be the same approach to take in professional communication. In approaching the question of when, we can draw on our new understanding of why we are communicating and the emotional state of the audience, so we can choose our moment and the pace of our communication. When we are in a hurry or short of time to achieve our goals, we ought to recognize we too have an emotional state – it is one of anxiety, perhaps agitation or impatience. This mood or emotion becomes apparent to our audience, and they in turn may take on our emotion or react negatively to it. Either way, we have commenced our communication by demonstrating our emotional state. Ideally, we want to set up our communication to find the right approach to the emotional state of our audience. Often, we do this naturally when giving people some bad news. We use tone of voice, a pitying expression on our face and other body language that send out clues already that the audience is to expect something bad has happened. In choosing our 'when', we are exploring the optimum time for communicating, a time when our audience will be most receptive. We are also looking for a time when the audience can optimally absorb information that goes against their interests or desires.

How we communicate

A great deal of our communication is now electronic, and thus remote. However, it lacks the power of the body. When delivering communication face-to-face, your body language can help or hinder. Your audience is reading your body language before you even say anything. Your dress is a form of body language, but so is how you walk, your mannerisms, your culture and your physical attributes. People may think you look typically British, or typically 'foreign' to them. You can't change these attributes, but the reality is that people are reading your body, and this is one of those ways. This can work positively or negatively. Looking 'foreign' is attractive or interesting to some people, while to others it may be taken as being less interesting, serious or authoritative. It is these dynamics that come into play when we look at racism, but we also need to look into various aspects of the person and their personality. There can be other cultural aspects and norms to consider. Time and again on body language you will hear the opinion that you should always make eye contact to show sincerity. However, in some cultures this causes embarrassment, so don't do it. Looking stiff and formal can make you seem less approachable, even if you are happy to engage in discussion. Looking relaxed makes people happier to approach you. Body language can also appear as confrontational body language, even if we do not intend to behave this way. We can try to avoid sending mixed messages through our body language, but sometimes we may not even realize how our bodies are being perceived, and hence we have to assume there are many ways our bodies communicate and find ways to read by observing and questioning the body language of the audience.

There are many means of communication for us to choose from, and these means are usually called channels of communication. Channels include our body, our voice, electronic and physical means. Not all means are suited for all messages or effective for all audiences. Different channels are appropriate to different sizes and type of audience. A mass email can get information out to a lot of people, but it has weaknesses as well, such as people not reading it. However, you may need to communicate to people who cannot read, either through illiteracy, access to technology or disability. You need different channels for them. For a smaller group of people, more face-to-face communication may be more effective. Posters are good ways to communicate in factories, because workers there may be on production lines rather than sitting in front of computers. We can have a wonderful message, but it will be of little use if people are not receiving it through the channels they have ready access to or which they like to use.

3.1   Contest, persuade, consult or resolve?

After figuring out the why, what, when and how of our communication, the lawyer can then delve deeper into understanding what to do specifically with their legal communication. This depends on who the lawyer is, and what the context is in which they are operating. In court, the barrister or advocate is defending or prosecuting a case and seeking to persuade judge and jury alike, balancing the non-legal understanding of one with the legal expertise of the other. The court is a place of dispute, and the barrister is seeking the 'winning argument', as Stanley Fish terms it.[4] The barrister seeks to persuade by means of the stronger argument. The solicitor or in-house counsel plays a more consultative role, advising the client or internal management, setting out the legal landscape and suggesting the range of legal options open to decision-makers. This relationship is changing, as client expectations change and the tools and knowledge easily at the disposal of clients become more sophisticated. The automation, and to some extent commoditization, of law presents a new business challenge for legal professionals which calls for more sophisticated communication. When general counsel is advising the C-suite there can be frustration that there appears to be a lack of clear advice or direction. This may be because the C-suite is labouring under the misapprehension there is a clear 'law' on the problems they face or the decisions they need to take. The general counsel is trying to lay out the legal options and balance this with precision. The outcome is the C-suite and legal team risk talking past each other. The why, what, when and how need to be set out clearly in these various contexts of communicating law.

This means lawyers are becoming more embedded in business processes, and in turn playing 'trusted advisor' roles rather than being seen as having a compliance or policing function, which is not to say they do not continue these roles. Indeed, contentious litigation is on the rise and communication plays a critical role in contentious issues, with a drive toward exploring alternative strategies to manage disputes. Research from Norton Rose Fulbright, in its 15th annual Litigation Trends Survey, identified two major trends that began impacting the industry more intensively in 2019 and were predicted to accelerate:

> More organizations than ever before anticipate dispute volume to rise in the year ahead, and they are putting in place more preventative measures in order to manage the increased risk. Despite the increase in proactive risk mitigation, the findings show that companies are still underutilizing one of the most effective measures available – embedding lawyers in business operations.[5]

This research reveals that $1.5 million is spent on disputes per $1 billion of revenue, with 2.5 disputes lawyers for every $1 billion of revenue. We can expect that Covid-19 will lead to even more disputes. These trends

---

[4]   Stanley Fish, *Winning Arguments* (Harper Collins, New York, 2016).
[5]   https://www.nortonrosefulbright.com/-/media/files/nrf/nrfweb/knowledge-pdfs/final---2019 -litigation-trends-annual-survey.pdf

require lawyers to improve their communication, and step outside of legal language and more into speaking the business language. People and technology are driving the rise in disputes, according to the research, which reveals 35% of respondents expect the volume of disputes to rise and only 9% expect the volume to decrease. Common causes for disputes are the areas of labour and contracts, which are further impacted in declining economic circumstances because people are laid off, changing jobs or feeling under pressure, including mental health issues, in the job. Equally the business is under pressure from customers or clients, raising new contractual problems. There are also a number of technology pressures, with much uncertainty as to where the technology is going. Cybersecurity raises the prospect of increasing risk, which may become a greater cause for disputes. Regulatory demands and intervention continue to increase and create greater regulatory burdens, leading to the prospect of disputes, including the high-profile big tech and GDPR cases. The research reveals that 38% feel regulators are becoming more interventionist, while 17% felt they were less interventionist.[6] As big data and Internet of Things (IoT) increase, so too does the need to balance data protection regulations in one jurisdiction with discovery obligations in another.

While contentious issues rise, and pressure grows on the court system, automation is being developed to expedite and smooth processes. However, this simply speeds up problems, and perhaps like building a new motorway that just gets filled with more cars, we will simply end up with a busier court system that is not necessarily fulfilling the needs of society. More is needed, and effective communication is a key part of the solution. One way in which communication can have a positive impact is in the use of negotiation, mediation and arbitration. These are communication-based approaches that are closely related activities, which, at different levels and through different sets of channels, help to bring about an agreement, suggesting we don't need to rely on the idea of winner takes all. The role of persuasion is important here, but there is a greater attempt in these methods to bring about an understanding of a neutral space for dialogue and a possible meeting of minds. One dimension of communication in how these different ways to deal with legal differences are used is the role of formality. Implicit in much legal communication is the notion of formality. The language is precise; the style is formal. It is about conducting formal, regulated or official communication of rela-

---

[6]   Ibid.

tionships between people, institutions and objects. It is about delineating roles and responsibilities, titles to ownership, and other legal precision. You don't want to open a door to ambiguity, the oft unspoken enemy of legal communication.

However, your client is not legally precise and is not always certain. Much business communication is informal rather than formal. In the legal process, we are trying to some extent to shoehorn imprecise and informal detail into a formal structure, process and language. Clients are also often not basing everything on the facts. Lawyers can speak past their clients because the lawyer is expressing what are the facts, while the client wants to express how they feel about the facts, or what they believe the facts to be that are important. However important many facts may be in a situation, they are not all legal facts. The lawyer knows this, but the client does not necessarily see this. Thus, how effective the lawyer makes that connection, and draws the client into a fuller legal understanding of their situation, is what effective legal communication is about. The lawyer is dealing with 'what is' and 'what could be', while the client is often dealing with what they feel 'should' be or what they believe 'ought' to be.

Bridging the gap is at the core of playing a consultative role, and there is a growing demand in the legal profession for lawyers who can embrace effective communication and technological understanding. In the commercial context there is increasing demand for lawyers to advise beyond the risk-averse limits traditionally drawn by practitioners. To illustrate, I recall when working with a CEO and general counsel how the CEO would complain to me after the general counsel left the room: 'Bloody lawyers – all they do is come in and give a whole lot of options and never any answers!' I coached him that he and the general counsel were talking past each other and explained 'the general counsel is setting out what your legal options are, and the balance of risks, leaving you to make the decision. You just want to know what you can do or can get away with!' The point was put slightly humorously, but it underscores a key approach that is changing, because there is now greater expectation that the lawyer will participate much more directly in the making of the decision, based on their legal expertise. The difficulty for the lawyer is that this suggests they need to move away from their risk comfort zone. In deploying the Dialogue Box, however, we can explore how it is possible to maintain a risk-averse approach and still give what the client or organization wants. Box 3.2 invites you to go step by step through communication modes to add more SPICE! By SPICE, I mean taking on board: Speech, Pace, Information, Context and Engagement. Box 3.3 highlights ways in which you can adapt your thinking to the context you need to address. A final aspect of emotional lawyering remains to be addressed, namely mental health and the wellbeing of individuals.

BOX 3.2 ADDING SPICE

Speaking

We can start where lawyers generally tend to be comfortable: with the word. Our language can be used to connect or disconnect – it depends on the speaking voice we adopt. Tone of voice can be inviting, or it can throw up barriers. Jargon terms or language belonging to a particular generation can be useful when shared language, but if it is crossing boundaries, you are making your audience at worst confused or unillumined, and at best having to work harder than they need to. Communicating clearly means avoiding jargon and technical language as much as possible. As noted in Chapter 2, in training around the world, one of the most common communication problems class members have flagged is their difficulty in communicating their technical expertise and needs to a non-technical audience. This is a difficulty because they are speaking in the wrong language. To communicate your legal knowledge effectively, you have to reverse the polarities and speak in the language of your audience. After all, you understand what you need to communicate; it is your audience that does not understand. You should also help them by not making them work so hard. Even if your audience knows some technical terms, you may be forcing them to pause while they translate in their own minds what you are talking about, and they then fall behind in the understanding, and perhaps ultimately become disinterested. You know what the terms mean or what the law is, but your audience may not, and you need to draw them into this understanding.

Using examples of your own culture or experience can be inclusive, again if shared experience, but you can exclude your audience if they do not feel connected to your language, experience and terms of reference. Second-language speakers are always at a disadvantage if not fluent, and the words chosen, sentence structure and pace of speaking can all create problems for second-language speakers. Some people speak very fast, and some regional accents – whatever the language – can be more difficult than others to decipher, in part due to speed and in part due to words chosen and sentence structure. This is not to say regional accents should be dismissed, but to recognize the reality they are difficult for second-language speakers, and even some native speakers. This is why in the early days of radio and television, along with the creation of the BBC World Service, the UK-based BBC developed the 'BBC accent'. Mannerisms can be distracting, and again these mannerisms can be verbal and non-verbal. Some are cultural. Glaswegians, for example, start and end sentences with 'but' and 'you know' a lot. Canadians often end sentences with 'eh'. Some people have a nervous cough, others tut, many scratch and so on. Mannerisms relay information to your audience or can be perceived to relay information. Are we nervous, unsure, overconfident, lying? Your client is picking out these, often unconscious, mannerisms and paying attention to them, and they themselves may also be doing this unconsciously. This is not to say mannerisms have to be eradicated, but they may need to be managed. This means you need to ensure you are aware of what your mannerisms are. If you are not sure, ask someone very close to you, like a partner or spouse, and they'll soon tell you!

Pace

They say in comedy that timing is everything. This is true in all effective communication, and having a sense of timing and pace can be very rewarding. Choosing when to communicate can be as important as choosing what to communicate. The time you take to communicate communicates something different as well. We can say something at one time and people respond, whereas on another occasion it is met with complete disinterest. This ebb and flow of communication means that at times we ought to be rapid in our response, and on other occasions a little patience is a better approach. Sometimes we can stay silent and wait for new developments or data to prompt us in a certain direction. The obverse is that failing to react can create a vacuum, and rumours and fake news love a vacuum. If you are not communicating, someone else may be doing it for you, shaping the discourse and undermining any communication you may subsequently offer. Hence, we should look first at our reaction times and determine what pace we should have for our communication. The form of communication plays a part in the timing. Emails suggest immediacy, demanding our attention regardless of its true urgency or quality. Texts and WhatsApp are also instantaneous communications. Using literature posters and other physical communication is more about informing and influencing, based on relationship rather than the more transactional nature of instantaneous communications. Another dimension of timing is tone. Choosing words, using capital letters and flagging the importance of an email are ways of importing a tone of urgency into the communication. Delivering bad news with due speed, or without unreasonable delay, is critically important. Often people sit on bad news, hoping that things will improve, and indeed sometimes this is a legitimate approach. However, delaying giving bad news can be costly, as it allows conditions potentially to worsen. Bad news delayed can be bad news compounded, and there is a risk that other stakeholders will hear about it from other sources before you speak to them. When we hear bad news from other sources, it tends to amplify the negative response to the news. Yet, giving time to explore a response or not responding immediately may communicate the opportunity for reflection. These are judgement calls we need to make, and we do this effectively when we consider the pros and cons of timing before we communicate.

A last note on timing to offer is the length of time we take to communicate. Giving long speeches may just be long-windedness, but it also risks silencing your audience because there is little space for interaction. Audiences today, especially younger generations, have different attention spans, and if they have a low attention span, you quickly lose your audience. Constant repetition may be a distraction, whereas for others it may be required because they are not really listening. There is much to be said for creating, even if just in your own mind, a timing matrix for your communication.

Information

Ensure you have all the necessary information to hand in advance and be clear about what you are going to say and why you are saying it. Anticipate any questions or concerns that your audience may have. These are tried and tested axioms of legal communication, and ones most lawyers are probably comfortable with. Where there may be room for improvement is in explaining how a situation has arisen or a decision was made as far as possible. Taking clients through the reasoning may be time consuming, but it may also be something you find harder to do, because it may mean stepping outside of legal reasoning and language to translate into the language of your client. Be clear and deliver the information or news in a clear and confident way. In dealing with clients, armed with your legal opinion, you are trying not to change your mind or back down if challenged. Using the Dialogue Box, you can better prepare yourself for those challenges and to deal with the difficulties your client is facing. It is important that a consistent message is delivered across the matter with authority, but this requires keeping control of your communication as well as maintaining the legal integrity of your message. The Dialogue Box can help you navigate any difficult waters you may have to travel through.

Part of navigating these waters involves understanding the role of empathy, which is the pitch – to use a musical analogy – of the context in which rational decision-making takes place. This means taking into consideration the nature of the advice, news or information you are communicating and trying to think about how it will affect your audience. An essential act of empathy is listening, which means giving your audience the time to ask questions or raise any concerns, and this equips you to address them in a more considerate way. On certain occasions, the difficulty people are having is not an intellectual one, but an emotional one. Hence, the need to develop your emotional intelligence skills, which doesn't mean sugar-coating things, is about giving the space to explore the experience. This requires a patient approach to supporting your client through the thinking process and ensuring they have understood the full implications of what you are communicating. This may take a little longer but will save time later if confusion or misunderstandings are successfully avoided. To do this effectively means checking back they have understood in some detail, not just a casual check. Clients can have a habit of leaving a meeting thinking they have understood, but in fact have used their selective hearing – or lack of understanding – to drive their thinking process and end up perhaps drawing unrealistic or inaccurate conclusions.

Context

Particularly when delivering difficult news, it is important to be as open and honest with your audience as far as possible. This is important in combatting misunderstandings, distortions or rumours. Open communication will demonstrate trust to your audience. Hiding behind words or actions is often seen as a purposeful action against your audience. Another related step is being explanatory – being clear on what will happen next so that you can lead the client through the process. This also includes setting down markers or points which you can remind them of when they come back to you with a different understanding of what has happened to date. Explaining what will happen next allows the client to understand so they can be prepared and deal with what the impact will be on them as matters move forward. Transparency about this will reduce their anxiety and reduce or minimize the likelihood of them getting the wrong end of the stick. Knowing the law is great. Knowing what is good for the client is wonderful. However, communication makes the difference as to whether you are being heard and if people are responding appropriately or acting upon your legal intelligence. If they aren't, it is not as effective as it might be. The law may be treated normatively, but it is received contextually by your client, and connecting the two is the role of effective communication.

Context is critical to using the Dialogue Box successfully and developing the kind of mindset needed to help lawyers today respond to the ways the profession and business of law are changing and innovating, and supporting the changing role of the lawyer. Lawyers are expected to be leaders and managers more than partners; yet the ethos of partnership as a collaborative approach needs to remain. This is the collaborative leadership that is increasingly essential in the legal profession, which is achieved through effective communication. Effective communication means the new emotional lawyer needs to be:

- emotionally attuned;
- visually aware;
- communicative;
- clear.

The great disservice of communications professionals has been the attention paid to the superficial, spin and selling aspects of communication. It is little wonder that lawyers have traditionally been suspicious of the role of communication, but this is an attitude that needs changing as well. As a profession the communication practitioner, in the context of the world of business and organizations, remains largely juvenile, but there are signs of a progression into adulthood. While this explains in part why lawyers have been rather wary, they have also been misinformed about how communication can work effectively. Now we have the need and opportunity to make communication a core competency and a critical legal skill focused on behaviours.

Engagement

Law societies now encourage solicitors to impress upon their clients the options of negotiation and mediation at the first stage of exploring the legal strategy for a client's problem. This is to be welcomed. Lawyers can go further in supporting their clients in dispute prevention. Yet, as the chief executive of the State Claims Agency in Ireland said, 'Some lawyers are implacably opposed to mediation.'[7] Being a communicating lawyer involves being closer in dialogue with clients, and negotiation and mediation are closer, healthier forms of engagement than confrontation and litigation. Why then is our system so confrontational? As noted earlier, the court system could benefit greatly from better communication, and this goes for the whole legal profession. Our public discourse, especially in social media, has become more fraught with bad communication, which is affecting the fabric of society. There has also been a trend of 'weaponizing' speech. The recognition of 'assaultive speech' or 'hate speech', which is part of triggering and other trends in the regulation of speech, all deserve some discussion. These are trends we will need to pay close attention to if we are to create better public and legal discourse.

Fish writes, 'argument is everywhere, argument is unavoidable, argument is interminable', and triumphantly declares that 'argument is all we have'.[8] In making the arguments we advance, if we do so successfully, Fish suggests we deliver the world 'in a particular shape', and if we are to argue successfully, we must do so in ways that are 'context-specific'. A set of assumptions are at work in his mind that have great relevance to law. He tells us that argument may sweep away the politico-legal frameworks, or normative worlds, we make and inhabit and that invest our lives with a sense of significance and security. On this view, we are always vulnerable to the depredations of those who could prevail at our expense by means of argument. Thus, there is no 'oasis' or 'safe space' that is entirely secure.

---

[7]   https://www.irishtimes.com/news/crime-and-law/solicitors-settle-medical-cases-for-much-less-than
       -initial-demands-1.1818110.
[8]   Ibid, p. 3.

BOX 3.3   SIX DEGREES OF CONTEXT

There are six areas you can focus on in assessing your communication in context:

1. **Balanced motivations**: Public values and positive social impacts achieve currency through dialogue with diverse stakeholders and can result in a successful outcome for you.
2. **Transferable skills**: Understanding the nature of the problem will allow you to assess what skills are needed to solve the issues or challenges you face, and which are suitable for your audience so that you can work through appropriate channels of communication.
3. **Contextual intelligence**: By assessing the emotions and the broad range of diverse interpretations of your audience, you can develop empathy and encourage engagement and connections sensitive to language, culture and other aspects.
4. **Integrated networks**: Developing networks is done through connection, language and making effective use of connecting channels, whether human or technological. Working with these networks, rather than siloed elements, can make decision-making a more holistic process.
5. **A prepared mind**: Having a prepared mind is not the same as having a fixed mind. We should avoid turning our dialogue into an exchange of positions or trench warfare.
6. **Intellectual thread**: Assessing your data and intelligence, and understanding your audience's emotion and interpretation, allow you to define the narrative intelligently and communicate on that basis, rather than through wishful or fixed thinking. The intellectual thread is necessarily emotional.

3.2   Mental health

A growing concern in law and the legal profession concerns mental health, which links closely to emotion and collaboration. Working collaboratively relieves stress, but also understanding mental health requires we have a better understanding of collaboration. When I attended a global law firm's discussion in London about their mental health awareness day, I was not so much struck by their concern but by the strange whiff of a mixture that is PR, compliance box-ticking and smugness.[9] They gave everyone a brochure and a badge, talked about how they might do better and extoled their exciting plans of sharing cake on the day and asking people how they feel. This is not how you deal with mental health. Such activities are really not going to stop someone with a mental health issue from being depressed. Actually, it is more likely to increase their anxiety. It is well documented that there are rising levels of anxiety, stress and pressure at work, and there have been numerous reports of problems of mental health and stress in the legal profession,[10] so there is little excuse for not getting it right, but sadly progress is slow.

To start with understanding mental health, we have to see that an arc of mental health exists, from everyday stress through to mental illnesses such as self-harm. Emotional demands, bullying and harassment, and pressures on time are factors most common amongst those suffering from stress. However, too often for law firms and clients alike, mental health awareness provides a calendar opportunity to do internal PR about how nice the firm or company is to their employees, provides fodder for a corporate social responsibility report that nobody reads, and provides evidence with respect to compliance when it comes time to give someone with a mental health issue the heave-ho. And here's the dirty little secret: there is great awareness now about mental health, but it is largely trivialized by these PR efforts. To deal with mental health seriously, law firms and companies have to take the issue into a deep-dive review rather than see it as a cost, public relations or human resources exercise. Taking such a deep dive requires an understanding of how the individual facing mental health issues is dealing with these issues and the workplace environment. The sense of loss of control, or barely hanging on, are hallmarks of a mental health condition. The problem for people with mental health

---

9   https://www.rte.ie/brainstorm/2019/1209/1097923-do-employers-really-care-about-staff-mental
    -health-issues/

10   *The Bellwether Report 2019: Stress in the Legal Profession – Problematic or Inevitable?* LexisNexis
    https://www.lexisnexis.co.uk/research-and-reports/stress-in-the-legal-profession-problematic-or
    -inevitable.html. See also Jonathan Koltai, Scott Schieman and Ronit Dinovitzer, *The Status-Health
    Paradox: Organizational Context, Stress Exposure, and Well-being in the Legal Profession* (March
    2018), Journal of Health and Social Behaviour, Vol. 59, No. 1, pp. 20–37; and Patrick R. Krill, Ryan
    Johnson and Linda Albert, *The Prevalence of Substance Use and Other Mental Health Concerns
    Among American Attorneys* (January/February, 2016), Journal of Addiction Medicine, Vol. 10, No. 1,
    pp. 46–52.

issues is that the mechanism I mentioned is not working properly, if at all. The problem with mental health is its lack of visibility, and people suffering from issues may be disguising their behaviour very effectively by appearing almost happy or even exhibiting great bravado in their actions. However, they are acting, because deep inside are the demons at work within them. Concerns also exist for practitioners who are exposed to distressing material and situations in the course of their work. Criminal law and family law practitioners in particular can find themselves exposed to distressing materials, cases and situations in the course of their work, thus impacting their wellbeing. US research even suggests that lawyers may experience significantly higher levels of vicarious trauma and burnout than US mental health clinicians and social service workers.[11]

Do I have any solutions? Yes, I do actually – in outline. Law firms and departments need to look at their complicity in the real mental health issues. What is the management system, the working environment and the HR mentality in the company? How are you working collaboratively? What are the mental health impacts of performance metrics and the billable hour? In other words, to what extent is the company or management causing or exacerbating a mental health issue in respect to a real person with real problems? To what extent are the problems systemic, rather than simply the problem of individuals within the firm or department? I do have three policy options for firms and organizations to consider:

1. Remove anything to do with employee engagement from the HR department. HR's primary duty is to take care of compensation and benefits. The clue is in the term 'resources'. People do not think of themselves as resources, and people with mental health issues are not defective or underperforming resources. They are people in pain. So, leave HR to be a finance and control function, because that is what it is, however the HR industry tries to dress it up.
2. Develop in this new function people well trained in care issues, and train them to be effective communicators who can listen and see

---

[11] https://nysba.org/why-burnout-is-so-pertinent-in-lawyersand-how-to-recognize-it/. For a more in-depth look at the issue, see G. Maguire and M.K. Byrne, *The Law Is Not as Blind as It Seems: Relative Rates of Vicarious Trauma among Lawyers and Mental Health Professionals* (September 7, 2016), Psychiatry, Psychology and Law, Vol. 24, No. 2, pp. 233–43.

things from the employee view. Then they can negotiate the space between the person and the work needs.

3. Change how people are managed. Instead of simply fitting people into boxes that makes them 'easier' to manage – and easier to tick boxes against for the HR, finance and legal function – try understanding what fits the employee. They may fit better elsewhere in the company or may equally need better support to help them find another company where there is a fit.

These three policy options require a more collaborative and understanding approach to the problems, and they also call for a long-term view of performance and the workplace. With technology and disruption in the legal profession, the situation can only become worse if not challenged within each firm and organization. The Covid-19 pandemic raised a number of mental health issues, and there is an opportunity to reflect on this period and create better paths forward. Personally, I'm not optimistic that many senior partners or company executives will listen, though I hope I am proven wrong. Changing leadership culture is like trying to turn around a big ship, and I am not confident this is going to change any day soon, regardless of the 'good press' law firms and companies generate through their PR efforts. Mental health will remain a performance issue and a compliance problem for management, masked by PR campaigns. As the campaign smiles fade into the daily grind of work priorities, and the whiff of mental health cake wafts away, the stench of poor management of mental health issues remains. But then again, there's always next year's mental health day.

4   Collaborative lawyering

If lawyers are to succeed in a world of legal technology, disruption and commoditization, it will be necessary to embrace another future dimension, namely collaborative relational lawyering. The notion of client relations has always been part of lawyering and has been well explored in the notion of relational lawyering.[1] However, there is much room for improvement through effective client, employee and stakeholder communication, hence extending the term to collaborative lawyering. Before doing this, we will look at building relationship and the need to hone communication skills, which has not been a staple in legal education but needs to be so for the future lawyer. Building on our understanding of the emotional lawyer, we can move on to look at engaging your 'audience'[2] and how to create an emotional heatmap of an audience. I use the term 'audience' as a handy catch-all term for the various individuals and stakeholders with whom you need to communicate. Relational lawyering is about exploring and understanding your audience – whether this comprises one person or a multitude – as part of the communication process, how this affects you, and vice versa how you affect your audience. At the heart of relational lawyering is the need to engage in dialogue with legal and non-legal audiences and to do what I call reversing the polarities. This starts, as discussed in the previous chapter, with listening. However, we need to take seriously Susan L. Brooks'[3] criticism that lawyers are

---

[1]   S.L. Brooks, *Listening and Relational Lawyering*, in D.L. Worthington and G.D. Bodie (eds), *The Handbook of Listening* (Wiley-Blackwell, Chichester, 2020). Brooks (Associate Dean for Experiential Learning and Professor of Law, Drexel University Thomas R. Kline School of Law) has written extensively on relational lawyering and communication, and is a pioneer in the emerging field of therapeutic jurisprudence. Particularly useful is her essay Susan L. Brooks, *Using a Communication Perspective to Teach Relational Lawyering* (2015), Nevada Law Journal, Vol. 15, No. 2, Article 5.

[2]   The term 'audience' usually refers to a collective of people, and often that matches with the idea of stakeholders, but can also be a singular consultation with an important person. Thus, while I am aware I am stretching the term a little, perhaps it is justified as capturing the importance of the formal engagement between a lawyer and client?

[3]   Susan L. Brooks, *Using a Communication Perspective to Teach Relational Lawyering* (2015), Nevada Law Journal, Vol. 15, No. 2, Article 5.

notoriously poor listeners, whose only education on listening has tended to be instrumental and linked to an individualistic and adversarial legal culture. A fundamental notion in using the Dialogue Box is that listening is where you get to the heart of drawing your audience into your legal understanding, in order for them to benefit most from your advice, insights and expertise. Relational lawyering also moves you from being a transaction lawyer to a relationship lawyer, and I would also extend this meaning of relationship to include not just working with people, but also working with technology in what I propose to be an emerging world of augmented reality. I am not talking here about augmented reality in some fanciful flight of futurology. I intend it as a working term to cover the emerging relationship between humans and technology, and we are already working in this way even if it is not commonly described this way. In talking this through, we should not let the technology disguise or distort the human dynamics of life in the law. To this end, we will look at a range of dynamics that are forcing the pace towards disruption of the legal profession and law and link these dynamics where appropriate to technological change. To understand these new dynamics, we will take a two-step exploration. First, we will look at relational lawyering and then we will build on this to explore the augmented lawyer. These two steps will take us to a well-rounded view of collaborative lawyering.

4.1   Relational lawyering

Relational lawyering for the future requires change in two central ways: social dynamics and technological innovation. Social dynamics focuses our attention on how we relate to persons, whether they are clients, victims or professional colleagues. This requires understanding, adapting and participating in communication with a variety of shifting audience perspectives, frequently in relationship with each other. This includes clients, witnesses, legal administrators, law enforcement, media, political bodies, the general public and colleagues. This is critical on the day-to-day level of getting things done. However, it is also critical to have improvements in interdisciplinary and broader relations and collaborative efforts – how we relate to persons in other professions and disciplines. It also demands we look through the lens of changes in culture, addressing diverse audiences, communicating gender, and how areas like bias, harassment, bullying and racism can be better addressed and changed through effective dialogue. To do this effectively requires improving legal communication to connect with all audiences and building relationships. We can seek to bring people together, not necessarily in a lockstep agreement, but at least into a neutral space in which we can find ways to collaborate – not just on the private level but also on the public level. The latter is problematized by the eruption of social media, which has created a new social space in which we operate with increasing polarization, where it seems we are locked in a battle of 'common sense' individualism tinged with nostalgia, and 'progressive' social change tinged with idealism – with bullying characteristics on both sides. To what extent social media amplifies such discord in society is a moot point, but it does highlight the struggle between received tradition and change, which takes place at both a societal and individual level. What people call their common sense is perhaps filled with bias and does not have inclusive concepts or language as part of their interpretative lens, and so one person's common sense is another person's need for change. However, in driving social change there is a tension between those changing and those content to stay as they are or remain satisfied that the existing state of things is fit for purpose. Progressive change is also a move into the unknown and may not necessarily be for the good. Law and lawyers have an important role to play in how we get beyond this discord to a better integrated world of social diversity, economic fairness and environmental care.

Technological innovation focuses our attention on the relationship between persons and technology – the augmented reality I referred to above. Technology is changing the profession and how things are done, as I have sought to establish in previous chapters. We need to delve deeper into the relational aspects of communication and technology and discover more about how lawyers can best augment their work, understand the optimal use of technology tools and pursue collaborative approaches with people in other units, areas or various disciplines. This opens up new and exciting opportunities for lawyers, and law students thinking about their future career, but also changes what it means to be a lawyer. The question is not if, but when and how this change will evolve. The reason to tie people and culture to the technology is that this is where we need to understand the established idea of 'GIGO' – garbage in, garbage out. We are building evermore complex communication and technological ecosystems, particularly with technologies like AI and blockchain, and in the process we are coding culture and bias into these systems. We are building a new legal environment in which the augmented lawyer, a practitioner who combines their talent with technological support, will become the norm.

4.2   The augmented lawyer

Our relationships are increasingly being filtered and mediated through data, demanding that we have a better understanding of how we can analyse change in the data economy. The 21st century is an extremely crowded communications space. We live in an era where we are transmitting information at 1/1000th of the cost in 1970, while the volume of digital information is increasing ten-fold per five-year period. According to the 'Data Age 2025' white paper published by the IDC, the world's data will grow from 33 to 175 zettabytes by 2025.[4] You're probably used to gigabytes, maybe terabytes, and a few of you may be familiar with petabytes; but, what are zettabytes? To illustrate, storing 175 zettabytes on DVDs would require a stack of DVDs that would be enough to circle the earth 222 times. Downloading 175 zettabytes, at the average current internet connection speed, would take you 1.8 billion years, though if everyone on the planet pitched in it would take a mere 81 days. The 21st-century communications environment has changed greatly and is more fluid and challenging. The outcome is that we will never be less transparent, have less information and be less connected than we are today. The hallmarks of this data age are captured in Box 4.1.

BOX 4.1   HALLMARKS OF THE DATA ECONOMY

- **Interconnectedness**: We are all interconnected and interdependent, as nations, organizations and individuals.
- **Speed**: Everything is considerably faster, and our deadlines, attention spans and the lifespan of information and products have become considerably shorter.
- **The transparency paradox**: We have to communicate transparently, both in the legal sense and in the cultural sense.
- **Privacy**: The flip side is that there are increasing demands on privacy as a result, and a feeling of discomfort that transparency has

---

[4]   https://www.forbes.com/sites/tomcoughlin/2018/11/27/175-zettabytes-by-2025/?msclkid=18 d37805d04911ecbf7d1019c3bbd8ca&sh=4b24ec315459

become intrusion, again highlighting the transparency paradox.

- **Surveillance**: Pushing this trend further, there is a great deal of surveillance, with CCTV, online tools and various other technologies tracking our physical and electronic moves.
- **Low-entry cost**: To get into new business areas or public spaces has become a lot cheaper, and innovation from idea to product is cheaper and faster.
- **Transience**: The rate of change and flexibility of attitudes and trends mean there is greater transience in our society, with people moving places, relationships and jobs more frequently.
- **Diversity**: Closely linked to this transience is the trend in recent decades of our society and workplaces becoming increasingly diverse.
- **Globalization and glocalization**: Diversity and interconnectedness are part of an increased awareness of the world, while glocalization[5] points us towards how we might strive for a better balance between our localized environment and the needs and values of the world globally.

An overarching change that runs throughout these hallmark trends is how our communications approaches have become increasingly experience-based. As noted, our ways of interacting in society and communication have become much more related to our experience of each other. Our interest in a product or service thus becomes more based on how we experience it, and so we will pay more or less as a result. Look at all the coffee shops and baristas, for instance. Is it only a cup of coffee, or is it an experience? When in court, what is the experience of the court for a plaintiff or a victim? The question we need to relate to is what is people's relationship with the law, and thus not just asking 'what is the law?' but also asking 'what is our experience of the law?' Technology is radically changing our experience by creating new user environments.

---

[5]   Glocalization brings together the terms 'globalization' and 'localization' to explain the balance of global and local, or domestic, needs. The term was popularized by the sociologist Roland Robertson, who explained the term came from Japanese economists seeking to explain Japanese global marketing strategies. In international law, one could say that legal directives and treaties, for instance, are global on one level and 'glocalized' by incorporation into domestic law.

4.3   Context

There are many channels we can use to connect to people, and technology has increasingly powered up these connections, so we can connect quickly and at distance. Context will determine which channel can be best used. Taking an obvious example like an email, which allows us to communicate a lot of information instantaneously and globally: what it gains in reach it lacks in body language and often contextual meaning. Precision in language can help, but there is more than just stating the facts, because emails and their wording lack nuanced language. You can manipulate emails to be more effective communication, but it can still lead to a lack of close meaning or event clarity. Emails have become ubiquitous in the legal profession, as they have in other areas of work and commerce. Commercial necessity is one of the influences of this ubiquity, but increasingly so too is social media, which is creating a global dialogue far beyond what previous generations could imagine. This creates transparency, one of the hallmarks noted above, but it can also create confusion and communication overload. People complain they get too many emails, but part of the problem is that when we complain about this, we are complaining about use, which means in fact we are complaining about the behaviour of others. People send without thinking, forward things without explanation, copy bosses to make a point or cause trouble, and so on. All these frustrations about email as a communication channel are a frustration with the bad behaviour of others, and ourselves. AI and other tools may help to lessen the load, but a more radical solution would be to have better rules of the road for online activity, and not tolerating abuse of these rules.

Physical communication remains the most powerful form of communication. Voice is powerful, but it is voice combined with body language that makes for better understood communication, and a more fulsome embrace of the message being communicated. The way we communicate visually offers more than the simple written or said word. We tell someone something and they perhaps say they understand, but their face may equally reveal their incredulity. We read into faces, actions and bodies as much as we do into words. However, we are not just reading out of what we see; we are reading into what we see, and there can be bias on both sides of that equation.

4.4   Tackling bias[6]

When someone asks 'where are you from?' it can be an obvious and interested inquiry. However, in some contexts it can also mean in fact 'where are you (really) from?' An English white person may ask a non-white English person this question, because they are assuming for some reason the person is not really English. If someone has a 'foreign' accent, the question may be less challenging, but even then we risk causing offence. Yet many people ask this question, and it is sometimes classified as 'unconscious bias'[7] as the person doesn't really recognize that they are asking a question in a biased way. We all have biases, and some of these biases are built into language and systems. To communicate effectively requires understanding where such biases and emotions exist, in order to communicate them. The role of the lawyer, and the Dialogue Box, is not necessarily to judge the emotion and biases, but simply to recognize they exist, how they impact your audience, and how you need to frame your communication. It is important to start fixing this problem now, because as we have seen with facial recognition technology, for instance, these human biases are built into machines. They are biases of today and tomorrow. Machine learning depends on data training sets, but these data sets have biases. I am not just discussing gender or racial bias here, for instance, but also the bias of many values and our perception that skews our communication in a particular way and can be a problem for our audience. What we are trying to do in the Dialogue Box is to explore dialogue in as neutral a way as possible, but also as emotionally connected as possible. You may have thought neutral and emotional are almost opposites, but in fact it is when we understand the neutrality of a situation that we find ways to make the best emotional connection.

---

[6]   https://biglawbusiness.com/lawyers-are-uniquely-challenging-audience-for-anti-bias-training

[7]   Harvard psychology has been a pioneer in this thinking: see M.R. Banaji and A.G. Greenwald, *Blindspot: Hidden Biases of Good People* (Delacorte Press, 2013). As well as a more generalized discussion in legal circles, this topic has become a significant topic in law and technology thinking, particularly around AI coding, black box technology in sentencing and facial recognition systems. Alexandra Wilson discusses her experience of bias as a bar pupil in her autobiographical work *In Black and White: A Young Barrister's Story of Race and Class in a Broken Justice System* (Endeavour, 2020); my review of which can be found in the *Times Literary Supplement*, https://www.the-tls.co.uk/articles/in-black-and-white-alexandra-wilson-review-david-cowan/

Taking bias out of the equation – or at least minimizing it – makes for better collaboration. Taking bias out of the equation is itself, in part, a collaborative process. Most people and cultures, I venture, do understand that we make mistakes or don't realize our bias, or we simply don't understand the place of the other. In most instances, people are prepared to forgive an initial error or faux pas. What is problematic is when it is repeated, repetitive and systemic. When mistakes are made, or biases conveyed, we can have dialogue to correct this. There is a caveat to this, which the Dialogue Box helps us with, and that is whether we expect people to be prepared. If we don't understand, there are ways to prepare us for an encounter or dialogue where we can explore the other, and explore ourselves, so that we reach a basis of mutual understanding before we go to the next step of dialogue or activity. This paves the way for better collaboration across whatever boundaries there may be, real or perceived.

4.5   The collaborative process

Nick Lovegrove and Matthew Thomas, writing in the *Harvard Business Review*,[8] identified six distinguishing characteristics of collaborative leadership (Box 4.2), and their insights are helpful to understanding the activity of collaboration more broadly. In understanding the communicating lawyer approach, we can see how each of the listed characteristics can be designed into collaborative efforts in a legal context. Starting with balancing motivation, the modern business mission – typified by corporate responsibility programmes – is to strike a balance in fostering public values, wielding influence for the better, having social impact and generating wealth. These are possibly metrics for the future successful company, but they are also common interests that can form the basis of collaboration. To forge a shared sense of common interest, we have to look for a fair engagement and mutual outcomes. The lawyer can do this in daily work with clients, but also inform the legal, regulatory and ethical debate amongst clients, other stakeholders and colleagues.

---

[8]   https://hbr.org/2013/02/why-the-world-needs-tri-sector.html

BOX 4.2 SIX CHARACTERISTICS OF COLLABORATIVE LEADERS[9]

1. **Balanced motivations**: They have a desire to create public value no matter where they work, combining their motivations to wield influence (often in government), have social impact (often in non-profits) and generate wealth (often in business).
2. **Transferable skills**: A set of distinctive skills valued across sectors, such as quantitative analytics, strategic planning and stakeholder management.
3. **Contextual intelligence**: A deep empathy of the differences within and between sectors, especially those of language, culture and key performance indicators.
4. **Integrated networks**: A set of relationships across sectors to draw on when advancing their careers, building top teams, or convening decision-makers on a particular issue.
5. **Prepared mind**: A willingness to pursue an unconventional career that zigzags across sectors, and the financial readiness to take potential pay cuts from time to time.
6. **Intellectual thread**: Holistic subject matter expertise on a particular tri-sector issue by understanding it from the perspective of each sector

A significant impact of technology in the disruption in the legal profession is the necessity to develop transferable skills. In the modern economy it is now much easier to change jobs, make career changes in one's own discipline and also move into other disciplines. It is common enough now to have more than one job description at one time, but also to have a number of careers in a lifetime. There is another aspect of importance to lawyers specifically, and that is the broadening of range of positions young lawyers out of law school can take up rather than simply thinking about qualifying as a solicitor or barrister. It is increasingly likely there will be a reimagining of the work that someone with a legal education will pursue. Richard Susskind has helpfully outlined ten kinds of emerging, or reimagined, jobs we can expect to see (Box 4.3), and these will certainly require more effective communication.

---

[9]   Ibid.

BOX 4.3 TEN NEW JOBS FOR LAWYERS[10]

1. legal knowledge engineer;
2. legal technologist;
3. legal hybrid;
4. legal process analyst;
5. legal project manager;
6. legal data scientist;
7. R&D worker;
8. online dispute resolution practitioner;
9. legal management consultant;
10. legal risk manager.

Perhaps there will be other jobs as well, but this seems like a fairly comprehensive list at this stage. What the list demonstrates is that, first, there are many ways we might slice up the legal role demanding a legal education, and second, there might be much more interesting or appealing jobs for some law graduates than being a 'lawyer'. The job of lawyer itself will likely evolve, and we may see the end of what has effectively been a 'closed shop' with unionization that has been tighter and more enduring than any association of Liverpool dockers or Durham miners ever achieved. These roles also reflect parts of a legal machinery that is evolving, and success in the future will likely involve greater collaboration between these roles or functions and other more traditional legal practitioners.

Lawyers may move in and out of these roles, but they may also move across to other specialist areas of law. When there is a property market crash, lawyers might jump over to bankruptcy law, which is not a new idea in terms of transferring skills in search of work. However, this list suggests there are new alternatives whereby traditionally schooled lawyers may seek one of these new roles. Whatever move the lawyer makes, it falls under the rubric of 'transferable skills', and this is a communication process more than it is a legal one. Certainly, a change in legal specialism requires learning of new law or revisiting law you have studied before. However hard or daunting this may seem, it is actually the easier bit. Just learn it. More tricky is when we move into a new legal ecosystem, with its

---

[10] Richard Susskind, *Tomorrow's Lawyers: An Introduction to your Future* (2nd edn, OUP, Oxford, 2017), p. 133.

own network of people working together, speaking their own language and operating within a different frame of reference. This is not so easy, and to transfer your skills means learning to communicate in this new ecosystem and exploring ways to collaborate to become part of the ecosystem. Part of this transfer is honing new contextual intelligence. This requires embracing a deep understanding towards the differences within and between sectors, legal and non-legal, especially those of language, culture and other key performance indicators. By this, I mean the way things fit together on an intellectually coherent level. Speaking in our language of law does not help in speaking to other disciplines, and if we are to gather this contextual intelligence, we need a more connected approach to language and ideas.

This is what deepens our understanding of the context and connects our expertise to the context of the other, so we can then in turn connect that context to the context of the law, courts and legal practice. This contextual approach is what makes the transfer of skills and understanding more productive and helpful. When we reach this contextual understanding, we are better able to create integrated networks with other disciplines and individuals. It creates a set of relationships across sectors to draw on when advancing our legal solutions, building collaborative teams, or bringing decision-makers on a particular issue to seek common ground and mutually beneficial solutions or outcomes. This approach also allows us to negotiate our way around networks more easily, which also requires that we have a prepared mind. Whether we are seeking to transfer skills or foster collaboration, we need to be prepared with a willingness to pursue an unconventional path on occasion. This may mean being adaptable in how we think of our career, so we can move in a more frictionless way across sectors, and have the mindset to make concessions which may be financial, temporal or otherwise challenging. Preparing a Dialogue Box is how you can better prepare your mind – it is a long leap before you look or act. Lastly, on this helpful list, is the intellectual thread. A holistic subject matter expertise is best achieved by understanding it from the perspective of each viewpoint, sector, discipline or, as structured in the Dialogue Box, each zone. This is how we can develop more effective collaboration.

4.6   A collaborative LegalTech ecosystem

If we are to have a more collaborative approach, we also need to look at the entire legal ecosystem, and within this the LegalTech ecosystem that can support genuine change in relationships. It is recognized that there is a need for a multifaceted understanding of the LegalTech eco-system, which involves exploring the potential and limitations of using new technologies, especially artificial intelligence (AI), natural language processing (NLP) and machine learning (ML), to support legal services and to tackle a range of innovation, economic and governance issues. Researchers note AI's capabilities have made enormous leaps in recent times and many expect it to transform how the economy operates. In par-ticular, activities relying on human knowledge to create value, insulated until now from mechanization, are facing dramatic change. This has led to in-depth research into the career trajectories and typical skillsets of start-up founders, law firm innovation leaders and others. A University of Oxford research project[11] is looking into these issues to assess the role of funders and buyers in the market, on the basis that such information is crucial to start-ups chasing scale. Rather than undertaking research into the barriers to adoption, the university is looking at the prospects and networks of the entrepreneurs themselves. The project has looked at six interlocking work packages – complementarities that support imple-mentation of AI, respectively, at: the firm level (strategy and governance); the sector level (skill investment and technology transfer); the country level (comparisons of national skills and innovation policies); the indi-vidual level (technology-driven education, skills and training); mapping the constraints of legitimacy and current technology for digital dispute resolution; and work on semantic systems at the technological frontier of AI in legal reasoning. These packets of work offer a useful matrix for anyone looking at innovation within their own organizations in human relationships.

---

[11]   *University of Oxford team to study LawTech 'ecosystem'.* October 29, 2019: https://www.law.ox.ac.uk/news/2019-10-29-university-oxford-team-study-lawtech-ecosystem

4.7 Women's LegalTech problem

Women are perhaps making greater progress in LegalTech than more traditional areas of law, and with more women pursuing careers in LegalTech, they have an important role in the disruption of the profession as a whole.[12] One might have thought this provides women with an opportunity to find improvement in gender balance in the profession, but the situation is by no means straightforward. Delivering the keynote address at a legal conference I attended, Christina Blacklaws, a past president of the Law Society of England and Wales, said LegalTech was weighed down by systemic bias and 'cultural and social expectations of what women can and should do'.[13] She urged more women to pursue careers in technology, and said the stakes were particularly high due to the danger of data containing gender bias being used to train AI, warning: 'In a computerized world, diversity should get better', but it could get a lot worse if bias in society gets 'hardwired into decision-making'.[14] A LegalTech specialist, Olga Mack, CEO of San Francisco-based contract management platform Parley Pro, told me: 'LegalTech combines the worst of legal and tech. Historically, and even to some extent today, investors dread investing in LegalTech. This relative scarcity of funding makes the existing networks of mostly men even tighter and harder to penetrate for women in LegalTech.'[15] She calls for the creation of more LegalTech-focused funds generally and more funds specifically focused on increasing 'diversity of thought' in the industry, and also urged buyers of LegalTech to put pressure on suppliers to improve diversity.

---

[12] A useful overview is provided by K. Munisami, *Legal Technology and the Future of Women in Law* (2019), Windsor Yearbook of Access to Justice / Recueil annuel de Windsor d'accès à la justice, Vol. 36, pp. 164–83. https://doi.org/10.22329/wyaj.v36i0.6418. On women in the workplace more generally, McKinsey started a useful annual report in 2015 which traces developments in the US corporate market; the 2021 report is the most recent: *Women in the Workplace*. McKinsey, September 27, 2021: https://www.mckinsey.com/featured-insights/diversity-and-inclusion/women-in-the-workplace

[13] Author's speech notes. Global Legal Forum, February 2020, *More women must enter male-dominated legal tech to guard against AI bias, conference hears*, The Global Legal Post, https://www.globallegalpost.com/news/more-women-must-enter-male45dominated-legal-tech-to-guard-against-ai-bias-conference-hears-95730357?msclkid=1ebfbd9fd03811ec955afa1d721f74d2

[14] Ibid.

[15] Author's interview notes.

One problem for women is the perennial complaint about compensation. A typical example is an Equilar General Counsel Pay Trends study,[16] which reported that male general counsel earned 18.6% more than their female counterparts, the largest pay gap since Equilar began reporting figures in 2014. The report reveals that from 2017 to 2018, median compensation for men increased from $2.52 million to $2.63 million, while median pay for women decreased from $2.44 million to $2.21 million. Compensation is not the only measure that law firms and departments are tracking. Thomson Reuters' 'Transforming Women's Leadership in the Law' research[17] sheds light on the steps law firms are taking to improve gender diversity. The research shows that law firms are making significant progress in addressing the disparity in the gender make-up at senior and junior levels by introducing a raft of initiatives.

On the last point, the research showed that 'women-only networks', for example, can be damaging for gender balance, but opening those networks up to include men can result in them having a positive effect. This can help to overcome the difference between the perspectives of men and women, which are most visibly pronounced on issues such as sexism in the workplace and the gender pay gap. Women tend to see a diverse and inclusive workforce as a priority and are more critical of law firm culture, compensation structure, and business model.

4.8   Sexual orientation

The GDPR: Capturing data on sexual orientation and gender identity under the GDPR in the European Union report from Stonewall[18] highlighted that sexual orientation and gender identity data monitoring can help employers understand the barriers that their lesbian, gay, bisexual and transsexual employees face. Capturing LGBT data is commonplace in some countries and complemented by a supportive legal framework, while a number of countries have legal limits on the types of data that can be collected. Likewise, the European Union's General Data Protection Regulation (GDPR), introduced in 2018, places additional requirements for the

---

[16] https://marketing.equilar.com/08-29-2019-gc-pay-trends
[17] https://blogs.thomsonreuters.com/legal-uk/2019/06/25/are-some-diversity-initiatives-actually-making-gender-diversity-worse/
[18] https://www.stonewall.org.uk/resources/gdpr-guide

collection and processing of special categories of personal data, including sexual orientation and gender identity. Many employers are concerned about the legality of introducing diversity monitoring programmes, and in particular about data privacy requirements. Understanding compliance requirements of the GDPR and relevant national legislation across the EU, and how they relate to sexual orientation and gender identity data, is an important step in creating greater understanding. There is also increasing attention to supporting people with gender dysphoria, a medical condition whereby a person experiences discomfort and distress from a mismatch between their biological sex assigned at birth and their gender identity. Firms have included this in their insurance and healthcare coverage, which also includes pre-authorizing surgery in line with health service protocols that require the individual seeking treatment to be under the care of a gender identity clinic and specialists. Mental health support from specialists is provided to help deal with gender dysphoria, including counselling and speech therapy. Firms are also involved in charity work to raise money in support of those who need legal services. However, managing these issues remains contested.

4.9   Disabilities

Mental health is a form of disability, though it is only recently that it has been seen as such – and still law firms and other employers seem to struggle to understand how to move from it being an internal public relations or wellness programme to a meaningful part of management care.[19] Disabled people with various conditions working in the legal profession continue to face a less understanding culture and outmoded practices that hamper efforts to build successful careers. According to a UK study,[20] a cross-section of legal professionals say they hide their disability when applying for training places or jobs, and encounter hostility and discrim-

---

[19]   David Cowan, *Do employers really care about staff mental health issues?* RTE Brainstrom, updated February 19, 2020: https://www.rte.ie/brainstorm/2019/1209/1097923-do-employers-really-care-about-staff-mental-health-issues/

[20]   *Legally Disabled? The Career Experiences of disabled people working in the legal profession*: http://legallydisabled.com/research-reports/. The report's research team worked with the Lawyers with Disabilities Division of the Law Society and drew on focus groups, interviews and surveys of solicitors, barristers, trainees and paralegals. The research was commissioned by DRILL (Disability Research on Independent Living and Learning), a £5 million research programme led by disabled people.

ination in their jobs. The report states, 'Disabled people in the legal profession face – on a daily basis – rituals, practices and attitudes that exclude
or undermine them in their roles as trainees, advocates and employees.'[21]
This includes situations when they seek 'reasonable adjustments' to their
working environment or practice, which they are entitled to under the
law. Some requests for – often inexpensive – adjustments were met with
ignorance and resulted in ill-treatment or discrimination, and their problems or difficulties are often handled as performance-related problems.
The report reveals that more than half (54%) of disabled solicitors and
paralegals involved in the study thought their career and promotion prospects inferior to their non-disabled colleagues. Some 40% either never
or only sometimes tell their employer or prospective employer they are
disabled, while just 8.5% of respondents who were disabled when they
started their training disclosed their disability in their application. Some
60% of solicitors and paralegals said inaccessible working environments
limited their career opportunities, while 85% reported pain and fatigue
associated with their disability that could be made worse by inflexible
working arrangements and long hours.

A significant proportion of disabled people in the profession have also
experienced forms of disability-related ill-treatment, bullying or discrimination. The same report explained, 'A poverty of imagination, bureau-
cracy, belligerent managers and outdated working practices prevent often
minor adjustments that would make a huge difference for disabled people.'[22] Its recommendations include a proposal that law should become
the first profession to introduce disability pay gap reporting. The report's
lead researcher, Debbie Foster, professor of employment relations and
diversity at Cardiff Business School, highlighted the impact that line managers and supervisors can have on the working lives of disabled people
in the profession. She said, 'Line managers and supervisors play a pivotal
role in the reasonable adjustment process and in the management of
sickness absence, performance management and promotion.' However,
she added that, in practice, improvements 'often depended on "good will",
"luck" or personality rather than a good understanding and professional
training'.[23] Project researcher Dr Natasha Hirst, an independent pho-
tojournalist and researcher, said, 'Often exclusion or discrimination in

---

[21]   Ibid.
[22]   Ibid.
[23]   Ibid.

the legal workplace is not intentional but comes from behavioural codes, rituals and assumptions that date back to when few disabled people were working in the profession.' The report stated that 'a generous interpretation' of the findings suggests employers and recruitment agencies are 'risk averse' in the hiring process, which is clearly unsatisfactory a quarter of a century after the Disability Discrimination Act first guaranteed the right to reasonable adjustments in the workplace.

4.10   Generational differences

Generational differences are revolutionizing how law firms are structured and how lawyers, business development, finance, operations and IT staff collaborate for success. New generations of entrants into the profession are challenging and demanding change more than any previous generations. I don't intend to go into the dynamics of each of these generations (Box 4.4), but suffice to say there is a need for firms to have a generations strategy, developing talent and being flexible in how generations collaborate. What is important is to understand the communication implications of the intergenerational workplace of today. It should not be assumed, however, that the younger generations are tech-savvy, as they may be used to technology without necessarily understanding what lies behind it – to which I should add that the earlier generations built much of the technology used today by the young.

BOX 4.4   THE GENERATION GAME

The current generations today are commonly defined as follows:[24]

- Gen Z, iGen, or Centennials: born 1996–2012;
- Millennials or Gen Y: born 1977–1995;
- Generation X: born 1965–1976;
- Baby Boomers: born 1946–1964;
- Traditionalists or Silent Generation: born 1924–1945;
- The Greatest Generation (or GI Generation): born before 1924.

---

[24] A useful compendium of these categories can be found at: https://edition.cnn.com/2013/11/06/us/baby-boomer-generation-fast-facts/index.html

4.11   Boundaries of collaboration

Context has boundaries, often disciplinary boundaries, but also boundaries of language, identities and other ways that define the context. People also refer to this as pigeon-holing, 'oh, you're the lawyer', or 'ah, you're French'. These contextual boundaries can also be formal, and implicit in much legal communication is the notion of formality. The language is precise, the style is formal. The law can be communicated by means formal, regulated or official, but it is also the communication of relationships between people, institutions and objects. In the pursuit of precision, the lawyer is looking to delineate roles and responsibilities, titles to ownership, and such like. You don't want to add to the list 'such like' – as I just did – because it opens a door to ambiguity, which is often the unspoken enemy of legal communication. In this way we have a deep texture in understanding the context, which mixes boundaries, formal spaces and persons as roles, and this may be fine most of the time in a legal context, because there is a shared language for this context. However, your client is not precise, not certain. They are also often not basing everything on facts. Lawyers can speak past the clients because the lawyer is expressing what are the facts, delineating boundaries, while the client wants to express how they feel and romp around the context, jumping from one point to another, one feeling to another. The lawyer is dealing with 'what is' and 'what could be', while the client has a tendency to deal with what they feel 'should' be or what 'ought' to be.

4.12   Broken business model?

Collaboration and diversity, along with other trends of disruption, raise questions about the evolution of the legal business model. The great pursuit of 'making partner' may be less desirable than it has been for past generations, though Millennials remain interested in becoming partner despite this. There is some debate whether the partner model is best, and in many quarters a growing belief that the law firm business model itself is fundamentally broken. A US study, 'New Expectations, Evolving Beliefs and Shifting Career Goals',[25] conducted by Major, Lindsey &

---

[25]   https://www.mlaglobal.com/en/knowledge-library/research/2019-millennial-attorney-survey-new
-expectations-evolving-beliefs-and-shifting-career-goals

Africa, reported that the Millennial generation operates differently than their predecessors, and suggests that successful law firms of the future are those that challenge the status quo. This means firms need to work with Millennials to address their concerns. If not, they risk losing out on attracting and retaining talent in what remains a highly competitive market. The survey also reveals key differences in the experiences of male and female attorneys. When asked how long they would like to work at their current firm, 33% of male respondents said they want to make partner at their current firm, compared with 26% of female respondents. Meanwhile, after partnership, men are more likely to see themselves as in-house counsel in ten years, whereas women aspire to go into non-profit and government work. Career satisfaction also requires striking a work–life balance, which again differs according to generations and gender, and is a top priority. There is much evidence, in surveys and industry reports, that many legal professionals would trade a portion of their compensation for either more time off, a flexible work schedule, or a cut in billable hours. One way of improving the working environment, rooted in good communication practice, is the use of mentorships. These are more successful and meaningful when kept as an informal process. An informal mentor can play a significant role in a career, and the report suggested women tended to value informal mentorships more than men. Younger workers can greatly benefit from informal mentoring, but this requires knowing how to communicate across generational lines, and ensuring it does not imitate a parental or authority relationship.

The diversity issues discussed above form a core element in understanding how the business model is changing. Law firms regularly publish ambitious diversity targets, using technology to measure and model more accurately impacts and trends. This allows firms to set new targets to increase the diversity within its senior leadership positions over a set period – a limited number of years, usually three. The targets are focused on ensuring that a diverse group of people have access to senior management roles within the business. Yet firms also have to admit regularly that the total gender pay gap persists, and has even crept up at times. The areas where diversity is a struggle are in gender, sexual orientation, race and disabilities. This in turn impacts how different generations are managed within the firm or law department. Becoming diverse is not something that happens by accident but can be achieved through requiring change and commitment, and by ensuring colleagues have access to opportunities to grow and progress. Technology, as the various reports cited suggest, is increasingly able to track and trace developments on diversity and other needs and makes analysis more nuanced. This can be a positive move if firms take the data seriously and develop more tools to support the diversity of the firm or organization. We have the collaborative technology, but frankly, I suggest, the jury is out in some respects on whether we have the collaborative attitude to match.

BOX 4.5 A FIVE-PILLAR STRATEGY TO BUILD A LEGALTECH ECOSYSTEM

Drawing on interviews with a number of leaders in law, I have devised a brief overview of a successful strategy for building an improved LegalTech ecosystem within firms or law departments. This centres on managing generations within the firm or department and is founded on five pillars of development.[26]

Pillar 1: Leadership

Partners need to drive change, but can also feel the most threatened by it. Law firms are changing slowly, but equally are under extreme pressure to change. However, equity partners have differing levels of appetite for radical change. The lawyer's worth and role is changing as they become more consultative, internally and externally. Work increasingly done by using technology will command lower salaries, while the trusted advisor role, utilizing judgement and expertise, will be the focus of high demand. This means leaders need to draw on greater competitive intelligence and creativity, which are innate human characteristics. Leaving younger lawyers to sink or swim in paper to develop their talent is no longer viable. Nor is it viable to leave anyone behind. Leaders need to embrace and reflect more diversity and inclusiveness as they manage the generational transformation of their firms. Leadership is increasingly an individual competency, rather than simply the attainment at the pinnacle of the firm or a particular department.

---

[26] A version of these five pillars was published in David Cowan, *C-suite culture change needed to shake up tech investment*, The Legal COO Report, Raconteur/*The Times*, February 25, 2019, pp. 4–5.

Pillar 2: Support and operations

Legal operations need to be better integrated. Firms need to make good technology choices that genuinely help lawyers and clients, rather than just chasing a fashion for feature-rich tech solutions that do not meet the specific needs of lawyers and their clients. Amongst support services, legal secretaries are amongst the fastest declining occupations, and their tasks are being taken over by those they serve. There is a greater appetite for self-serve approaches. Things which used to be done for lawyers are now done by themselves using smartphones and apps. Support staff are managing hotdesks, health facilities and comfort places as pit stops which are now seen as support rather than benefits, turning the formal regime of offices, dress and reporting lines on its head. The IT function has a dual role of managing the technology and consultatively supporting everyone in the firm to use the technology more effectively.

Pillar 3: Innovation

Incubators and labs within law firms are flourishing. These are places where tech experts and lawyers collaborate with other teams, and younger generations can play a key role. Law firms that understand the innovator's dilemma and worry about the timing and execution of reinvention will be more successful. Many firms also know there are internal innovators, or 'intrapreneurs', who can create projects designed to deliver tangible benefits to their firms. Such projects can build buy-in and momentum for more ambitious change. Innovation is not just coming from tech people; it is more holistic and solicited from everyone, whatever their age, role or function. Bringing these elements together promotes a more effective collaboration.

Pillar 4: Dialogue

Younger generations expect to be communicated to, as do clients. Serving clients means integrating business development, client communication and marketing functions, thereby fostering open, diverse and creative dialogue. Firms need to prioritize improving communication. Different language is needed to describe needs and desires, including recognizing diversity, avoiding alienation and acknowledging cultural differences. Firms have a variety of subcultures, which are generational, functional and social, and dialogue as activity and language is how they can break down siloes between various parts of the firm, promoting greater collaboration with shared aims. Using workshops tackling implicit bias and fostering open dialogue, and breaking down barriers and silos, within the firm helps attain both business and diversity goals.

Pillar 5: Coaching and mentoring

Law firms have a tradition of getting smart new entrants to do repetitive tasks, often burying talent in a sea of paperwork. Now they can focus on providing value. Younger lawyers want to learn and be challenged; otherwise they will move on. Training needs to focus on coaching and mentoring to do more interesting and creative tasks. This is essential to maintaining work–life balance, integrating gender, diversity, cultures, and tackling mental health issues. These were areas once shunned by law firms. Structured mentorship and advanced training support the recruitment and retention of attorneys with diverse backgrounds. Management can build a culture that is collaborative and meaningful for all levels of the firm and generations, which may mean creating different types of workspaces and practices to suit different ages, experience and cultures within the firm and build a more collaborative culture.

5 Changing channels

Communication can be done through a variety of channels to reach difference sizes of audience, ranging from one-on-one communication through to mass communication, including the now ubiquitous social media. To use channels effectively requires creating a matrix of the best channels to use, in order to create a more holistic communication platform ranging from general awareness down to a specific message. Your audience may have a general awareness of your organization's reputation, which may affect why they chose to approach you, or they may have done an online search and gained some comfort from your online profile before approaching you. They come with some preconceived ideas of who you are or what you can do for them, and your specific messages and communication will be measured against this. Equally, you may need to influence one audience that has influence over another. People may trust the advice of people in other sectors and take that as a reason to approach you or trust you. How you build this platform effectively depends on accessing the right channels to reach these various influences. What channels you use is a matter of selection, which involves evaluating what the more effective channels are based on a full understanding of the audience you want to reach. This in turn involves an assessment of how all the moving parts of a contextualized situation are to be understood.

Creating and managing your communications strategy involves drawing up a stakeholder communications map, which will in turn form the bases of the channel matrix that suits the relationship between your audience and the channels available. What channels work will also change, as new channels become available, while other channels fall out of fashion. Equally, what channels will work at one point of your strategy may change and lead you to make use of other channels or desist from using a particular channel. Channels also need to be understood in relation to the formal versus informal lines of communication discussed in Chapter 1. Face-to-face communication is the channel of choice for informal communication, and gossip. It is the most persuasive channel, as we will discuss, but it leaves fewer traces. People can always deny the contents of a one-to-one conversation, the so-called 'he said, she said' case. Further than that, the hints in tone of voice and body language can leave people with an impression without really saying anything specific, which can be influential. A lot of our communication today is direct electronic communication, such as email; text and other such channels can be used for informal communication, but they also tend to lack nuance. Social media, as we shall see, is a powerful mix of informal and formal communication. In organizations the primary focus is on formal communication, and there is an established process of using channels to reach throughout the organizations and across sectors and geographies to reach stakeholders and influencers.

5.1   Infusion ... not cascading

Before we get into the most effective way to use these channels, it is best to dispose of the most common but least effective way of thinking about managing communication within your organization, and that is 'cascading'. The term cascading is used a lot in companies and law firms to describe the act of communicating within the organization. Well, stop cascading, now! What cascading is in practice is a passive, hierarchical and uninspiring word to describe a process whereby managers, partners and others pass on the information until there is no one left to pass the information on to – the buck has stopped. Someone in this chain could be asked if they have communicated some information or a message, and they can respond they have cascaded it, which makes it sound like they have done something. A cascade may conjure up an image of water flowing with energy, but in reality, organizational cascading all too often stops at the level where the buck stops at a common level of the organization – and have you ever had a shower that only reaches your chest?

Another aspect of cascading that is concerning is how it involves breaking down the information hierarchy. In the past, as noted in Chapter 1, information has historically been about power because it referenced the position you had in the hierarchy. To know something was a way to show you had power, and whom you shared it with demonstrated power relations. To let someone in on the secret could be a way of showing you had greater power. This is all very much a top–down approach to communicating. A more collaborative approach, which has a different and arguably more positive understanding of power, is an approach I call 'infusion'. This approach creates a communication process that promotes sharing and a healthy flow of information throughout your organization. Information is thus not power; rather, sharing is power. Linked to hierarchy, the currency of communications is information, and this was traded on a need-to-know basis. The beloved maxim of 'information is power' really meant information was held and filtered rather than spread. The exercise of communication was akin to a command-and-control approach, as organizations sought to control the message and the spread of information to maintain command over events. Towards the end of the 20th century, the shift was to information cascades and this idea still persists today, but in truth it is still old-style communications thinking.

To illustrate, here is a cascading question you can ask about your organization: is your management a herd? Cascading as a term was originally used to explain the cascading effect of when individuals in a population make their decisions based on actions and information almost passively provided by others. This is instead of relying on their own information, and results in herd-like behaviour amongst the individuals. It usually occurs when the individuals do not have sufficient information on a particular problem or are unable to properly process the information they have access to. This leads to a situation where we can look at whether what you choose is what is popular or what is best. Take for instance somebody trying to decide on what smartphone they should purchase. Often people will go for the same smartphone everybody else has, because they have little knowledge of what is actually the best smartphone. They rely on information from friends and observing what is the most popular smartphone with others. The buyer is led to believe that if everybody else owns this smartphone, and says it is the best, then it must be the best. However, this information is not always necessarily correct, and another less popular smartphone could actually be the best for you, or even 'the' best. In both instances, the cascade process replaces intelligent handling of information.

Cascade is thus a poor process. However well intentioned the idea of cascade as a means to spread information, leadership and managers in fact often end up creating blockages. What an organization does in practice is a process along the following lines. Take the example of campaigns that are run throughout the organization, whether it be a mental health awareness week, a health and safety day, or some other top-level concern

– these are said to be 'cascaded' through the organization. This is basically what happens in four steps:

1. An internal project manager gets told 'we need a campaign' for all employees.
2. They figure out a campaign to show how 'we care'.
3. They launch the campaign telling them 'we care'.
4. This then 'cascades' down the organization.

And the result? Surprise, surprise! Nobody actually cares. It doesn't work, and largely it breeds cynicism. Employees frequently complain of initiative fatigue, and this is the reason why. Employees are flooded by initiatives, programmes, inspirational messages complete with fridge magnets or water bottles and the like, expertly generated by the campaign project but somewhat lacking in merit or effect.

Do you still want to cascade? Or do you want to engage, infuse and enthuse your audience? Start thinking infusion. Think how tea infuses. Now close your eyes and think of communication working through infusion throughout your organization – get the image? Infusion offers a more dynamic way of thinking about your communications. Infusion recognizes how successful communication within an organization is 'up, down and across' and requires active engagement at all levels and in all directions. This is why I call this process 'infusion'. So from here on, whenever you see or hear the word 'cascade' in internal communications, insist on replacing it with 'infusion'. Using the Dialogue Box and having an effective understanding of your audience, and matching the right channels to your message audience, is how you will achieve infusion. Let us now turn to choosing the channels that will be most effective.

5.2 Embracing training

Ongoing education and training are an important aspect of creating infusion, bringing about a commonality of approaches. Effective training should be collaborative and task-oriented, and can be deployed in person, virtually or in a blended environment. The Dialogue Box is a tool for training that is collaborative and workshop-based, which produces an outcome of the Dialogue Box. Perhaps an issue for some in having to do training is that they feel it is taking up time when they could be getting on with business, and billable hours. Good training can, indeed should, result in learning that creates efficiency, so the time can thus be made up by the new learning and the costs recouped many times over. However, this is where there are problems in how firms can operationalize their training and learning programmes. There is also the issue of commitment by participants, with one of the challenges for any learning and development person being how to keep people in the room and focused on the classroom task, rather than the 'comings and goings' of the average class and the attention diverted by doing other business tasks in the learning time. Good and engaging content can help, making learning also a communication issue.

This said, law firms have increased the amount of in-house training offered. A 2019 report from the Solicitors Regulation Authority (SRA)[1] noted that since introducing 'continuing competence' requirements in 2016, 40% of law firms report that they have increased the amount of learning and development support offered to their solicitors. The SRA noted the introduction of a revised approach to maintaining and developing skills among solicitors was positive. Half of firms (52%) say that levels of learning and development have remained unchanged, with just 9% reporting a reduction in the focus given to this area. All solicitors are required to make a declaration on what training and development they have undertaken over the past 12 months as part of their annual renewal application. To help better understand the impact of the new approach, the SRA also conducted an online survey of 500 firms and solicitors and visited 20 firms.[2] The most popular internal training methods were reading, research and discussion (75%), informal and on-the-job training (69%), and peer-to-peer learning (58%). Training courses on specific topics and areas of law (70%), e-learning and webinars (59%), and conferences and events (58%) were the main external methods. Other key feedback on the continuing competence approach included that the new regime was implemented without significant problem and is seen as more flexible and able to adapt to individual needs and specialisms. Most firms reported a reduction in the cost of learning and development by better focusing activity on specific roles and teams. However, some solicitors

[1]   SRA, Annual Diversity Report (2019), Solicitors Regulation Authority: https://www.sra.org.uk/sra/equality-diversity/archive/annual-diversity-report-2019/?msclkid=de97c54ed04911ec8bb7da7da04166ad
[2]   SRA, Press Release (2019), Solicitors Regulation Authority: https://www.sra.org.uk/sra/news/press/2019-press-release-archive/continuing-competence/?msclkid=c19b374fd05f11ecbb596a63a4ffdf7d

claimed it is difficult to make time to reflect, identify and address their learning and development needs.

5.3   Choosing channels

All channels have positives and negatives in their deployment (see Box 5.1). For instance, emails maintain consistency and integrity of the message, but an email is not always read and is not always accessible to the audience. In a legal office, emails are an efficient means, but this is not the case for a machinist in a factory. Likewise, if an email campaign has managed to convert a large proportion of its audience to switch over an administrative tool to another platform, it is successful, but if some are not making the switch, clearly email, or at least in the form used hitherto, has been less optimal for a sector of your audience. The size of audience is one measure of suitability – after all, one person cannot have one-on-one meetings with thousands or millions of people. From the individual to the mass communication tool, there needs to be a heatmap of the audience that can target the people who need to be communicated to, and what communication they need. This audience can be broken down in the Dialogue Box into much more defined audience groups.

BOX 5.1   USING CHANNELS EFFECTIVELY

Visibility: You want to ensure your communication is highly visible, over a variety of channels, and gives time to discuss the issue at hand, change or further developments.

Toolkits: For more complex communication, creating toolkits can be very effective in maintaining the integrity of key messaging, providing standardization of information and messages by maintaining a set of FAQs and talking points to help others involved in the communication process – though they should not be used as a crutch or be a parroting exercise.

News updates: By use of regular emails, newsletters, videos, podcasts and other collateral for certain issues, such as a longer-term change, it is important to maintain updates on your communication issue.

Direct communication: Roadshows, lectures, brown-bag lunches and other channels can be critical to maintaining direct physical communication. This is the most powerful communication, but time and logistics can make it impossible for you to engage directly all the time. However, you can use other people and fora to create powerful direct communication. Use of events and 'ambassadors' are such channels, though they need to be handled with caution, as events fill diaries and people can be weary of the plethora of 'champions' taking up their time.

Consider what are the communication channels to deliver your communication, which will vary according to the level of difficult information or news. Where possible, try not to have an over-reliance on email. The matrix of channels will help you understand their pros and cons. You will get further with your audience by using face-to-face communication much more, and the effort will be appreciated. For longer-term change or projects, think about the best way to keep employees or your audience updated on a regular basis. Social media has made a huge impact in choosing channels, given its immediacy and ability to reach large audiences with both formal and informal messages. Box 5.2 offers a framework of five questions you can ask yourself to create a channel matrix, based on defining your message and choosing the channel that fits best. Let's take these in turn.

BOX 5.2 CREATING YOUR CHANNEL MATRIX

1. Why am I communicating?
2. What am I hoping to achieve?
3. Who do I want to reach?
4. What do I want people to do as a result of receiving my communications?
5. How will I know if it has made any difference?

Often communication is done without thinking why we are doing it. We may assume we have to communicate, where in fact it can be the case we ought not to be communicating. In the Dialogue Box you will discover why you are communicating, because what your legal or business objective is may not be the same as your communication objective. You may be communicating because you have legal advice to dispense. However, your communication objective more specifically may be that someone is in an emotional state where they may not be able to listen to your counsel, so your first communication objective is to find a way of supporting them to be receptive to your counsel. This may mean communicating around the issues rather than directly, and also requires choosing the most appropriate channel. To take an obvious example, missing this step may lead to you sending an email when a phone call may be more effective. What then are you hoping to achieve? You want to give legal advice, but what is your objective in giving that advice? It may be simply to give specific advice, but it may also be to create a relationship. In business terms, if we are too transactional in our communication, this may make the communication too narrow to open up other opportunities for upselling or cross-selling. You may want to give advice that solves a specific problem, but how you do it may open up a dialogue about other potential issues. Sometimes, dare I say it in the environment of the billable hour, you might want to give a certain amount of advice freely as it may lead to deepening trust and relationship. The legal version of a loss-leader product.

Turning to who you want to reach means understanding who your audience is, which in some cases will be straightforward. You have a client and they want advice. However, this may be too transactional in some cases. You may want to reach others who can influence your client or client organization. You may need to lobby people internally to reach your ultimate audience. Take a legal strategy in-house, for instance. Your audience may be the C-suite, but you may want to lobby individuals within certain departments who will in turn influence the decision-makers. The ultimate decision-maker has people they turn to for advice, and perhaps you can identify them as influencers and communicate to them either directly or by building awareness. This process can mean choosing channels such as an internal magazine that features the legal department, or a brown-bag lunch where you invite a broader audience to a talk on a subject of mutual interest or related to the strategic point you are trying to make.

What then do you want people to do as a result of receiving your communications? Do you want them to make a decision? Do you want to influence someone else close to the decision-maker? Do you want to make an audience aware in case events turn in such a way that they become impacted, so they are not surprised because you have already created a level of awareness? The channel you use has different impacts on responses. Sending an email may work for some of your audience, but not all, because they need more support. A poster can create awareness, but does not necessarily get someone to respond to your message. If awareness is all you want, that is fine. If response is what you want, you may need to have a number of channels for different segments of your audience, or at different stages of your communication strategy. Using channels for awareness can be the prelude for more direct engagement, such as a townhall or email blast. Do you have any other matrix, apart from response, to define what you want your audience to do? You may want them to act in a very specific way in response to your legal advice, or you may want to change a behaviour. In compliance initiatives within organizations, for instance, often what is wanted as a result of communication is a change in behaviour, which then creates compliance actions.

The last question is the hardest, though it can be answered if you have precision around the previous question. How will you know if your communication has made any difference? Henry Ford famously said that he knew half of his advertising worked; he just didn't know which half. Awareness, which is what a lot of advertising is about, is difficult to measure. If you give an instruction and it is carried out, you have a very transactional measure of success. The more we look at relationship and patterns of behaviour, the harder it is to measure the impact of communication. We can tell someone something that impacts them much later, sometimes years later. If you use communication agencies, this is the hardest part of the relationship to manage, as there is much work done around creating awareness that agencies cannot measure for you. This is not to say you should not work with them to create effective metrics, but a lot of the work is still based on confidence in the agency and trust in what communication does for you. Having asked the questions, let us look at the specific channels at your disposal.

5.4   The ubiquitous email

The most pervasive channel of communication is the email, but it is highly problematic. Certainly, it gets set information to a lot of people instantaneously. However, getting a message to someone is not the same as communicating it. That would be data processing, and sometimes that is the appropriate thing to do. Communication is where you add some value to the message or information.

It seems that everyone has a dirty little secret about why they are communicating, because all too often they don't tell the receiver of their email. You are the one who has decided to send the email, so you have the duty to make clear to your audience why you are sending the email, and what you expect them to do as a result of receiving your email. Awareness of this process will help you as much as it will help your audience. If everyone did this, we would have less email traffic for a start. Much email traffic is generated by lacking this clarity and direction, as people ignore, query or pass on unprocessed messages. Here is what you can do in emails. Break them down like a newspaper or news website. Your subject line is the headline. The headline is not written to state a fact or push your point of view, rather it is used to draw the audience to the story, and that is done by understanding what is of interest to the audience. The more relevant and engaging your subject line, the more you prepare your audience for your message. Thus, emails with 'FW:' or 'RE:' before them may be ignored because the subject line was written by someone else for reasons that may be different from the original purpose, or written for the interest of a different audience. It may also just be spammed out. Emails with 'FYI' or 'FAO' in them may be fine if it is clear why this is of interest or for action; but may be less interesting if someone doesn't understand why you are sending the email. The key here, like using language, is to ensure you are not making your audience work any harder than they have to, and to remember you know why you are sending the email, but at point of receipt your audience may not know the why or the wherefore.

Once into the body of the email you can structure the information, to make clear any segmentation of your audience which may be helpful. This starts with an introductory sentence explaining why you are sending the email. This step is often overlooked, as people launch into why they are sending the email, rather than identifying the interest of the reader as to why they ought to read your email. If there are attachments or information that only applies to a certain segment, this should be clearly flagged, so only those who need to will look at what you want them to look at. In terms of who is included or copied on the email, this also needs sound judgement and is fraught with difficulty. When you complain about getting too many emails, you are complaining about people's behaviour, and this aspect is the most revealing. People copy to say 'look at me!', or to get someone else in trouble – 'look at them!' – and so on. We all know the issue, and it takes individual and organizational commitment to stamp out this behavioural problem. The problem is not particularly new. Even in the bad old days of handwritten memos, the observation was made that memos were sent to protect the sender rather than inform the receiver. Emails have exacerbated the problem greatly, and it is less productive and more problematic. At the heart of the problem lies a fundamental lack of trust in our colleagues and our processes, and perhaps as an organization the issue ought to be given some attention.

Checking emails, according to a McKinsey study,[3] leads to the average professional spending 28% of the work day reading and answering email. The study explains for the average full-time worker in the US, this amounts to 2.6 hours spent and 120 messages received per day. On average, professionals check their email 15 times per day, or every 37 minutes. In terms of response expectations, only 11% of customers/clients and 8% of co-workers expect a response within less than an hour. About 40% of people expect a response in about an hour. If people checked their email hourly rather than every 37 minutes, they could cut six email checks from their daily routine. More concerning is the finding from a Loughborough University study[4] which found that it takes 64 seconds for people to return to work at the same rate they left it. Rather like an athlete recovering from a 100-metre race, recalibrating their breathing, the brain needs this time to change its attention from one email to the next. If the study is right, this means for every 60 emails to read, you are losing an hour of your life, and even more if we take into account important, stressful or amusing emails that may hold our attention longer. There are a lot of necessary emails, so I suggest this needs attention in your life. However, it is a shared responsibility, and if we all work in our various communities or ecosystems to write better emails, we will reduce traffic and be more effective. There are other aspects of a psychological nature to take into consideration,[5] in respect to how emails create pressure and are more of a distraction than a source of multitasking, itself being a suspect notion as well.

---

[3]   https://www.mckinsey.com/industries/technology-media-and-telecommunications/our-insights/the
     -social-economy
[4]   T. Jackson, R. Dawson and D. Wilson, *The Cost of Email Interruption* (2001), Journal of Systems and
     Information Technology, Vol. 5, No. 1, pp. 81–92.
[5]   https://edition.cnn.com/2005/WORLD/europe/04/22/text.iq/; https://www.apa.org/research/action/
     multitask; https://www.ics.uci.edu/~gmark/CHI2005.pdf

5.5   Social media

Social media is the most dynamic and ubiquitous of channels in use today, but organizations are still struggling to create effective strategies for making the best use of social media. There is a specific reason for this, namely fear. Organizations are fearful of the security issues, but also of dealing with the responses received – often more of a backlash – in social media. Such backlash, which mutates into hate speech on many an occasion, is an area where there is both a concern for lawyers in how it should be treated legally, as much as how they should make best use of the channels. Cardiff University and Mishcon de Reya co-authored a report[6] on online hate speech entitled 'Hatred Behind the Screens', which highlights the nature, scale and impact of online abuse as well as the existing legal framework and potential routes for redress. The authors call for tougher internet regulation and a statutory duty of care – enforced by an independent regulator – to make big tech companies take more responsibility for the safety of their users and for dealing with harm caused by content or activity on their services. The report explains how online hate speech had risen over the previous two years and how certain 'trigger' events, such as terror attacks, general elections and the Brexit referendum, can lead to spikes in the volume of online hate speech. Covid seems to have since highlighted this problem even more. This environment is the same environment, or ecosystem, that lawyers are stepping into when they make use of social media. Online hate speech is on the rise, and damaging to its victims, and there is no clear mechanism in place to address it. Lawyers need to be aware of these concerns when going onto social media for themselves, though there is still a need to find a coherent approach for stakeholders and society as a whole.

The interesting thing about social media is how it blurs the lines of formal and informal communication. World leaders have taken to social media to bypass a whole apparatus of communication controls and gatekeepers to communicate directly with citizens. The most dramatic example of this is former United States President Donald Trump, whose famous early morning tweets kept his communications people, diplomats and party

---

[6]   Matthew Williams, HateLab, Cardiff University and Mishcon de Reya, *Hatred Behind the Screens: A Report on the Rise of Online Hate Speech*, https://www.mishcon.com/upload/files/Hate%20Crime%20report.pdf

members busy every time he decided to tweet something. His approach was very informal, often to the extent of appearing abusive, but they were also very effective on occasion. Not only did he bypass the apparatus, but he often used language and conveyed thoughts that had been largely unprocessed, shooting from the hip as the saying goes. However, it is also a formal kind of communication, because he was still tweeting as an office-holder, and often referred to formal processes, even if it was often done to undermine them, and thus it had consequences.

5.6   Face-to-face communication

When meeting in person, before you say anything to anyone, you have already communicated. Your very appearance and mannerisms are immediately interpreted. If someone is surprised by what you say, do or respond, that has been communicated before they say a word that seeks to rationalize their response. People have different thresholds in this respect, and some are fortunate enough to have good 'poker faces', but even then they are read, there is an interpretation. Whether the interpretation of your body is accurate is another matter, and change in that interpretation becomes negotiated through the ensuing encounter via body and words spoken. There are any number of videos and courses tackling body language, and it is not within the remit of this book to detail this material. Suffice to say, such training is well worth going through. Of particular value is role-playing within training, which includes filming the role-play exercise. It is valuable to play out how you are communicating on the issue, and very instructive to see how your body performs on film. I have seen many an executive believe they did a good job, but when the film rolls they see just how problematic their performance was. This is because they focused on what they thought were the right things to say, but didn't pay attention to what their bodies were saying. The added difficulty is that people may be interpreting your body language wrongly. In this case you have to have greater awareness in difficult contexts to ensure you minimize the room for misinterpretation and find ways to address any misapprehension by learning to read other people's body language effectively.

Lawyers need to have a good understanding of these face-to-face dynamics, and indeed many certainly appreciate these points in reference to the court as an environment sensitive to face-to-face communication. The point is also crucial to client relations. If you are advising a client, you can manage the relationship better when you are judicious in the meetings you have. Building a client list means building client relationships, and that is a communication skill. Yes, you give them the law and you may have a better grasp of the law than the next lawyer the client could consult. However, particularly in cases where clients are dealing with emotional issues, they may find it hard to deal with the law.

5.7   Death by PowerPoint

Formal presentations are a necessary part of lawyering, and the best presentations ensure they have a balance between style and substance. It is easy to listen to an entertaining speaker and then afterwards not remember anything they have said. This is a triumph of style over substance. A boring speech, where the audience is looking at the back of the head of the speaker as a slide is being read, fails to get attention and can lead to the audience tuning out. PowerPoint is one of the best, yet most abused, tools for effective presentation. There are some practical considerations in how to use PowerPoint, and how to manage the overall presentation effectively. The main problem is one of over-presenting. This occurs because there is over-preparation. While in-depth preparation is important, it should not dictate how you will in fact present the material. What is needed is brevity and editing. Overall, each PowerPoint should only use images and short points. It is there to highlight what you are saying, and to act as an aide-mémoire for you as the presenter and to hold the attention of your hearers, by reminding them what it is they are hearing. This also involves deciding what you don't want your audience to hear, or being prepared to have certain material at hand should the need arise.

Presenting at conferences is important both for professional profile and for the organization, yet not everyone is comfortable with doing this, and not everyone has been trained. A little training can go a long way in this respect, and again seeing film of yourself is useful. Equally, a person close to you – such as a spouse or long-term partner – can be your best critic, as they will pick up quickly on any personal tics in your presenting. There are different styles of presenting which suit different personality types. Some prefer a formal look, standing behind the podium. Others prefer to wander around stage, though technical set-ups may not always allow this. I would counsel that the latter style is always the most effective. Appearing informal and conversational creates a great sense of interaction. The more formal style is rather like the 'chalk and talk' style of a university professor, which is not always the best pedagogy either! Reading off a speech, lecture or a prepared paper is much rarer today. Some high-level speeches, particularly in political and bureaucratic settings, remain carefully drafted and read out. Many business leaders remain loyal to this format as well, in the belief it gives them and their thoughts some gravitas. However, it has limited appeal to audiences, who can now sit engaging with smartphones and laptops rather than listening to the supposed pearls of wisdom being dispensed. This is not to say such speeches should be done away with; rather it is a case of being sure that such a format will work with the audience and the message. What this format allows is control over what is said, word by word, crafted by speech writers or the presenter. It takes more gifted presence to turn a static page into a moving message, which can partly be done by the quality of writing but still requires effective delivery.

Another important aspect of presenting is editing. How often have you, or someone you have seen present, run out of time and speed up the presentation or stop prematurely? This is an issue of editing your material and pacing out how it will be delivered. You can do this on a simple basis by looking at how many slides you have and how much information each slide contains. Clearly it takes time, and 40 slides will not work for a ten-minute presentation. In some circumstances, like a board meeting, you may be rushed by having your time cut or the priorities of the board changing as they learn from what you present. A more nimble approach is required here. If you have all the important slides in your preparation carefully targeted to keep time, and then have appendices that can be drawn upon as and when required, you can keep up better. This technique is often used, but the editing process still leaves many presentations too long. The secret of board meetings is that members just want to know you have done your homework and have tested your data and done your lobbying in the right places. Members usually don't want to hear you, and if they ask a question, you can say you have that data and turn to that if they want you to, but most of the time members are likely to be satisfied. You have the slides if they decide they do in fact want to take a deeper dive into the issue. If that happens, you ought to question your preparedness, and whether you have communicated, or failed to so do, in such a way that you left a gate open to a conversation that derails your presentation. If you present on the basis of what you want to say, rather than what the board wants to hear, you may well fall into this trap. This is another way in which the Dialogue Box can be used to prepare you for a specific occasion.

5.8   Meetings mania

One day people in organizations will be brave enough to admit that the vast majority of their meetings are rambling, 'small p' political or just plain ineffective because they lack clear agendas, get hijacked by particular people or have the wrong people attending. They also reveal behavioural traits in organizations, including the lack of trust between people and the lack of preparedness by people, partly caused by having to attend too many meetings! They can be used to coordinate matters effectively or to generate creative ideas, but probably only about 10% of the meetings you attend in your career ever fall within that category. Shorter meetings with fewer participants and more focus using a defined agenda could go a long way to making meetings more effective and collaborative. However, another problem with meetings is they are not always connected to other communication channels or to the objectives. All these defects leave many meetings to be mainly an information exchange, rather than meaningful and productive dialogue.

Townhalls and roadshows are a common form of meetings that are used to engage larger audiences, though falling short of mass communication. If well staged and purposefully targeted, they can be very effective channels of communication If, however, they are a parade of top people pontificating, they are less than optimal. The usual test applies as to who comprises your audience and what it is we want them to do. If you just want the audience to listen, the disappointing outcome is that few will. Well-focused panels, involving peers of your audience, are much more effective. For leaders, often less is more, but sadly events get constructed around the idea that more is more. It should also be understood that an audience has a memory. They have heard many of these messages before, and it is just a cold dish reheated – the outcome, again, is less than optimal. Hearing a company CEO say 'our number one priority is our people' and then ignore discussing the people's concerns breeds cynicism, especially since health and safety is a number one priority, or financial performance; how many number one priorities are there? Your audience also comprises individuals in different emotional places, and so a roaring speech will fall flat where there are deep concerns regarding the content. Your audience also comprises a transient congregation, with some new people who have not heard the messages before or who are missing vital references. Holding a townhall or roadshow needs to take all these differences into account and create a heatmap of the emotions and a stakeholder map of interests and knowledge. On a smaller scale are focus groups, brown-bag lunches, presentations and lectures. These are all good means to communicate when they are focused on a theme of interest to an audience, rather than simply about you or your organization.

5.9   Print versus digital

A regular concern is whether to use print or digital, with much support for the latter and going all-electronic. This is one of those situations that devolves into being an either/or situation. The best solution is to do both. If we think back to the early days of colour photography, everyone wanted colour, while black and white was seen as old-fashioned. Likewise in recent times, everyone wanted to go digital. Yet, in the photography market, black and white came back with power because it offered contrast, and so we are used to seeing both types of photography in use. Likewise print versus digital. There is in the UK magazine market a plethora of magazines targeting the young. The logic of all-digital is to save money and the environment, but also assumes the young prefer digital and it is only older generations that want print. The magazines targeting the young are amongst the most hip and cultural areas, such as music. What is best is a balance between print and digital, linked to each other as well.

There is a place for brochures, posters and other communication collateral, and again the same rules apply of relevance and appeal. As a rule of thumb, if you need to reach blue-collar workers in an organization, print tends to be more effective, while for office workers it is more likely to be digital. A good option is to do both. We have seen how newspapers have managed to survive by offering both print and digital packages. The smartphone has made digital even more appealing, but even then people see the smartphone as a personal space, and companies may be crossing boundaries for some users. One important aspect of these forms of communication collateral is the visual element. Making things look nice is an obvious point, but it is also about making the visual meaningful. Lots of pictures of generic scenes or senior people in the organization may be less effective than having readers and their peers pictured.

Digital platforms obviously provide powerful channels, and lawyers spend a lot of their time working via such media and use them as primary communication channels, but this requires care. Making communication disruptive, by interrupting people's work or being distracting, does not help. Having a logon announcer is useful, but again needs to be used purposefully and with relevance. Intranets and the internet, along with video, radio and podcasts are all powerful means of communication. However, like social media, you have to feed the beast. Links need to be maintained, and new content has to be in a constant flow. The rate of flow will also differ, in terms of daily, weekly, monthly and so on, but also the mix of content substance has to be carefully selected to ensure these media are engaging. Messaging services, such as texts and WhatsApp, can also be very useful when used properly. It has a conversational and informal feel to it. Such messaging is done on smartphones, so you have the same issue of crossing boundaries. A WhatsApp group can be productive, but started as a novelty, the channel use can quickly fall away if it is dominated by the few to the irritation of the many.

5.10   External media

Last but not least is the external media, meaning television and publishing outlets. These are important stakeholders for any lawyer to understand, and that they should, at some level, engage with. Most organizations have policies and control mechanisms for dealing with the media, including who can speak to the media. There are corporate communication specialists and departments on hand in most organizations acting as advisors and gatekeepers. There are many courses in media training, and doing these usually pays off. They are best done practically rather than from a book. However, there are a few things that it is useful to briefly highlight.

The media follows a narrative, and you may get caught up in the narrative without really trying or even realizing what is happening. You may be doing business with a company in the news, or someone may make baseless allegations against you or your company. If the media comes to your door, being silent is rarely a good move. A holding statement or giving a story that trumps the one against you are ways the story may be closed down. Off-the-record briefings are a powerful way of dealing with stories, as most professional journalists are reasonable, and if you explain a situation, they may be convinced there is not a story. Hiding from them will fuel their suspicions. If there is a 'bad' – but also true – story involving your organization, it is best to find ways to work with the media through the narrative. You might not stop things, but you can make them less damaging. However, be careful not to give oxygen to a story. There are many times when a story dies down only to be inflamed by someone who feels they have been ill-treated. Seeking exoneration may lead to building the story, and may be counterproductive. Advising your client on media work is a useful piece of legal work as well, which involves sensitivity to timing, impact and rationale.

Away from such big-picture stuff, there is much you can do to engage productively with the media and build your reputation. Such engagement can be via writing blogs or an op/ed for top publications, which can associate you with a major media brand such as *The Economist, New York Times*, the BBC or other such media. This builds your profile, and also helps you demonstrate thought leadership in your practice area. Building relationships with journalists can be helpful too, as they will discuss story ideas with you and include you in their articles as a contributor to the debate. On this level you are being part of the news, by offering quotes via interviews or other such participation.

A last word of caution on media work: the biggest problem for lawyers in media work is verbosity and the need for precision. This is not to make an insult, rather it is to again reverse polarities and see what priorities journalists and editors have in order for you to access the media effectively. When offering quotes, the lawyer needs to be concise. Offering full-paragraph answers is not fit for purpose. Mastering the art of the soundbite is not easy, because it does not leave much room for legal exactitude. It leaves too much open for the reader. Crafting quotes, or doing interviews, is fraught with difficulty as you are trying to balance legal correctness with the needs of media and consumers of the media. The Dialogue Box can help you in this process as well.

6   Changing paradigms – confront or collaborate?

6.1   The legal pyramid

To be provocative: less than 5% of cases end up in court, so what are you doing 95% of the time? The figures are commonly accepted,[1] and in being provocative the intent is not to be crass, but the figures do beg the question posed. One way of answering is to explain what is happening in legal terms. In criminal cases, the other 95% of cases are either dismissed or a plea bargain is arranged, leading to eventual dismissal or a lesser charge.[2] In the US, for instance, only 2% of federal criminal defendants go to trial, and most who do are found guilty.[3] In civil cases, the other 95% settle out of court. Notably in America, reputed to be the most litigious population in the world, there is a falling rate in filing lawsuits. Fewer than 2 in 1,000 people alleging civil wrongs filed tort lawsuits in 2015, in analysis of data collected by the National Center for State Courts. Back in 1993, the figure was 10 in 1,000.[4] The way I want to answer the question, without minimizing the importance of the more formal legal answer, is that 95% of the time there is a significant portion of activity involving lawyers negotiating, mediating and advising. The 95% of the time also

---

[1]   Marc Galanter and Mia Cahill, *'Most Cases Settle': Judicial Promotion and Regulation of Settlements* (1994), Stanford L. Rev., Vol. 46, pp. 1339–40; G.K. Hadfield, *Where Have All the Trials Gone? Settlements, Nontrial Adjudications, and Statistical Artifacts in the Changing Disposition of Federal Civil Cases* (2004), J. Empirical Legal Stud., Vol. 1, pp. 705–6; Frank E.A. Sander, *The Obsession with Settlement Rates* (1995), Negotiation J., Vol. 11, pp. 329–31. A useful review is offered in Daniel P. Kessler and Daniel L. Rubinfeld, *Empirical Study of the Civil Justice System*, in A. Mitchell Polinsky and Steven Shavell (eds), *Handbook of Law and Economics* Vol. 1 (Elsevier, 2007), pp. 381–3.

[2]   https://www.nytimes.com/2012/03/23/us/stronger-hand-for-judges-after-rulings-on-plea-deals.html

[3]   https://www.pewresearch.org/fact-tank/2019/06/11/only-2-of-federal-criminal-defendants-go-to -trial-and-most-who-do-are-found-guilty/

[4]   https://www.wsj.com/articles/we-wont-see-you-in-court-the-era-of-tort-lawsuits-is-waning-1500930572

involves a lot of communication. Legal activities involve a range of communication-based activities, but I contend that contentious litigation and ending up in court is often a failure in communication somewhere along the line.[5] Legal procedure is obviously understood by lawyers, and this is not a textbook chapter on the topic; rather I want to run through the various modes of legal procedure with a focus on the role of communication. The role of communication highlights the collaborative side of a process and profession that is often pictured or perceived as primarily adversarial.

Looking at legal activity as a pyramid allows us to explore an interesting dimension in respect to communication (Figure 6.1). As we move towards and through the court system, thereby heightening the contentious nature of proceedings, the level of transparency increases and the degree of control the parties have decreases. This greatly impacts communication and also calls upon different styles of communication and collaboration.

Figure 6.1   The legal pyramid

At the base of the pyramid, everyday legal transactions are quite straightforward, with the involvement of a lawyer being integral to the legal work of creating terms and conditions, contracts and other activities that make a bus ticket or a grocery bill – doing some business together – for the large

---

5   R.E. Miller and A. Sarat, *Grievances, Claims, and Disputes: Assessing The Adversary Culture* (1980–81), Law and Society Review, Vol. 15, pp. 525–66.

part non-contentious. Where differences or exceptions occur in such everyday legal relations, or where there is more transactional complexity, lawyers may need to get involved. Even then, most of these actions can pass by with relative ease – which is not to say it does not involve much skill and hard work. A client needs to buy a house, and the norm is for the conveyancing to proceed relatively smoothly for most buyers and sellers. A lawyer may offer advice, testifying wills and undertake other legal administrative work, again quite smoothly. These two levels of the pyramid don't concern us in this chapter, except to say the focus of attention at these levels is still to ensure clarity in expression by drafters and a focus on the need for lawyers to communicate awareness and education on such transactions proportionate to their scope. The focus in this chapter is where there is some form of dispute, resulting from something going awry, whether it be in an everyday transaction or broader areas of legal advice.

When things go wrong, or there is a disconnect, matters can quickly escalate or devolve, and dealing with this can be as much a communication issue as a legal problem. If, as this book advocates in proposing a more communicative approach for lawyers, a more collaborative space is needed to engineer a better future, there has to be less room for contentious approaches. Alternative dispute resolution (ADR) is preached, and many law societies have sent out notes promoting the use of ADR before court, but in practice the question is, as the saying goes, moot. As an aside, law schools have traditionally promoted moots as the highlight of legal engagement, and hold many moots competitions, but few law graduates will ever argue in court. They will, at various points and in various ways, negotiate, mediate and advise, and it is good to see the emergence of more competitions in these areas – which is not to denigrate or belittle moots; they are a specialized and impressive skill. What it does suggest is that legal education is skewed in the way it presents the law, with courts as the pinnacle of achievement, but divorced from everyday legal reality. This is not to say the courts are less important; obviously they remain hugely important. However, perhaps it is time to give a better place to ADR alongside moots to highlight that the court is ultimately a failure in law rather than a great success.

Having offered a provocative start, let us then move on to look at communication through the arc of resolving disputes in the legal context, from client meetings through to the courts. Developing the communicating lawyer means assessing communication in court and other formal situations, and in turn to look at alternative dialogue such as negotiation, mediation and arbitration. The role of neutrality, persuasion and manipulation forms a central theme in this discussion and sets the scene for using the Dialogue Box in Part II.

6.2 Changing courts

The courts are under great strain in every country, and the legal profession is pushing for change. The Covid-19 pandemic has become a catalyst for change in the courts, with many moving to remote courts and rolling out online courts. The desire to innovate the courts predates Covid-19, and there have been some innovative developments. One area where reform and innovation are being pushed, apart from in the commercial courts, is in family law. In 2020, the Saudi Arabian Justice Ministry launched a programme for divorce by text for women, which allows Saudi women to receive a divorce notice by text message, ensuring they know about their marital status change. The Saudi Justice Ministry said the move is 'aimed at protecting the rights of female clients'. Before this reform, women in Saudi could be the last to know they have been divorced, since men often registered divorce deeds at the courts without telling their wives. It is now mandatory for a woman to be notified by text message when a court issues her husband's divorce decree, allowing women to get their alimony rights when they're divorced, and means any powers of attorney are issued before the divorce to avoid misuse. Women will be able to confirm their marital status through the ministry's website or at their local court.

In contrast, the UK has also made use of enhanced technology and communication to improve the, often emotional, process of divorce. The online divorce service that was rolled out across England and Wales on 1 May 2018 offers prompts and guidance to assist people in completing their application, and uses clear, non-technical language. The whole process can be completed online, including payment and uploading supporting evidence. More than 1,000 petitions were issued through the new system during the testing phase – with 91% of people saying they were satisfied with the service.[6] Under the old system, court staff spent 13,000

---

[6] https://www.gov.uk/government/news/fully-digital-divorce-application-launched-to-the-public

hours dealing with complex paper divorce forms, but the online service has quickly contributed to a 95% drop in the number of applications being returned because of mistakes, when compared with paper forms. Between January and the end of April 2018, from the circa 1,100 applications, only 0.6% were rejected. Feedback from users of this service has been largely positive, according to the Ministry of Justice, which provided stories of success. Rebecca, who did not want her last name to be used, received legal confirmation of her divorce 11.5 weeks after submitting her application – the paper process takes around six months. She said the service made the process 'so much less painful than it could have been, especially as a disabled person. The service was a lot easier because I use a wheelchair and didn't have to go out, and I also found it very easy as an autistic person to get support from the team when I had questions.' Elaine Everett, who was separated for more than two years before applying for and getting her divorce, explained, 'It was marvellous, pain-free and less stressful than the paper form, which I tried several years ago to complete but got fed up of it being rejected.' The online divorce service is part of a £1 billion programme to transform the court system and make it quicker, more accessible and easier to use for everyone.

Speaking on the launch of the service, Sir James Munby, President of the Family Division of the High Court, said, 'The online divorce pilot has been a triumphant success and shows, to my mind conclusively, that this is, must be the way of the future.' These changes in the court are focused not just on access to justice, but also to cut the cost of the legal system by making it more efficient. This service has made the divorce process more transactional, and thus disintermediates a few steps for lawyers as well, meaning revenue has to come from somewhere else.[7]

Such change can do a lot to reduce costs and raise efficiency, but effective communication is also a way to reduce pressures on the court system. Changes in how we communicate can ease the problem by stopping many cases from entering the court system in the first place, and can help stop the process getting out of control when it does so. The solutions developed in Saudi Arabia and England and Wales, as well as elsewhere, are technology solutions that are also in part communication solutions. They create a level of transparency and clarity that helps avoid some of

---

[7] R.H. Mnookin and L. Kornhauser, *Bargaining in the Shadow of the Law: The Case of Divorce* (1979), Yale Law Journal, Vol. 88, pp. 950–97.

the messiness and misunderstandings that come along with many legal disputes.[8]

BOX 6.1 TAKING SMALL DIGITAL STEPS ...

There are other examples of government court reforms in train, aiming to make access to justice easier. UK steps taken include:

- **Small claims**: A digital system that makes it quicker and easier for people to claim money owed, resolve disputes out of court and access mediation.[9]
- **Tax appeals**: A new service that allows people to submit their tax appeals online – drastically cutting the number of applications being returned as incomplete or inaccurate.
- **Fare penalties**: A paperless system, in operation at Lavender Hill Magistrates Court, which means thousands of offenders caught dodging fares or using fraudulent tickets can now be punished more swiftly and effectively.[10]

6.3 Negotiation

In a successful negotiation you are trying to get the most out of a situation, but not in a vacuum. You are involved in a process where individuals have shared and opposing interests, and they recognize there needs to be an agreement to work towards a settlement that works for all. To achieve this involves a dialogue that works toward carving out a space for producing an agreement. All relationships operate in a negotiated space, and the process of negotiation is a purposeful act aimed at finding a neutral space for dialogue in order to reach an agreement where each party gets something. This is partly done by exploring a situation and relationship, and partly by persuasion. Communicating lawyers must hone the art of being exploratory and persuasive at different points in their work. You

---

[8] For further discussion of online courts, I refer the reader to Richard Susskind, *Online Courts* (OUP, Oxford, 2019), opportunely, as it turned out, published at the outset of Covid-19. My review of the book was published in the *Canadian Journal of Law and Technology*, https://digitalcommons .schulichlaw.dal.ca/cjlt/vol18/iss2/5/

[9] https://www.gov.uk/government/news/quicker-way-to-resolve-claim-disputes-launched-online

[10] https://www.gov.uk/government/news/swifter-justice-for-london-fare-dodgers

need this art in order to bring clients into the realm of robust legal advice, as this is a space you are in fact negotiating. You also need it if you are involved in formal negotiations, which may be over a contentious issue or a business merger deal, for instance. This can be done more effectively when you position a solution that clients and other parties believe strikes a reasonable balance of risk and reward. In a negotiation you are looking to identify and utilize appropriate styles and tactics, and then to conduct the negotiation in a systematic and logical manner. This requires effective communication, which includes how you handle yourself professionally and how you understand and engage with your negotiation or dialogue partner.

There are constraints to your negotiation. One is that a negotiation is managed within a professional code of conduct and based on ethical standards. There are also emotional constraints, where you or your dialogue partner may find it difficult to discuss certain topics easily or even rationally. There may be emotional responses to certain words or structure of language, such as how something is phrased or explained. There are time constraints, which may be because there are pressures to get a deal done or some other deadline, with timelines for various steps in the process as well. Some of these temporal aspects may be within your control; others may be imposed by your negotiating partner, or sources external to the parties. In preparing your negotiation you may need to do a fair amount of coalition-building, which might be done internally, with others in the industry or other influencers, or even with your negotiating partner. If you are to be successful, you need to explore your own bias and that of others and seek to create an atmosphere of inclusivity. Failing to do so can easily alienate your negotiating partners, which can be an emotional response or a reasoned disdain towards your perceived lack of understanding. Some of this bias may be unconscious bias, so work has to be done to understand your dialogue partners in the first place and to question assumptions you might be making. This is especially true of cross-cultural communication, which is not just a geographical but a demographical challenge. As an answer as to what it takes to pursue a successful negotiation, the checklist in Box 6.2 serves as a useful set of needs.

BOX 6.2 NEGOTIATION CHECKLIST[11]

- good interpersonal skills;
- willingness to prepare;
- ability to deploy tactics;
- knowledge of strengths and weaknesses;
- knowledge of client needs and interests;
- knowledge of opponents' needs and interests;
- inner confidence;
- ability to decide fundamentally what the other side wants;
- understanding of what client is willing to give up to get other side to settle;
- your personality, questioning ability and responding to patterns and changes.

Traditionally, negotiation texts have regarded emotion as an impediment to reaching constructive agreements. For example, in *Getting to Yes*, Roger Fisher, William Ury, and Bruce Patton say, 'separate the people from the problem'.[12] The authors tell us we need preparation to identify core interests, walkaway options, assess how other parties see their choices, running the numbers, scouting the marketplace, and having a plan B. However, and this is a big however, I would add to this that emotions count in real-life deal-making and dispute resolution. You need to understand, channel, and learn from your emotions in order to adapt to the situation at hand and engage others successfully. This means being emotionally prepared to negotiate as well, and thus separating the people from the problem is an aspiration to be taken with caution, because we cannot treat the emotion and rational actions in a disconnected way. There are many, often trivial, events that trigger reactions which can affect negotiations. A bad trip into work, a sick child at home, news that your pay rise didn't come through – these are the kinds of event, minor and major, that can spill over into behaviours in a negotiation. Awareness of this possibility will improve your odds of recognizing the effects of such triggers in the heat of the moment, as the temperature of the discussion rises or pressures on time impact discussions. Not managing these trig-

---

[11] John Burwell Garvey and Charles B. Craver, *Alternative Resolution: Negotiation, Mediation, Collaborative Law and Arbitration* (LexisNexis, New York, 2013).

[12] Roger Fisher, William Ury and Bruce Patton, *Getting to Yes* (3rd edn, Penguin, New York, 2011).

gers may cause you or your dialogue partner to crack under a strain that has been growing, rooted in earlier or exterior events, as you were negotiating. It is important therefore to recognize any emotions, so you can act to defuse an incidental emotion in your counterpart, by being aware that their mood may have nothing to do with you. If you suspect that the other side's feelings are incidental to the negotiation, encourage them to connect to the source of these feelings. Open-ended questions such as 'Terrible day out, isn't it?' or 'How was the drive over?' can go a long way toward minimizing or neutralizing the influence of negative emotions on judgements and choices.

There are various stages to negotiation, and different authors and educators use different names and number them differently. My intent is not to go through the various stages in detail; instead I want to highlight aspects of negotiation in terms of communication and how the Dialogue Box (Figure 6.2), which you will learn to use in Part II of this book, can help you. In using the Dialogue Box, we start with the Intelligence Zone, where you will want to prepare yourself to state what it is you want to achieve. In the Emotion Zone you will want to express how you feel about the situation you are negotiating about. In the Interpretation Zone you will want to explain the reasons for your needs and emotions. You will want to go through the same process to understand your dialogue partner. You will also be dealing with both positive and negative thoughts and feelings. This way you can then create an effective narrative for the situation in which you are negotiating, and to find the dialogue language that will allow you to create a negotiating space to create solutions and reach optimal outcomes in your negotiation. After learning how you work through the Dialogue Box, you may want to come back here again later. The Dialogue Box will give you the preparation step that can help you navigate the other three stages of negotiation.

1. preparation;
2. opening and proposing;
3. bargaining;
4. closing.

As you progress your negotiations, you will evolve your Dialogue Box in an iterative process, because as the negotiation makes headway, the variables in each zone I have mentioned will change, and this impacts the narrative – the negotiation itself – and the dialogue language, until such time you reach an agreement. The Dialogue Box is a tool you can use to

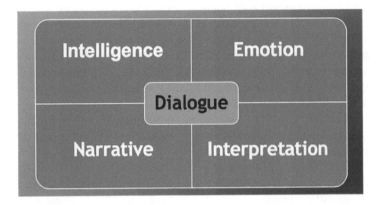

Figure 6.2   The Dialogue Box

mediate the situation for yourself. It brings the process into a framework you will find helps you through each of the negotiation stages.

There are three more aspects of negotiation to flag. First, negotiators pay attention to climate setting, trying to get the atmosphere of the negotiation to be favourable to having positive dialogue and reaching agreement. The communicative needs here include the physical language of the climate, which means where you sit and how you sit. There is the need to manage the language you use, and what language you want to avoid. You want to set a certain temperature and tempo for the dialogue, which means looking at the language again, the use of pauses and being responsive to negotiation partners. The Dialogue Box will help in this process as well. Second, you are in a bargaining situation, which means communicating and listening to what the other negotiator wants. If you are intent on getting what you want, that is fine, but you also need awareness and responsiveness to what the other side wants. This process can be derailed by misunderstanding or having preconceptions in your mind about what the other side 'really' wants. The level of transparency and willingness to be open in words and body language become pivotal here in communication terms. Third, you want to close, which is not just closure in the sense of what deal is done, but how negotiation partners feel about the agreement in terms of reaching emotional closure.

A last note on mediation before moving on is to be aware that in negotiating you have a higher level of autonomy than you will have in subsequent means of dealing with contentious matters. You have more leeway to move your position, and more effect in your efforts to move the position of your negotiation partners. The major reason for this is that it just involves you and your negotiation partners. You, and they, may answer to people internally, but you have more autonomy in that process as well, as you are the appointed negotiator and seen to be in control. The negotiation that does not reach agreement is one over which you have lost a degree of control. Once you leave the negotiation room without a deal, you are opening the door to others to intervene or play a role in reaching agreement, and you will not be in a direct negotiating relationship but one mediated by another. You may at some point return to the negotiating table, but the relationship will have changed, and the threat of further mediated steps may curb your sense of freedom to negotiate. Bear this in mind as you prepare your negotiation approach, and remind yourself before you get to a stage where you think you have to leave the room, as you may later regret you did so.

BOX 6.3 GETTING IN THE ZONE

Like athletes and other competitors, you need to get into the zone emotionally, and these are the questions you can ask yourself to prepare and set yourself emotionally for the negotiation ahead:

- How do you, and how do you want, to feel going into the negotiation?
- Why are you feeling the way you do?
- What can you do beforehand to put yourself in an ideal emotional state?
- What can throw you off balance emotionally during a negotiation?
- What can you do in the midst of a negotiation to regain your balance?
- How do you want to feel when you're finished?

Much of what is discussed in this section on negotiation applies to other forms of dispute resolution, but there are some specific aspects in these other realms to highlight, starting with mediation.

6.4   Mediation

In mediation we move on from having Party A and Party B to involving a mediator, because the situation is such that insufficient progress has been made, though there is some residual form of willingness to nego- tiate. This changes the communication dynamics, though, as stated, many of the same insights in the previous section apply here as well. In mediation, as in negotiation, the law is a constant, and both sides know this. They may have different interpretations of the weight of the law and undergo legal risk analysis as to their chances should the dispute go all the way to court. However, there are a variety of reasons why the parties might want to avoid going this far. Aside from the cost of a more con- tentious dispute, perhaps the primary reasons are the desire to maintain some sort of ongoing relationship with the other party or the desire to avoid reputational damage that could affect other relationships and their place in the market. The same sort of preparation is required, so you know what you want from the mediation, and know what the other side wants, but the outcome is mediated because neither side knows how to break their positions down to meet at an agreeable point. Again, similar tactics are involved, such as taking breaks and timing when to reveal your points. If the mediation has arisen out of a negotiation, many of these points are already known, so a major part of the mediation strategy involves trying to understand the role and impact of mediator.

Mediation is a communicative process of facilitating and channelling negotiations between the parties where they have come into difficulties in dealing directly with each other. How the positions of the parties are formulated is also done in a different communicative way, whereby the mediator is able to suggest potentially mutually acceptable proposals for settlement in a way that may be more neutral than the parties themselves have been able to attempt. The mediator can also use more manipulative communication to cajole or influence the parties in a particular direction to move towards an agreed outcome. The Dialogue Box, if used success- fully, should have already given you insights into the answer to this, and perhaps if used successfully you would have found an outcome without need of a mediator to bring one or both sides to their senses. Specifically, the Dialogue Box can map out your strategy in the following five-step process:

1. **Intelligence**: Statement of the problem by the parties to frame the issues factually.
2. **Emotion**: Information-gathering, time, taking the temperature and understanding relationships.
3. **Interpretation**: Identification of the problems, insight into common goals.
4. **Narrative**: Understanding the settlement landscape, bargaining scenarios and generating your options.
5. **Dialogue**: Moving towards a solution and reaching an agreement.

In this process the key note is the impartiality of the mediator, acting as a channel of communication. The mediator as a facilitator does not act as a judge, nor do they give legal advice or make decisions about the dispute, and of course the parties can choose whether to accept or reject the outcome. However, they do influence the outcome in their act of 'shuttle diplomacy'. The mediator is entrusted with the 'true' position of each party as to where it will settle and uses this to work with the other side in attempts to bring the parties closer together. This takes much judgement and tests the communication skills of the mediator themselves. Like any channel, how the communication is framed or reframed between the parties is open to distortion. The better or more experienced the mediator, usually the less the distortion, but even with the best of motives distortion can and does happen, for all the usual reasons of communication dynamics. The basis of the agreement is fundamentally a voluntary process, which retains a level of confidentiality and a degree, albeit lessened, of control over what works best for them. Though this is an indirect process, it is also forward-looking, as how the process is communicated and the eventual settlement arrived at can allow the parties to maintain their business relationship if they wish, and they can also strike agreements on solutions that could be beyond the scope of a judge or an arbitrator.

Mediation works as a communicative process because of its consensual nature, leaving it open for either party to walk away. It allows parties to engage more indirectly, thus avoiding concerns of being seen to lose face. It is still a relatively collaborative process, and hence more cost-effective, particularly when compared with litigation. The parties set the timetable, which may also be mediated for them, so there is a higher likelihood of a speedy and efficient resolution. As a confidential process, and without prejudice (up to the point where agreement is reached), mediation keeps the dispute out of public view. Once agreed, the agreement is legally enforceable, and because it is a mediated agreement, the possibility of default on payment, which is a distinct possibility, is less likely because the parties have a stake in the agreement they have arrived at rather than feeling it has been forced upon them. The process is essentially non-legal, with the mediator informally putting forward proposals that may work to resolve dispute, but not necessarily based on an analysis of their legal positions. The process is non-binding, and thus legally the parties retain control of the outcome of the mediation, and they can always move up the legal pyramid of dispute if they believe it is required at any point. While these last points describe the law, they also say something about how the law is communicated and how communication affects the choices parties make in law.

6.5   Arbitration

Over the last 60 years there has been a vast increase in the number of international arbitrations. Arbitration has been chosen over other methods of dispute resolution due to the enforceability of awards, flexibility, and the ability to avoid specific legal systems or national courts. However, this is weighed against increasing costs, a lack of effective sanctions and a lack of power in relation to third parties. The inherent flexibility and adaptability of arbitration is also countered by increased efforts to increase regulation and structure around the arbitral process. There is some concern that there could be an 'over-regulation' of arbitration, which is in turn met with concerns that the privacy of arbitration is contrary to public interests. This debate will rumble on for the foreseeable future, and a lot may depend on your worldview in respect to the balance between private and public interest. Technology has also come to impact arbitration, especially in document review, presentation of evidence and document security.

There are important cross-border dynamics in disputes that correlate to communication. In a mediation there is little difference in choosing mediation in respect to international versus domestic disputes. However, there is a marked difference when it comes to arbitration and litigation. In cross-border disputes, there is more of a preference for arbitration, while the reverse is true in litigation. This is due in part to questions of enforceability, but it is also a question of communication. In a domestic dispute, dealing with similar cultures is easier, whereas a cross-border dispute may take the parties into less familiar territory, where they want a more formal process to get them through the dispute, where the different language and cultural issues may also be mediated for the parties.

Another aspect that impacts communication is the choice of arbitrators, who can be either lawyers or non-lawyers. Some have been judges in the public courts, while others are non-judges who have been solicitors or barristers. Arbitrators are commonly chosen because they possess specialist knowledge and expertise that is more valuable than strict legal knowledge. Some arbitrators are naturally a combination of these. Judges turning their hand to arbitration often remark they find moving from being a judge in the public courts into arbitration as a culture shock for them and have realized they had a lot of new things to learn.

Choosing arbitrators is thus a matter of negotiation for the parties, and they can be named at the beginning or decided later. This illustrates there is a residual collaborative approach to solving the problem. This has given rise to Med/Arb, a flexible approach whereby parties may move back and forth between mediation and arbitration. One constraint on the choice of arbitrators is that one of the three, and there are commonly three, is neutral and the decision often turns on the neutral member. This in itself is thus a matter of negotiation, because if the parties cannot agree, a neutral may be chosen by another interested party to avoid impasse and frustrate the parties involved. Once past this step, the parties decide on how matters are to be conducted, the arbitral seat, how the process will be financed, and detailed provisions such as pleadings, orals, and time limits. The *Compromis* may detail the evidence, experts, visits, provisional measures, languages, how the decision is taken, separate opinions, and publication. Parties can be ad hoc or follow established practice. Hence, we have a fair degree of control in a consensual process that is private in nature and operation, and it still remains a somewhat closed communication. The incentive to arbitrate is that the alternatives are either to return to mediation or go to court, and thus the communication dynamics are a tipping point towards a more private and collaborative process or a public and contentious process.

The advantage to arbitration is that it extends across all industries, whether it is banks or builders, parties can go to arbitration together. It is cheaper or more cost-effective than litigation, though increasingly not as cost-effective as in times past. It is faster with fewer delays, though again not as much as previously. There is perceived minimal judicial bias, which is a concern when a case goes to court, where parties may feel as a company they may be made a public example of, or there may be an unconscious bias on the part of a judge based on the type of business an organization does or when it has come up against civil society. An arbitrator experienced in a particular sector may understand more the nuances involved in that sector, and be able to reason more fairly on this basis. Arbitration also allows greater scope for confidentiality and protecting trade secrets, whereas a public court may demand disclosure as a matter of course or for specific reasons. There are thus a number of commercial control issues at stake, and more may be lost going into court – that is a risk management decision the parties have to weigh. All of these aspects require different approaches to communication, and also offer clients different reputational challenges. These are aspects lawyers need to take account of in the legal strategy

Turning to relating the use of the Dialogue Box in arbitration, this is how we can map out the five steps outlined earlier to explore the issues and questions in play:

1. **Intelligence**: Mapping the formal process, business environment, framing the issues factually.
2. **Emotion**: Still room for negotiation, but more use of manipulation and persuasion?
3. **Interpretation**: Less clarity on common goals, may involve more dealing with experts and disputed or complex evidence?
4. **Narrative**: Ensuring a compelling picture to move towards a solution.
5. **Dialogue**: Reaching an agreement that may be more based on persuasion and manipulation than on neutral territory.

BOX 6.4 THE DIALOGUE BOX GUIDELINES

Here are some helpful guidelines based on the Dialogue Box:

- **Intelligence**: Create and maintain a consistent communication strategy by defining your facts and objectives. Develop your messages with consistency, so that in briefing to media and others they all match, whether they are on or off the record, or for purposes of background. Journalists will exploit the gaps. This a zone of the Dialogue Box lawyers are traditionally comfortable with, but they are not so attuned to what comes next in the Dialogue Box.

- **Emotion**: Have a keen sense of your audience and their emotional make-up, and create a heatmap of specific audiences, both internal and external, which will give you a better sense of how you can emotionally manage and influence.
- **Interpretation**: To deal with Q&As and do effective scenario planning, you want to know what other stakeholders think and relate this to how your client and their opponents think. You want to capture as many points of view as possible, positive and negative, for and against you. This can be done by interview, public meetings, focus groups. You can also include other disciplines into the mix to understand these dynamics, including evidence from neuroscience and behavioural economics, for instance.
- **Narrative**: Your public presentation must avoid thinking you have control and that all you need to do is just keep telling people only what you want them to hear. People are not stupid, and they will react to what meets their interests. An effective narrative will help you understand the behaviours you want to influence.
- **Dialogue**: The narrative you develop will keep your strategy on track, and prepare the ground for creating a vocabulary of words and a grammar that can best guide your strategy and frame your argument to match the emotion as well as the legal facts of the case.

There are nuances in the differences between how you might develop your Dialogue Box in mediation versus arbitration. However, the paradigm takes a rather more dramatic shift when we come to litigation.

6.6 Litigation

Litigation takes communication to another level, distinguished by the use of public communications,[13] which has been in the background with other

---

[13] See: Thomas Beke, *Litigation Communication: Crisis and Reputation Management in the Legal Process* (Springer, 2014); D.S. Bailis and R.J. MacCoun, *Estimating Liability Risks with the Media as Your Guide: A Content Analysis of Media Coverage of Tort Litigation* (1996), Law and Human Behavior, Vol. 20, pp. 419–29; B.H. Bornstein, B.L. Whisenhunt, R.J. Nemeth and D.L. Dunaway,

dispute mechanisms. While arbitral decisions may be publicized, there is not as much media interest around the other dispute mechanisms. After all, the purpose is to be low key. In litigation the dynamics change quite dramatically. Public relations consultancies will also be involved as professional communicators, and there are a number of them that offer this as a specialist service. The current trend may be traced back to the end of the last millennia and the Woolf Report. *PR Week* reported on the rising trend of litigation PR in 2000:

> The Woolf reforms to civil justice – which came into effect last year – place great stress on lawyers trying to settle disputes before wasting court time. As that becomes a requirement for the legal profession, the battle to capture public opinion and save or protect corporate and individual reputations is becoming an increasingly open field.[14]

The article noted that one of the founders of the genre is New York's Howard J Rubinstein, a lawyer and PR advisor to Rupert Murdoch for 26 years, who said, 'When we started it was not an accepted method of building support for a legal case. Now every high profile case has PR people on both sides talking to the press.'[15] The idea of just saying 'no comment' is not sustainable, which is not to say it is never appropriate. You need an active communications strategy that is adaptable, because the speed of the communication environment is never to be underestimated. You can lose your company or reputation in a day or become beholden to an individual in a David v Goliath struggle.

Communications outside the courtroom puts your dispute into the public glare, and you may find yourself and your client fighting on multiple fronts.[16] In this instance, what is said and done in one place can impact

---

Pretrial Publicity and Civil Cases: A Two Way Street? (2002), Law and Human Behavior, Vol. 26, pp. 3–17; F.L. Cook, T.R. Tyler, E.G. Goetz, M.T. Gordon, D. Protess, D.R. Leff, et al., *Media and Agenda Setting: Effects on the Public, Interest Group Leaders, Policy Makers, and Policy* (1983), Public Opinion Quarterly, Vol. 47, pp. 16–35; J.V. Roberts and A.N. Doob, *News Media Influences on Public Views of Sentencing* (1990), Law and Human Behavior, Vol. 14, pp. 451–68; D.L. Rhode, *A Bad Press on Bad Lawyers: The Media Sees Research, Research Sees the Media*, in P. Ewick, R. A. Kagan and A. Sarat (eds), *Social Science, Social Policy, and the Law* (Russell Sage Foundation, New York, 1999), pp. 139–69.

[14] https://www.prweek.com/article/102271/opinion-news-analysis-uk-litigation-pr-upsurge-set-mimic-states-litigation-pr-well-established-us-corporates-aware-reputational-impact-legal-issues

[15] Ibid.

[16] V.P. Hans and J.L. Dee, *Media Coverage of Law: Its Impact on Juries and the Public* (1991), American Behavioral Scientist, Vol. 35, pp. 136–49.

or influence what is said and done in another place. Therefore, the communication of your case demands the same level of thought, discipline and depth of research as other parts of your case management. It is not an add-on or an inconvenience; it is part of the litigator's armoury. Litigants that take their battle into the outside world – and deal effectively with the 24-hour news cycle mentality and social media-led debate – can be more successful in their pursuit. It is not just the public courts you are testing your case in, but also the more fickle courts of public opinion. As Justice Anthony Kennedy in *Gentile v State* opined:

> A defense attorney may pursue legal lawful strategies to obtain dismissal of an indictment or reduction of charges, including an attempt to demonstrate in the court of public opinion that the client does not deserve to be tried.[17]

A major concern outside of the legal issues is that of reputation. Being part of litigation can impact business and stakeholder relationships. This can influence the course of litigation, which – like true love – is a course that does not run smoothly. You need to prepare for and manage your communications around the legal issues in fora that play by different rules and use different language, and this means communicating differently to position persuasive arguments and reach key audiences. There is a range of other functions you will deal with, including journalists, lobbyists, political advisors and corporate spokespeople.

In a collaborative relationship, the essential function of a communication professional is to be the storyteller, telling the client's 'story' to various constituencies and stakeholders. This cannot be done disconnected from the legal strategy, as to do so could spell disaster for the case as a whole. The communication will link this contingent event to the long-term activities, aspirations and reputation of the client. The sooner you can make this connection, and get ahead of the story, the better. It is all too easy to think communication comes later in the process, and find you are playing catch-up all the time. If you are not framing your case and talking about it, someone else is doing this for you, and you don't want that. In doing this work there can be a tendency towards 'spin', a beloved technique of recent vintage, but one that in the longer term is not really productive. The 'spin' may well return to haunt you at a later date.[18] The Dialogue Box will help

---

[17] Justice Anthony Kennedy, *Gentile v State*, Bar of Nevada, 501 U.S. 1030, 1043 (1991).
[18] C.A. Studebaker and S.D. Penrod, *Pretrial Publicity: The Media, the Law, and Common Sense* (1997), Psychology, Public Policy, and Law, Vol. 3, pp. 428–60.

you to gather all the variables in the mix and define a narrative that can guide you through some tricky and often controversial waters.

It is not just the media and public discourse at stake; there is the role of opposing counsel, judges and juries.[19] Different lawyers will take differing approaches to engaging with the media and other audiences outside the legal process, but ignoring the problems can as noted be disastrous.[20] This is not just being in the battle, but being above it and looking at what biases may already be in the public space before your particular case came along. The reputation of the client, the industry or sector they are in and public sentiment are all aspects that can bias the jury and the public at large. These biases can work for or against you, but either way you need to know what pervades the public ether. Another aspect to be aware of is what the opposition is doing, as some counsel can be more aggressive and adept than others in using communication professionals.

The stakeholders and constituencies you are dealing with extend beyond the actors in the legal case itself, and include customers, shareholders, regulators, employees, local communities and others. A stakeholder map or matrix should be developed to understand what they are all feeling and thinking in relation to your case. It will also detail what messages might resonate with them and what channels of communication will be most effective in reaching them. For example, as noted about blue-collar worker channels, if your case involves communicating to factory workers in a dispute, emails won't be all that effective. The matrix will also assess risk, in terms of who is affected and who might be affected as the case grows in public awareness. Knowing when to target an audience is critical, and usually you want to frame the debate before they are too aware or influenced by other framers. Your individual audiences should be briefed in a timely manner, which may sometimes mean they are briefed first and at other times simultaneously. Your individual audiences, when well informed, can be great ambassadors in the fight to maintain client and customer confidence.

---

[19] E. Greene, *Media Effects on Jurors* (1990), Law and Human Behavior, Vol. 14, pp. 439–50; E. Greene and R. Wade, *Of Private Talk and Public Print: General Pre-trial Publicity and Juror Decision-making* (1988), Applied Cognitive Psychology, Vol. 2, pp. 123–35.

[20] S. Landsman and R. F. Rakos, *A Preliminary Inquiry into the Effects of Potentially Biasing Information on Judges and Jurors in Civil Litigation* (1994), Behavioral Science and the Law, Vol. 12, pp. 113–26.

PART II

The Dialogue Box for lawyers

In Part II, the reader will learn how to use the Dialogue Box as an effective tool for legal communication, management and leadership.

7 Introducing the Dialogue Box

Having discussed a range of communication issues for lawyers, Part II is the clinical heart of the book, as it teaches a tool and methodology that helps you to communicate as a lawyer more effectively. This chapter will provide an overview of the Dialogue Box, which has been taught and used as a well-established communications tool across multiple disciplines but is here applied specifically for lawyers. The Dialogue Box has five zones which will be outlined, and the reader will be led step by step through a process that will have a practical outcome to help the communicating lawyer engage in more effective dialogue, by defining either neutral or persuasive ground on which communication can best take place. In the previous chapters these steps have been highlighted in the various types of dispute, and the following chapters will take you in more depth through utilizing this process. The Dialogue Box is a revolutionary approach and is not about manipulating people or selling messages, which has often been behind communication tools and approaches. Instead, the Dialogue Box works on the supposition that facts are important rather than simply things to be twisted in one's favour. It is a tool primarily and ideally for use in a collaborative communication approach to find neutral ground, though it allows for persuasion as a positive force as well. However, like any tool, it can be used or abused, hence I forewarn that the Dialogue Box can be used to manipulate or push your audience in a particular direction. The value for lawyers is to communicate in ways that are factual and persuasive in their work and arguments. The Dialogue Box provides a practical methodology to communicate, which is essential for lawyers in today's changing environment. The Dialogue Box is rooted in the use of preserving the discipline of legal knowledge whilst creating more effective communication of this knowledge to connect to a variety of stakeholders.

However, what is needed first is a way to answer the fundamental question posed in Chapter 1: why are you communicating? There may be a general high-level answer to this question: I have a client. The client, who may well be an in-house client in a private or public organization, needs to understand the law on this or that point. The lawyer can offer more powerful counsel when their client actually understands what is said and done in the otherwise often opaque process that is the law, courts and legal language. These are high-level responses, but we can then drop down to a very specific level of the advice needed to be given to a particular client or internal audience in a specific context. However, this is not what I mean when I ask this question, and I want to push you further. The legal point, or the reason you have for communicating it, may not be your precise communication need. It may not be directly why you are communicating to this person in that context. We need to narrow the question down to a very specific audience or a range of audiences, which also means stakeholders, and you will need to map out these stakeholders.

7.1 Using the Dialogue Box

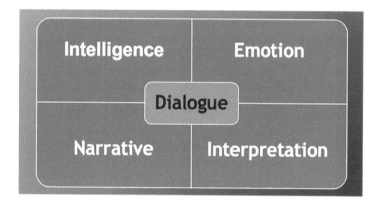

The Dialogue Box helps us to explore what kind of dialogue we need to have, and to address legal and cultural challenges, by breaking dialogue down into 21st-century zones:

- intelligence;
- emotion;
- interpretation;
- narrative;
- dialogue.

The Dialogue Box allows us to understand the intelligence and emotions of dialogue partners, and how these link to the different ways both we and our dialogue partners interpret events and information, thereby gaining insight into the narrative that emerges within the situation we face as a result, and doing this as objectively as possible. The outcome we want to achieve, by way of an objective narrative, is effective dialogue, which is the zone at the heart of the Dialogue Box. Hopefully you will – indeed you should – find much of what is discussed in this book to be intuitive. The process offers a way of seeing things you sort of know about already, because the aim here is to illuminate so you can make connections you may not have drawn before. The Dialogue Box is also highly contextual and contingent, with each Dialogue Box being created for a very specific situation you face to understand the variables involved. It is also an iterative process, because as the dialogue progresses, so too the variables change, and this process continues until the dialogue situation has been resolved to the required level of satisfaction. The objective, however, is not to make people happy, though it is always nice when that happens. The objective is to engage the participants in a dialogue that – overcoming what is highlighted in the Emotion Zone – brings people together in a rational process.

The Dialogue Box is constructed in five zones, consisting of four quadrants and a central zone. The four quadrants are:

- **Intelligence**: Here you can corral all the facts of the situation you face – the law, relevant cases, business events, timelines and other data. This involves stating the facts as plainly and objectively as possible. It can include decisions or reasons, so long as it is clear that the view is a fair representation of the parties or events being described.
- **Emotion**: This helps you to understand the emotional impact of the situation and facts. When you communicate the law, it is often not of interest to the parties involved. Often it does not seem to connect emotionally to some people. Likewise, there may be an inherent emotional impact that connects very directly with the concerns of an individual. Indeed, the mere fact you are a lawyer delivering legal information can contain an in-built emotion of fear.
- **Interpretation**: This is natural territory for lawyers and there is some incredible work done on interpretation of law. The process of legal reasoning involves deducing the legal facts and separating them from the interpretations, and of course understanding the important role

interpretation plays in separating out and deciding the legal facts themselves. Here we need to capture the full range of interpretations, so we do not become readily captive to any one dominant interpretation. The more emotional a situation is, the broader and more numerous the interpretations.

- **Narrative**: This should also resonate. Defining the narrative is to play the impartial judge, or the man or woman on the Clapham omnibus. It is taking a bird's eye view of proceedings, distancing yourself to be above the battle and gain as objective a picture of the situation under consideration as you possibly can. Only when you have grasped this can you truly gauge your communication to have effective dialogue.

At the centre of the Dialogue Box is the space where you can start to work collaboratively:

- **Dialogue**: Here you explore the words that will resonate with your audience and create a vocabulary with words that help and those which you should seek to avoid. Grasping this point should not require much imagination, as experience shows it can take only one word to alienate someone or to create an argument. In the Dialogue Box process, we will work to break down a huge legal complex into single words, to then build our communications approach.

One of the objectives of the Dialogue Box is to get definition around the many variables that exist in a communication process. As Frank P Ramsey noted many decades ago:

> … where there is a prolonged and persistent dispute …, it is often the case that the disputants … are really in agreement about an assumption, hypothesis, premise, fundamental to their argument, which is false. They share a common but false premise … the truth lies not in one of the two disputed views but in some third possibility which has not yet been thought of, which we can only discover by rejecting something assumed as obvious by both the disputants. Both the disputed theories make an important assumption which to my mind, has only to be questioned to be doubted.[1]

A core achievement of the Dialogue Box is to interrogate not just the assumptions of our dialogue partner but our own assumptions. It is on

---

[1] Frank P. Ramsey, *The Foundations of Mathematics & Other Logical Essays* (R.B. Braithwaite, ed.) (Harcourt, Brace & Company/Kegan Paul, Trench Trubner & Co Ltd., New York/London, 1931), pp. 115–16.

this basis that we can then work with the Dialogue Box to problem-solve and to manage legal issues such as governance, technical legal processes – from drafting statutes to the operation of courts – and, as we saw in the last chapter, managing client relations. It is to some of these specific applications we now turn, as examples of ways we might use the Dialogue Box to communicate the law more effectively.

The Dialogue Box starts with the facts. There are legal methodological and jurisprudential questions to be asked in respect to facts, rules, norms and values, and how they relate to and differ in legal reasoning and praxis. This is another fascinating debate to have, but it is beyond the ambition of this book to go into any greater detail than I have in the earlier chapters. In respect to the operation of the Dialogue Box, an overarching comment should be offered in respect to the issues that could be studied in this respect. The Dialogue Box operates in such a way that the facts, norms and rules reside in the Intelligence Zone, and do not need to change to use the Dialogue Box effectively. The role of values is important when we look at the Emotion and Interpretation Zones, because it is the values that people hold which act as the source of emotional and interpretative disruption. We are angry because we believe someone has acted recklessly, for instance, or transgressed our sense of values, ethics, decency or even our mood. The Dialogue Box can act as a very useful methodology to think through legal reasoning and discourse, but at this point I will stop short of going into the kinds of discussions we might have, as this requires engaging with a level of knowledge and expertise beyond the interest of the intended reader wishing to make use of the Dialogue Box as a communication tool. Suffice to say, whether one is a legal positivist, a natural law advocate, a legal realist or a critical legal scholar, the Dialogue Box can be a useful tool to facilitate discourse between these schools of thought whilst preserving the integrity of one's jurisprudential position. In short, the Dialogue Box essentially leaves the fundamentals of these scholarly positions theoretically untrammelled.

Facts, as the philosopher PF Strawson notes, depend on their expression through language[2] and the world that the language describes.[3] Facts are important, and they are stubborn. One of the problems with modern

---

[2]   J.L. Austin, P.F. Strawson and D.R. Cousin, *Symposium: Truth* (1950), Proceedings of the Aristotelian Society: Supplementary Volumes, Vol. 24, pp. 111–72.

[3]   Ibid.

communications and social media is that facts – along with truth – have all too often become casualties in public debate. Perhaps it is little wonder lawyers are often cautious in their approach to communication. This may be a consequence of postmodernity, but there is a mundane answer. First, the communications industry developed a way of behaving that focused on the idea that 'perception is reality' and so we have the invention of 'spin'. I say invention – it might be suggested it was old-fashioned lies, and there would be some truth to the point. However, there was a very marked turn in public communication that used spin to twist facts and even to fit a particular narrative. Twenty-first-century fake news is the natural successor to late 19th-century spin as a form of media manipulation. This makes the world of communication a fraught activity, but the Dialogue Box moves beyond such concerns by ensuring that in the Intelligence Zone the facts are preserved. This can be of much comfort to the lawyer, whose education and perhaps fabric is rooted in facts and precision, rather than perception and the 'fog of war'. For the lawyer using the Dialogue Box, the goal is not to learn to communicate through spin or 'good PR'. It is to find ways to effectively communicate knowing there are varieties of interpretations and emotions to be managed. The lawyer should be reassured that the Dialogue Box does not lead to obfuscation or misdirection. Quite the opposite – it will help you to navigate your way through a crowded communication space with participants having varying degrees of legal knowledge. To achieve this requires understanding, in communication terms, what the task is for the lawyer in a specific situation. The Dialogue Box will help you to discover what your communication issue is in context, and the rest of communication becomes considerably easier from this point of discovery.

The Dialogue Box is a methodology for this pursuit of precision, by assessing all the dimensions that go into dialogue, making the Dialogue Box an ideal tool for lawyers. It has been taught to and used by lawyers around the globe. In the training sessions I have conducted with participants from legal departments in partnership with other disciplines, the lawyers have been amongst the first to grasp its implications and usefulness. The Dialogue Box was created to help organizations to become better at communicating internally, which includes the in-house legal department. It has been used in training lawyers in law firms, chambers, in-house and the university classroom. A common response is that the Dialogue Box explores, in the legal context, the role and impact of emotion, which all lawyers trained in this methodology have noted was never something they learned in law school. This is understandable in the sense that law is very much about rationality, logic and the use of words and principles. It is odd in another sense. First, rationality is in a constant relationship with emotion, but has been decoupled in legal reasoning and education – except in very narrow terms, such as the examination of intent, for instance. The emergence of emotional intelligence, which is a response to a degree of reawakening of our emotional understanding of behaviour, is rebalancing this. Second, emotion plays a key role in law. A primary reason why cases are contentious and end up in court is in a fair part fuelled by emotion. Strip away the logical arguments, the contested points and the legal principles, and you will find at the base emotional behaviour. This is formally recognized in criminal law, where the *actus reus* and *mens rea* are considered hand in hand; yet still it didn't seem obvious to devote more time to emotion in legal discourse and teaching legal skills as a whole. Lawyers trained in this approach have welcomed the emotional insights they have gained from using the Dialogue Box.

A last dimension to highlight at this point is the conservative nature of law and language. Social language changes much faster than legal language. Judges may not 'get' the meaning of a word or phrase, as discussed in earlier chapters. Likewise, participants in the legal process may not understand the legal language. Just as the Dialogue Box is used to maintain the status of facts, it can also maintain the status of legal language, whilst allowing for translating colloquial language into the legal discourse and vice versa. This is important when we look at statutory language. There is a formality in the language, meaning and structure of statutes that can appear quite opaque to the bystander. We want to translate the statute into language that is meaningful to non-legal participants, and the plain language movement has indeed done much to create greater clarity around statutory language. There is a closing of the loop here that needs to be managed, since statutes and regulations are written to understand and interpret human activities and desires with a clarity that is useful to the courts. Yet traditionally the laws of the people are rarely used or even understood by the people, and so ironically lose touch with the people the law serves. Perhaps with more plain language and access, people may be better connected to the laws that serve them.

Language is, of course, a major consideration here, not only in terms of setting the tenor or context for change, but also more centrally and continually in the justice process itself, with all its communication flaws. Peter Goodrich explains:

> ... irrespective of the aura of rationality and of specialism that surrounds legal hearings, they are best depicted not in terms of the law's own image, that of impartiality and the inexorable necessity of the application of pre-existent rules of statute and precedent, but rather in terms of the uneven exchange that characterises the flawed dialogue or 'distorted communication' of the most contemporary bureaucratic discourses. What underpins and prolongs the unilateral monologue of most legal auditoria is not the exquisite precision of scientific expression but simple political expedience and the linguistic manifestation of the vested interest of economically and sexually dominant social groups.[4]

The Dialogue Box can help to isolate and address these concerns in this procedural set of needs and, if used well, can potentially satisfy the needs of all concerned. This is in keeping with the tendency of statutory language to become clearer, shorter and structured to make it more accessible to the non-legal participant. The resulting clarity can assist in everyday application of statues through to their interpretation in the courts. In short, the Dialogue Box assists those who are pushing the boundaries of the 'plain language' movement by answering the more conservative needs for precision and legal integrity in communication.

There is a set sequence assumed in using the Dialogue Box. The process starts with the Intelligence Zone, then proceeds to the Emotion Zone and into the Interpretation Zone. These three zones are quite straightforward. You are inputting data. As noted, the data in the Intelligence Zone is factual and stated as barely as possible and stripped of as much interpretation as possible. The emotions are recorded in both positive and negative states, and it is here you will do a lot of work discussing and trying to understand your audience. Then you go into interpretation, and you may find that in both the Intelligence and Interpretation Zones there is debate around when things happened or whether something can be agreed upon as fact. People often argue over something they take as a fact, whereas it is an interpretation. Hence, in this zone you may find yourself retracing your steps as you refine your Dialogue Box. This phase of using the Dialogue Box prepares you for creating the narrative, which is the attempt

---

4   Peter Goodrich, *Languages of Law – From Logics of Memory to Nomadic Masks* (Weidenfeld & Nicolson, 1990), pp. 185–6.

to describe the situation you are dealing with as objectively as you can. Moving into this zone is difficult, and it is commonly the case that users find this a trial and end up struggling to state the narrative. What happens is that users state a narrative consisting in what they think should be the case or what they want to say to their audience. What the Dialogue Box is trying to do is get you out of your point of view and truly engage with your audience in as neutral a state as possible. To create the narrative, you build it into three steps:

1. What is the situation you are dealing with, stated as factually as possible?
2. The 'but' factor, which means stating the following: but the response from your audience is that they feel X and believe Y; and
3. The 'so what?' factor, which is the impact of this response on the interests of all parties and how it frames the situation whereby all parties see what stake they have in finding a solution.

Once you have established your narrative, you then look at the dialogue you need to have to resolve the situation. You should find the narrative you have arrived at is at odds with the implied narrative in the Intelligence Zone. Once you have this new narrative, you can build a vocabulary of words for establishing an effective dialogue. Each zone, and building your narrative, is what we will work through in the coming chapters.

Understanding neutrality, as a communicative factor, is not an easy process, and the reason why people struggle with moving from the Interpretation to the Narrative Zone is partly why the Dialogue Box was created. Communication is often done in delivery mode, infused with our understanding and point of view, which blinds us from truly appreciating the other's point of view. If we look at work done on strategy, there can be a danger of developing an approach in terms of our strategy without much reference to understanding the strategy of the other parties in fact. We can be so busy persuading people about what we want or think that we fail to recognize we have lost the attention or engagement of our audience. We can speak in our own language and terms of reference, without realizing that this is lacking meaning for others. These are the polarities the Dialogue Box seeks to reverse, so that we understand the other's strategy, remain engaged with what our audience feels and thinks, and speak in a language that works for our audience. Then we have dialogue. Then we stand above the battle, using our new understanding of the narrative of the situation in which we are involved, and thus measure the language that will be effective, as well as what we need to avoid saying, thereby creating a neutral space in which to have shared dialogue.

7.2   Practical steps: ready to dialogue?

Each chapter in Part II will take you in detail through the zones of the Dialogue Box, so that you can make practical use of the Dialogue Box to help you in your daily work. There are five zones to the Dialogue Box.

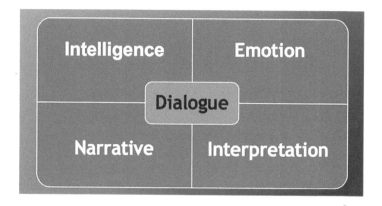

To use the Dialogue Box, you will move in this progression:

1. Intelligence.
2. Emotion.
3. Interpretation.
4. Narrative.
5. Dialogue.

From Intelligence to Interpretation you are collecting data and making sure the Intelligence is factual and stated as neutrally as possible, while the Emotion and Interpretation Zones will be subjective and include the positive and the negative feelings and views. In the Narrative Zone you are trying to get an objective picture of the situation. Having done this work, you can look at what the difference is between the situation and narrative in the Intelligence Zone and that in your Narrative Zone, having considered all the emotional and interpretative responses. Once you have this clear, you can decide what dialogue you need to have to bring alignment between the Intelligence and Narrative Zones.

Let's go through each zone in step and see the kinds of things you need to consider in filling each zone comprehensively. Each zone needs to assess a range of material and questions and find a way, in a sentence, to focus attention. This is a little like writing a headline in a news story. In each zone you will look to write your headline, piece these together to write your narrative, and then search for your dialogue word and effectively drive your communications strategy.

8   The Intelligence Zone

The great German writer Goethe said that to act is easy, to think is hard. Lawyers obviously do a lot of thinking, from dealing with cases through to organizing and developing their practice. In legal communications, it is the thinking component that communications work mostly focuses on: getting the law right, writing client advice, crafting presentations, and other intelligent tasks. This is why Intelligence is Zone 1 of the Dialogue Box. However, I want to extend this thinking process in the Dialogue Box to connect thinking of communicating the law emotionally, a step many lawyers find problematic and missing from their training as lawyers. The legal principle, the words used to explain the law and the strategy to connect the legal solution to the client's needs are all actions that involve crafting the right message. This work is also about matching the legal advice to the understanding of the audience, and this connection is both rational and emotional. Crafting the intelligence and facts is important foundational work that needs to be done, with awareness that while you want to preserve the integrity of your intelligence, during the process of communication it undergoes a process of distortion. It is possible to negotiate this distortion whilst retaining integrity. It is not easy, but the Dialogue Box provides a methodology to navigate your way. Aside from the distortion, all too often the thinking can stop at the point when the legal solution has been decided and the legal work is done, when in fact this is only the beginning. Getting the law right is essential for the lawyer, but communicating that law effectively is also essential to achieve an optimal outcome. Communication should carry the law through the process. This chapter will address how to understand and build the intelligence in the Dialogue Box to prepare for a more thoughtful and connecting way of communicating the law.

This Intelligence Zone looks at the facts as familiar territory for lawyers, but perhaps less familiar is to examine the role they play in communication. Analysing the legal problem is done by applying the law to the facts of the case, and deciding what are the relevant, irrelevant and key facts. Law students starting out on their path of legal study are soon asked to look at cases by separating the facts from the law, as though the difference is readily apparent. It is not, neither at the early stage in the lawyer's training nor when being considered by a judge or a seasoned professional. As Clarence Morris warned back in the 1940s:

> Since questions of fact are answered in one way and questions of law in another, the distinction between them is vitally practical. A question of fact usually calls for proof. A question of law usually calls for argument. The lawyer who confuses one with the other will look for evidence when he should be writing a brief or vice versa.[1]

The key facts will determine case management and whether a lawsuit should be filed. Understanding the facts given may be not achieved until the legal issues and governing law has been determined. The facts are assessed across a range of parameters, including parties involved in a dispute, persons or things that might be affected, actions that have been taken or failures in acting, and defences and remedies available. There are ethical implications in managing the facts, with a professional duty to be honest and represent the facts truthfully and accurately. The client's case has its own inherent narrative, based on a corralled set of facts. The facts in themselves, and the choice or omission of facts, may cause the case to be legally misrepresented. The inherent narrative is tested in court by determining the two sides of the case and what the court determines to be the narrative of the dispute in hand, and there will be discrepancies between what is, in effect, now three narratives, but the facts should deviate less, and the court will determine ultimately what defines the facts legally acceptable in the case and rule on the dispute. When new facts come to light there may be grounds to appeal.

Allen and Pardo[2] consider the nature of the distinction between issues of fact and issues of law, and argue that 'Courts in the United States and England have failed to articulate the distinction'. Rejecting arguments that a distinction may be drawn on ontological, epistemological or analytical grounds, the authors argue:

> ... the law/fact distinction involves a complex interaction between three variables: (1) conventional meanings of the terms 'law' and 'fact'; (2) structural

---

[1]   Clarence Morris, *Law and Fact* (1942), Harvard Law Review, Vol. 55, No. 8, pp. 1303–41.
[2]   R.J. Allen and M.S. Pardo, *Facts in Law and Facts of Law* (2003), International Journal of Evidence & Proof, Vol. 7, pp. 153–71.

relationships within the legal process; and (3) a distinction between matters of general import and specific, localised phenomena.

They concluded that 'this interaction is too complex to be reduced to simple rules and that the labelling of a particular issue as "legal" or "factual" is essentially a functional decision made on pragmatic grounds'. One simple statement of distinction was the Latin maxim offered by Thomas Littleton and Edward Coke, deriving from the 16th century – *ad quaestionem juris respondent judices, ad quaestionem facti respondent juratore*. This assigned questions of law to the judge and questions of fact to the jury, arguably the ultimate lawyer versus non-lawyer division. Apart from which, the saying is rather broad and not entirely accurate. As Isaacs mused, 'The delusive simplicity of the distinction between questions of law and questions of fact has been found a will-of-the-wisp by travellers approaching it from several directions.'[3] Allen and Pardo assert:

> The even shorter explanation for the chaotic legal landscape is that much of the effort to properly delineate matters as questions of law or fact is animated by the belief that the two terms, 'law' and 'fact,' specify different kinds of entities, that there is a qualitative or ontological distinction between them. This belief is false. Thus, the quest to find 'the' essential difference between the two that can control subsequent classifications of questions as legal or factual is doomed from the start, as there is no essential difference. There are only pragmatic differences, which are reflected in the three dichotomies of the conventional meaning of the terms, the judge-jury relationship, and the general-specific spectrum.[4]

In the Dialogue Box we are not isolating the facts or drawing such a distinction in this zone. We want to gather all the facts, regardless of how we might choose to categorize those facts. The zone draws the communicating lawyer into looking contextually at the law, gathering facts in a communicative way, and defining not just the legal principles but the social structures involved, the mass of data available and then a final step of distilling the intelligence in a way that leads us to take the next step into understanding the emotional responses involved. This zone is the starting point for a journey through the emotions and interpretations as they start to present a more objective narrative. You will find in the Intelligence

---

[3] Nathan Isaacs, *The Law and the Facts* (1922), Columbia Law Review, Vol. 22, No. 1, pp. 1–13, p. 1. See also the discussion in James B. Thayer, *'Law and Fact' in Jury Trials* (1890), Harvard Law Review, Vol. 4, No. 4, pp. 147–75.

[4] Allen and Pardo (n 2), p. 1770.

Zone that there is an inherent narrative that is buffeted, challenged and changed through the Dialogue Box process as you uncover this new narrative, which can then serve as the basis for a more neutral dialogue. Intelligence is our capacity to be rational and pursue a path of reasoning to reach a decision or conclusion about something. In legal reasoning, we are seeking specifically, for instance, to reach a conclusion that helps our case and our client. However, there is much intelligence in other contexts, such as advising the client so they can understand the legal intricacies of the case. Intelligence is also a collaborative effort, as we collaborate with colleagues to solicit opinions, gather data and analyse evidence. Intelligence has its formal content, often with predefined rules and language, such as a contract, a will, an affidavit and other legal instruments.

8.1　Facts, norms and language

Facts and norms in law hold a different status from how facts and norms may operate in other disciplines and have their specific uses and lines of enquiry, which is important in the context of law, where we are in search of legal certainty in regard to specific cases. There has been much inter-disciplinary discussion on the matter, and it has become a major theme in conversations between law and other disciplines, as well as within critical legal studies. In the context of postmodernity and the growing debate about the role of uncertainty in our society, this is an increasingly lively debate, but it is perhaps not an entirely new one. Professor Barbara Shapiro argues that for at least 200 years, the governing assumption of Anglo-American law has been that facts are uncertain and proving facts is a matter of probabilities.[5] Her argument draws on the idea of uncertainty in proof and probabilities that we find in the version of the relevance rule espoused by James Bradley Thayer in the 19th century.[6] The Dialogue Box embraces the idea that looking at the facts, and what comprises norms, should not be seen too parochially, but nor should we dismiss the idea that there are facts to be found. We do need to ensure we retain legal integrity in the Intelligence Zone. Within this, of course, there are

---

[5]　Barbara J. Shapiro, 'Beyond Reasonable Doubt' and 'Probable Cause': Historical Perspectives on the Anglo-American Law of Evidence, (University of California Press, Berkeley, 1991), p. xv.

[6]　James B. Thayer, Presumptions and the Law of Evidence (1889), Harvard Law Review, Vol. 3, No. 141, pp. 144–5. See also Peter Tillers, The Value of Evidence in Law (1988), Northern Ireland Law Quarterly, Vol. 39, p. 167.

disputes within the legal fraternity, and these should be recognized. The Dialogue Box offers an opportunity to assess these legal norms and facts, as part of the need to question the assumptions you are making. At the heart of this discourse lies language, which includes deep philosophical background. I want to set out some points that are deep in the literature and very much within the province of jurisprudence. As fascinating as the background academic debates are in what follows here, I want – no doubt to the consternation of some academic colleagues – to put these aside and leave on the table the practical aspects of these academic discourses. So, here goes!

To start with a non-lawyer, Willard Van Orman Quine, who argues, 'Language is a social art. In acquiring it we have to depend entirely on intersubjectively available cues as to what to say and when.'[7] In the legal context, language is still a social art, at least for the recipient of legal expertise, even if the legal expert believes that we have a language that is precise for dealing with the facts for the benefit of legal deployment. Quine suggests that all analytical questions depend on empirical evidence. Thus, in the legal context, we should understand that facts are not innocent or unproblematic sense data, and the legal apprehension of facts through theory and reasoning means that 'what the facts are' becomes tied to the theory 'about the facts', and thus fact and theory become entwined.[8] Hence, in the process of legal reasoning we may figure we have chosen, defined and managed the facts that are adequate for deployment in the legal process. However, these are enmeshed within a legal theory and framework, which your audience may not fully comprehend or accept, because they have a different apprehension of facts, and have a different theoretical framework within which they understand the language and facts you are relaying. In plain terms, the lawyer and client can end up talking past each other. Without going into a deep debate into his argument, we can see how this point becomes important in the Dialogue Box. Quine's point raises the problem that people argue over the facts, and in doing so are also arguing interpretatively. What we try to do in the Dialogue Box is to achieve, as far as possible, a division of fact and interpretation. Something may very well be normative in legal reasoning, but the normative aspects need to be translated into terms your audience can understand within their own framework of language and reference.

---

[7] Willard Van Orman Quine, *Word and Object* (MIT Press, Cambridge, MA, 1960).

[8] Willard Van Orman Quine, *Carnap and Logical Truth* (1960), Synthese, Vol. 12, No. 4, pp. 350–74.

This may not, in practice certainly, be fully achieved, but the mere attempt will help to clarify the situation you are being faced with. Often in discussion we argue about interpretations as if they are facts, and we need a mechanism to tease this complexity apart. We can look at the facts and norms, which we can retain in the legal context, and translate these into the non-legal context without coming to blows over interpretation. A strength of the Dialogue Box is that we need not change the facts or intelligence; it is about how we manage our social engagement with an audience. It is how we make the law, legal reasoning and potential courses of action meaningful in a way that your audience can understand, embrace and confidently act upon. The legal reasoning and language are be translated in terms more engaging for the client. I do not use the term 'layman's language' here for two very good reasons, both to do with exclusion. First, it transgresses gender neutrality – enough said there, I suggest. Second, the term brings the legal discourse back into the place this book starts with, namely the idea there is a secret world of the profession that is above the mere mortals seeking legal wisdom and attention. The Dialogue Box asserts that in communicating the law, the discourse is open and involves all. What is legal is not just the law and its professional actors, but all of us using and abusing the law. What we try to do in communication is to corral this into a dynamic discourse that retains legal integrity. In the legal process we are all doing law, rather than a world divided into the lawyer and non-lawyer.

Closely allied to facts, and again deeply influenced by theory, are norms and the relationship between norms. What we consider normative in a process is highly interpretative. In the legal environment there is the added problem that what legal reasoning and practice regard as norms, and how legal norms are understood and deployed, can be at odds with 'common sense' norms or the norms resident in other disciplines or cultures. Though it should be noted that when cases are decided, there are normative disputes, as Neil MacCormick writes, '[T]here may be more than one set of normative generalizations which can be advanced in rationalization of the rules which "belong" to the [legal] system.'[9] Again without going too deep into the theory, these are aspects in dialogue we need to address. In the Intelligence Zone we are looking to isolate the facts as far as we know them, which is crucial for the legal case. However, we are also looking to frame or describe the facts as neutrally as we can. This,

---

[9]   Neil MacCormick, *Legal Reasoning and Legal Theory* (Clarendon, 1978), pp. 69–70, 234–5, 246–58.

again, is something we try to do but can easily lead us into interpretation. An interesting political quote from the US comes to mind here. Democrat stalwart Daniel Patrick Moynihan wrote in a memo that 'everyone is entitled to his own opinion, but not to his own facts'. The more contemporary debate about 'fake news' brought Moynihan's words back into common currency when President Barack Obama told the story of how Moynihan said this in his autobiography,[10] as well as when quizzed on healthcare. The 2016 presidential candidate Hilary Clinton also used the quote when responding to a heckler on the campaign trail.[11] The divide of fact and opinion, like wheat from chaff, is an exacting process commonly problematic in political discourse and on social media, with the rise of 'fake news'.[12] As Ronald Reagan famously retorted, 'trust, but verify', though he was in fact popularizing an old Russian rhyming proverb *Doveryai, no proveryai*.[13] Our modern communication age, and the digital public square, highlight that as we solicit, recollect and record facts, we are writing them down, and into this act can creep interpretative ways of describing something that shows it in a particular light. In other words, we create our own 'fake news' or portrayal of a situation, which may be intentional or unintentional. Often when people are describing what they see as a fact, they are in fact putting an interpretation, even some spin, on the fact or facts. Hence, in contentious legal matters we need to be acutely aware of this division and vigilant about where the data falls, in terms of where we allocate data in the Dialogue Box. Does it really belong in the Intelligence or the Interpretation Zone?

---

[10] 'There's a wonderful, perhaps apocryphal story that people tell about Daniel Patrick Moynihan, the brilliant, prickly, and iconoclastic late senator from New York. Apparently, Moynihan was in a heated argument with one of his colleagues over an issue, and the other senator, sensing he was on the losing side of the argument, blurted out: "Well, you may disagree with me, Pat, I'm entitled to my own opinion." To which Moynihan frostily replied, "You are entitled to your own opinion, but you are not entitled to your own facts."' Barack Obama, *The Audacity of Hope: Thoughts on Reclaiming the American Dream* (Canongate, 2007). He also used the quote in various interviews and speeches.

[11] https://www.youtube.com/watch?v=ZdbfioKsxcY

[12] https://www.pbs.org/video/youre-not-entitled-to-your-own-facts-7cbvdd/

[13] 'Literally means that a responsible person always verifies everything before committing himself to a common business with anyone, even if that anyone is totally trustworthy,' see https://www.rbth.com/lifestyle/330521-reagan-trust-but-verify-chernobyl

8.2   Knowledge and unknowns

Having intelligence means we have a capacity for knowledge, and that we are able to take what we know and use our reasoning to systematize it in order to make sense of the data we have before us. It is also our capacity to be objective, to step outside of ourselves and see situations and events from a bird's eye view and make decisions that affect us and others; we are able to self-consciously think of ourselves as part of this whole process. Another crucial element of intelligence is our capacity to act ethically, and to make decisions on the basis of what is good, which may not necessarily be what we want to do but what we believe is the right thing to do. Which is not to say we will do what we should, however intelligent we are! We do not do this in isolation – there is both individual and group intelligence. This means that as individuals we can have intelligence and do all these things I have defined as intelligence, but it also means that as a group of people we can create intelligence and do all these things on a group basis, interdependently or in a supportive manner. All of these aspects can be the focus of our attention, and one aspect may sometimes take precedence over another in vying for our attention. This is a debate that becomes ever more important as we consider the complexity of the digital world. The way we live now shines a light on the necessity for collaboration, as we are all increasingly interconnected. Individualism is increasingly hard in this collaborative world, which raises many important intellectual and ethical debates. One of the foreseeable outcomes of Covid-19 has been the questioning over how collaboration and social measures work in our society, and existing norms are being reconsidered.

However, there are some significant drawbacks to the intelligent process of rationality and reasoning, not least the way that emotions and our subconscious influence the process, which is precisely what the Dialogue Box identifies as necessary to achieve overall success in our communication. There are many barriers to reaching intelligent conclusions, and one problem for intelligence is that the discernment of what is, or can be, known can be eclipsed by the unknowns, the things we don't know, cannot know or are only revealed to us by later information or events. This is often the source of fear, another dynamic that became quite apparent during Covid-19. Intelligence is also a process in which we discern what we can know and how we understand why something might be unknown. There was much derision when Donald Rumsfeld, serving as George W. Bush's Secretary of Defense, famously stated:

> As we know, there are known knowns; there are things we know we know. We also know there are known unknowns; that is to say we know there are some things we do not know. But there are also unknown unknowns – the ones we don't know we don't know.[14]

A convoluted sentence this may be, but there is a logic to it. The passage has been lifted out of context, and this is itself a context that has changed. The context in which the statement was made was a press briefing, and a discussion with a journalist about evidence. Perhaps Rumsfeld had learned something on dealing with evidence during his days at Case Western Reserve University School of Law and Georgetown University Law Center, though he didn't graduate from either place. The journalist said his reaction at the time was that he thought, 'Yeah, that's true. It's sort of self-evident, but it's true: the things that we know, and the things that we don't know, and the things we don't know we don't know.'[15] However, it took on a life of its own, seen as a gaffe, to the point *Unknown Unknowns* became the title of Rumsfeld's autobiography and a documentary.[16] As an aside, this is a good illustration of how a communication or message can take on a life of its own, as different parties struggle for ownership of the message and the ideas behind the message.

The reference to unknowns highlights that in our reasoning process we may suffer, or struggle, with insufficient knowledge. We also have certain biases and make certain assumptions. We try to fill in the gaps, and in so doing our attention can be steered in the wrong direction, or our eyes fall on the wrong element and our decision or viewpoint is thus faulty. There are occasions when we are unable to systematize to make sense, and hence we need to fill in the gaps based upon assumptions or by seeking out new information. In such moments we may well hold tentative or temporary notions of the complete picture and revise accordingly. There are occasions when we have a diminished capacity to be objective, and our intelligence is usurped by emotions or biases, leading to a triumph of a subjective over an objective view. In such circumstances we ignore the facts that do not fit and overvalue the facts that do fit to bolster our subjective case. There are occasions when we are challenged by the understood

---

[14] https://www.theatlantic.com/politics/archive/2014/03/rumsfelds-knowns-and-unknowns-the-intellectual-history-of-a-quip/359719/

[15] A partial transcript is reported in an opinion piece by documentary-maker Errol Morris, https://opinionator.blogs.nytimes.com/2014/03/25/the-certainty-of-donald-rumsfeld-part-1/

[16] Donald Rumsfeld, *Unknown Unknowns* (Penguin Group, New York, 2011).

ethical norms, and intelligence allows us to still make use of these norms or rules of thumb to achieve an equitable result. There are occasions when our intelligence is unable to appraise events fully for a number of reasons, which may be because there are key events not occurring that we would expect or had been told would be a precursor to the troubling event. It may be that key information we would expect is not established. Another reason may be that we are struggling with our approach to an event or information because the way is not adequately prepared, or simply because we have been kept in the dark. A daily humdrum example of dealing with this is business meetings and social gatherings, where there is the good practice of fully introducing people, rather than leaving people to try to figure who an individual is, thereby being distracted from the task of engaging with them. Of course, people may not introduce people exactly because they want to disconnect or marginalize their presence.

8.3   Rational decision-making

Ordinarily, when a firm or organization's management is coming to a decision, there is much intelligence at work, involving many intelligent individuals in the process. There may be many hours, weeks, months and more put into reaching the decision. The decision will be well researched, discussed in many committees, focus groups and involve multiple internal and external parties. Many presentations will be made, and feedback built into making the decision more robust. So far, so good. Why then can all this intelligent work be undermined in the blink of an eye? The answer is emotion, which we will explore in the next chapter. We take the common example of a company closing down a facility. Like many major decisions, let's assume this move is announced to the outside media, perhaps at a media conference or in a media release with various specific interviews. In this context, we can only admire the intelligence of the decision or plan, assuming the media portrays the decision in a sympathetic way. The media will ask questions, probe and discuss the decision or plan in a remote sense. Their objective is to see what the story is for them, asking if this is a valid approach, does it have great impact on the local community, will it send the share price up, will it lead to job losses, save the company or draw the wrath of politicians? In other words, is it newsworthy? Any number of news stories or narratives may emerge, depending on the size of the organization, the nature of the decision, and its interest to the outside world. The deciding question is simple: does the media narrative match the desired narrative?

The narrative battle you fight is that the decision or plan has its own narrative, the one the company or organization has based its own thinking on in order to reach the decision and the trajectory that is foreseen by the decision-makers. The media conference seeks to get that narrative reflected in what appears in the newspapers, on television and online, but the media will have their own ways of testing the decision and, as a result, form a different narrative. Internal media specialists and external consultants help to craft the message and materials to sell the organization's narrative, or at least to get the reported narrative as close as possible to the organization's narrative. Whatever the outcome, the media reporters are approaching the decision or plan intellectually. They don't really have any emotion vested, except in getting a story or being motivated by a big story or smelling a rat. The question is, are they convinced by the message and narrative they've been presented with, and will they more or less report the desired narrative? Hold this thought – we will return to it in the next chapter. The point to take on board here is that the work done on the decision or plan has been based on intelligence and it has been announced with this intelligence to an objective audience. We can admit that there has been some emotion that has gone into the planning, but again we'll hold that thought until the next chapter.

Intelligence is not simply about what it rational. We are also creative, spiritual and thoughtful, which are intelligent things to be and do. As human beings, we are not hardwired to act rationally, but our brains are wired in a particular way. Our brains are governed by the ability of neurons to forge new connections, to blaze new paths through the cortex, even to assume new roles. We can rewire our brain, and consciously develop our intelligence to learn new things. Our brains do a lot more than those of other species, and we have the capacity to rationalize about ourselves and our situation. We are also conscious of our end in life, and can seek spiritual paths to address our current existence and ideas of what lies beyond this life. We are, in other words, complex intelligent beings. While we often refer to what a rational and reasonable person would do in a situation, thinking through all the angles of a problem, we cannot get the full picture if we exclude the elements in the other zones we will discuss. But even in this zone, intelligence is not simply what is rational. In intelligence we use a lot of educated guesswork and rules of thumb. The brain also has the subconscious, which contains a lot that we, as the term obviously suggests, are not always aware of. When we calculate distance, for instance, we are subconsciously using a range of mathematical data and equations to make a judgement about when to apply the brake on a car or position ourselves to catch a ball in flight. Our brain has this built into it, and we barely pay attention to the fact we can do this and that we undertake a lot of work in the brain that goes on without us slavishly rationalizing step by step.

However, we also have to recognize that our minds are limited. Each of us, to varying degrees, has limited knowledge, intelligence and attention spans. Even a trained lawyer has limited knowledge of the law. The boundaries of our knowledge and expertise are tested when faced with choice and change, yet we usually hold onto our preconceived ideas in responding to change and this can lead to the ossification of our knowledge and expertise. There are neurological reasons why this is the case. Despite the widely held belief that more is better – in other words lots of choice reflects our independence and individuality – in fact, the human mind can only cope with so many choices at one particular time. Often for the brain it is less that is more. In making choices, our brains exclude data, trying to strip away the extraneous to get at the essential. However, in this process, our level of knowledge, assumptions and other factors come into play in excluding things, sometimes to the detriment of a good decision, which might partly explain why so many bad decisions are taken. Making choices is about making sense of a variety of data points and what we see before us. We have documents, cases and reports. We meet people and influencers. We have a range of assumptions and legal principles and authorities, which we work with to make sense of the possible trajectory for these assumptions in a particular case. All of these variables combine in coming to a decision, and all of the time involve us in seeking to make legal sense. It is not simply that we have all the data and just need to make sense of it; quite the reverse is often the case, as we find it hard to make full sense of a case because data is missing. The eye is a camera, with a lens for the mind to make sense of data. This extends to how we approach situations that at first don't seem to make sense. We fill in the missing pieces and try to complete the incomplete picture we are presented with. Again, we do not do this 100% rationally. We are influenced by a variety of factors, from rules of thumb to what we had for breakfast. In an organization we are surrounded by influencers – people who can have a say on what we think. The right or wrong thing said at the wrong or right time can have enormous impact, because it may cause us to fill in a gap we see and form the basis of what we decide we know about a person or situation. It may not, however, be the missing piece. In the politics of an organization or a situation, this is where vulnerability creeps in, as rationality yields to perception. In understanding perception, we see that knowledge becomes negotiable.

Knowledge is power – we've all heard that. It leads managers to hold on to information as a power play. It can be used at critical points to influence a decision. Organizational gatekeepers will guard knowledge or information to maintain their authority or control over a person or situation. Their possession of knowledge makes them attractive, and it seduces people into a particular power relationship with them. Here's the thing: Francis Bacon wrote that money should be like manure, effective only when spread about. Information and knowledge are the same. If knowledge is shared, it can produce teamwork and results – spread like manure to grow a nice crop of success. If it is hoarded like manure in a barn, it will soon begin to stink. How smelly is your organization? This is a seemingly silly question to ask, but I've asked it and you should be asking the question as well. Another thing about knowledge is that it is frequently observed that we live in a knowledge economy. The role and importance of knowledge are frequently talked about, as if it were purely something objective to be captured, stored and used. I contend knowledge is much more dynamic than this, because it is much more nebulous than this common picture implies. It is perhaps not surprising, then, that most organizations struggle with knowledge management. This is not a book on knowledge management, but there are some important aspects of knowledge that are relevant to discuss here. Knowledge is part of intelligence, since it impacts how we think. In situations of low knowledge, we are in learning phases, and more reliant upon external resources and consultants to create knowledge within the organization. The more we know, the more we can create and innovate new products, services and, of course, knowledge. This all contributes to the organization's knowledge capital, and the ability of your organization to be a learning organization.

8.4   Building the learning legal unit

A key reason for knowledge being difficult to grapple with is the speed of change. What we know is changing all the time, and we are constantly creating new knowledge and making old knowledge redundant. We can start a major project and quickly find ourselves in a race against redundancy. On one level we love technology, and all the possibilities of finding knowledge that it opens up to us. Let's look at how this plays out in the organization, whether it is a legal department or a law firm. While nearly everyone complains at some point about having to go to work, especially at the start of the working week, the truth is that people largely enjoy being at work, and it is important to them. What all employees need is to stretch a little at work, to avoid the repetitive. It is easy to get bored, lose focus with the repetitive and mundane and disconnect our attention. In the legal context, there are many mundane and repetitive tasks, such as going through contracts, but these are being replaced by automation. This has a double implication. First, it places the premium on our intelligence, discussed earlier, and second, it raises our boredom threshold. As we become more expert, our understanding of what is mundane or repetitive changes. These individual dynamics feed into the organizational dynamics of the law firm or legal department, which is an organization that is constantly changing and learning. The learning organization is one that keeps pace with the changing circumstances of its workforce and finds ways to stimulate people in an engaging way. We have seen that attention is key to human behaviour – which is about focus rather than skill or ability. However, an attentive workforce is a learning workforce.

To engage and get employees' attention, the common wisdom is that we have to survey employee attitudes, and so it is commonplace for companies to do employee surveys and other testing on a regular basis. However, I venture to suggest these are not really that useful. First, many of the most inconvenient findings go largely unconfronted, except at a very superficial level. If they were taken seriously, internal communications and human resources would be better resourced. Second, they are reflective exercises, in the sense that they call on employees to reflect on their experience, which is not as helpful as people think in terms of a survey. This reflection is already processed and mediated by memory and subsequent circumstances. Employees will often answer based on their feeling and situation at the time of the survey, not the time when various events were happening; in other words, they are not done in real time. Many of the best results can be achieved by simple polling exercises, done in a more fun way online or via an app, and with considerably less cost and interference. If there is one thing employees across all industries and professions say with some frequency, it is that they are surveyed too often by this consultancy or that specialist – and often without seeing any visible results at the end.

One method that may find itself more influential in the workplace in the future is the experience sampling method (ESM). Developed by psychologist Mihaly Csikszentmihalyi at Claremont Graduate University, ESM involves participants wearing a pager or watch that beeps randomly at two-hour points during the course of a set number of weeks. When the beep goes off, the participant writes down key aspects of their situation at that point, such as where they are, the specific act they are doing, who is with them and how they feel about what they are doing – in other words, recording emotion in real time. This is instead of filling in questionnaires at a much later point and reflecting on a range of times, places, people and feelings. The technique is some 30 years old and has produced data that supports the notion that people enjoy their work when they are focused on it and time is quickly passing. This and other research support the thesis that people are happiest at work when they are so focused that the day flies by, rather than drags on. When you are focused you lose sense of time, and you reflect less on yourself and actions; you cease to narrate internally and act instead. It is this activity that ESM measures. This understanding draws on the fact that reward comes from the joy of doing, not just the pay or getting awards, though they help! In a low-energy environment, people can spend time distracted and bored, alternating with moments of interest in their work or with their colleagues. A high-energy environment will have motivated people, working and learning together. It is unlikely that any environment exists that can sustain such high energy all the time, but on average it can sustain good energy levels. The goal is to keep stimulating employees as much as possible to be as high energy as consistently as possible, which is what an engaged workforce will be. You see this in well-written drama, which is a narrative. Comedy scenes break the pattern for a tragedy, and tragedy provides a counterpoint for comedy. In the legal workplace, this is not a question of making them happy, so for goodness' sake, never ask people if they are happy, and never ask an individual employee 'are you happy here?' Happiness is a reflection, a looking back, rather than a state of being. We realize we have been made happy by doing things that engaged us and by living in a state of being where we are absorbed by things, not happiness in itself. The real question to ask is this: are you engaged here?

One way to engage that is often suggested, and even been made into television shows, is to get people to do someone else's job for a day. To date I have seen little evidence of this happening in workplaces, but I have seen it done. This idea falls under the category of risk behaviour in a company, and so managers shy away from it. Yet companies take a lot of risks – it is inherent in business – but rarely do they take risks with their people in a positive way. We can learn a lot from doing someone else's tasks, seeing what they see and do, and perhaps this makes us more appreciative of the job we do. As the saying goes, the grass is not always greener on the other side of the fence. Perhaps I'm asking too much here, and it is just too disruptive for organizations to consider, but I would love to see companies make use of this as part of their work performance measurement – a few partners may well fail to make the grade! There are other low-level ways to achieve engaging results, and this is by finding ways to turn elements of work into a game, such as competitions, polls and quizzes. There are creative and fun ways to engage people and to educate them, and to help them grasp the organizational goals. However, this is not one-way traffic. By getting this engagement you can find people contributing ideas and stories that move the organization along. People will volunteer their ideas and stories more readily, from which the leadership can learn new things and directions as well.

In approaching the law, we can look at the formal process of the court system and the professionals working throughout the legal system. We should not lose sight of the fact that for the client, going through this system is only part of their life, and it is also only part of the whole construct of law in society. In looking to the facts, we need to be open-minded as lawyers and as people. We know we have some lack of knowledge and gaps in our perception, and we cannot contain a store of all cases and authorities in our head. Our legal education is in part a process of having learned paths through situations, so for whatever we don't know, we know where we can look or know someone who can help us in our case. Law is as much a case of how we do it as to what it is. Likewise, our client is not simply a person with a legal problem; they are a complex of variables from which we are trying to tease out the legal issues and solutions. Meanwhile, there are many variables constantly in the background, so that at any point an event or a single variable can change and cause a thought or action to break through the legal strategy and throw it off course. We are always only ever a step or two away from changing course. What often drives this process – and can throw matters off course or force them towards the courts – is emotion, and it is to emotion that we now turn in the next step of using the Dialogue Box.

8.5   Practical steps: Zone 1 – Intelligence

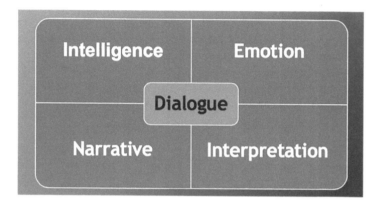

The Intelligence Zone is about the rationale and reasoning behind any decision, action or project that you might present to your audience. In using the Dialogue Box, the intelligence need not change, but you can choose to change the intelligence you want to work with, such as your advice or a decision. If that advice is difficult for a client, for instance, the Dialogue Box can be used to work through achieving a collaborative result whereby the client can embrace the decision. The point is to identify that this is what has been decided or what the best advice might be, and your role is to figure out how to communicate to clients, colleagues or other stakeholders in the most effective way. When you are in this zone you want to focus on making sense of the data and planning what steps are necessary steps, as well as making judgements about right and wrong. It is also a place to start looking to distinguish personal views from what is best in the situation, as they may not coincide. Note that we can be talking about the intelligence at either an individual or collective level. This is important to note, not just for self-awareness, but also in working with others. In collaborating with others, often a group is persuaded and guided by what becomes the shared rationale as individuals get behind the rationale, but on occasion this can result in the group going in the wrong direction!

8.5.1   In a nutshell

The Dialogue Box makes no assumption about whether the intelligence is good or bad, since often that is subjective. The point is to look at engagement once you have decided to do – or advise on – something. If this something is unpopular, as suggested, the Dialogue Box will help you to engage with others to get the best possible outcome. Going through the Dialogue Box exercise predictively, you may decide to change some aspects of your intelligence based on your conclusions. Equally, using the Dialogue Box after the event may help you to locate those aspects of your intelligence that can be reinforced or changed through dialogue.

8.5.2   Filling in the zone

Your headline should state neutrally what the situation or matter is about, having collected all the data together:

- Who is involved?
- What are the facts?
- Are there other stakeholders?
- What is the timeline?
- Who said what and when?
- If public, when and how did people first learn about the event?
- What reasons have people stated for their actions or statements?

Can you put the matter into a single, neutral sentence?

8.5.3   Key takeaway

Remember, we want to ask questions that help us to understand the facts and to state the narrative in this zone as simply and objectively as possible, so that any party to the dialogue would agree on the narrative as much as possible.

9   The Emotion Zone

Lawyers, as I have noted, are usually comfortable with the facts; they are less so when it comes to emotion. In the Emotion Zone of the Dialogue Box, we can explore the dynamics of emotion in communicating and dealing with clients and other audiences. We ought to bear in mind here that the law produces emotion as well, in terms of how people respond to legislation, compliance orders, acts of enforcement and a number of other ways the law impacts people and organizations. The reader will learn why emotions matter and how they influence and shape communication and dialogue in what may appear to be a counterintuitive approach. Emotion has become another emerging interdisciplinary field in law, bringing together scholars from law, psychology, classics, economics, literature and philosophy. This, I suggest, is a timely return to some basics of under-standing human behaviour and is not coincidentally linked to the rise of automation; indeed, I contend the question of emotion in society has an awful lot to do with the rise of new technologies. The focus on 'artificial intelligence' has put 'emotional intelligence' into a new focus, and how we manage the relationship between technology and the human is one of discovering a new world of augmented intelligence that cannot be under-stood without a better understanding of emotion.

The term 'emotional' is frequently used as a code word for 'unreasonable' or 'unreliable', based on the implicit assumption that emotion is incom-patible with reason. The law is based on rationality, but emotions and emotional intelligence play a much more direct and central role in legal communication than is traditionally recognized to be the case. The call for justice is often a call made emotionally, so we can quickly recognize that the notion of law as cold rationale fails to live up to that billing. It also fails to live up to the notion that lawyers and judges are working tirelessly with legally reasoned arguments, working in some cases with juries that deliberate calmly and dispassionately. Emotion is everywhere in the law, but let's just take a couple of core areas as examples. Contract law is rooted in the fact that people have made promises, and disputes arise because one or both have broken the promise. This is more than simply a rational deal, as the parties concerned are in part emotionally bound in the business they do, and in the business relationships they have enjoyed. Making a promise is not just a rational agreement; it is an emotional pact, one that gives deeper resonance to the agreement. When a promise is broken, there is an emotional reaction and not just a rational shrug of the shoulders. An emotional attachment to a supplier may impact business relationships, and lead to contract terms that were favourable when the parties were emotionally connected but have become a source of discontent when the relationship breaks apart.

Criminal law is an area of law where emotion is ubiquitous.[1] In its starkest view of emotion, as being contrary to reason, there are questions as to the extent to which rationality and emotion can be separated. The view that was long established in criminal law serves as a crucible for such discussion – which lies beyond the needs of this book – and that is The M'Naghten Rule (or test) established by the English House of Lords in the mid-19th century:

> Every man is to be presumed to be sane, and ... that to establish a defence on the ground of insanity, it must be clearly proved that, at the time of the committing of the act, the party accused was labouring under such a defect of reason, from disease of mind, and not to know the nature and quality of the act he was doing; or if he did know it, that he did not know he was doing what was wrong.[2]

Insanity is an emotional state, not just a breakdown in reason. We also see emotion being explicitly tackled in homicide, which is considered less culpable if it is committed in the heat of passion, instead of after cold calculation.[3] Posner explains how prejudicial evidence is excluded for reasons of emotion because it can excite bias or sympathy in the jury.[4] There is a great deal of emotion in the process of assessing evidence. Juries may try to suppress their horror or disgust when viewing photographs of

[1] Dan M. Kahan and Martha C. Nussbaum, *Two Conceptions of Emotion in Criminal Law* (1996), Colum. L. Rev., Vol. 96, pp. 285–89.
[2] M'Naghten's case [1843] UKHL J16 (19 June 1843) at 210.
[3] N.J. Finkel and W.G. Parrott, *Emotions and Culpability: How the Law is at Odds with Psychology, Jurors, and Itself* (American Psychological Association, 2006). https://doi.org/10.1037/11475-000
[4] Richard A. Posner, *An Economic Approach to the Law of Evidence* (February, 1999), University of Chicago Law School, John M. Olin Law & Economics Working Paper No. 66, pp. 21–4, http://dx.doi.org/10.2139/ssrn.165176

murder victims, or they may delight in the prurient details of misdeeds by celebrities once thought of as untouchable.

The International Society for Therapeutic Jurisprudence (ISTJ) states, 'Therapeutic jurisprudence (TJ) is an interdisciplinary field of philosophy and practice that examines the therapeutic and anti-therapeutic properties of laws and public policies, legal and dispute resolution systems, and legal institutions. TJ values psychologically healthy outcomes in legal disputes and transactions, without claiming exclusivity in terms of policy objectives.'[5] Abrams and Keren explain the pragmatic value of this school of thought, and how to enable broader application of law and emotions analysis to pressing legal problems. They note:

> Some legal analysts may never be persuaded that emotions should become a focal concern of the law. They may prefer to view law as an arena that answers to the standards of rationality, drawing on analyses such as behavioral law and economics to respond to rationality's limits. But for those who are prepared to understand emotion not simply as a departure from rationality, but as an affirmative mode of apprehension and response, the law and emotions perspective offers a way by which legal actors and institutions can both accommodate and influence crucial dimensions of human experience.[6]

Hence, the pushback at what they see as the ambivalent legal response to the law and emotions perspective.

Posner argues that there many issues in law which:

> ... raise questions about the relationship between emotion and law, but legal theory is unprepared to answer them. One reason for the neglect of emotions in legal theory may be that the dominant strains of normative legal theory – economic analysis, moral-philosophical analysis, constitutional analysis – rely on methodologies that are not well suited to analyzing emotion, or at least, for reasons of intellectual history, have simply not yet focused on the emotions. Another reason may be the primitive state of the psychology literature on the topic. Psychologists themselves admit that they do not have a good theory of the emotions, in part because research in this area is relatively new. Yet

5   https://intltj.com/about/
6   Kathryn R. Abrams, and Hila Keren, *Who's Afraid of Law and the Emotions?* (January 1, 2010), Minnesota Law Review, Vol. 94, No. 6, p. 2000.

a review of that literature reveals a number of insights that are sufficiently well-developed to be of value for legal theory.[7]

The Dialogue Box offers a methodology for analysing emotion in a very practical way and can also be of help perhaps in dialogue around the legal theory itself. It is also assumed that there are adequate psychological insights to help us practically in bringing emotional insights into legal practice and these are incorporated in the Dialogue Box, which illustrates there are productive ways where we can understand how law and emotion can be of immense support in the practice of law.

In the context of law, emotions are certainly present in various ways, but while they are to be weighted differently, they have been treated with little acceptance historically. As Susan Bandes notes, 'The legal system has long been inhospitable terrain for the study of emotion;'[8] we have to break down interdisciplinary hostility. In practice, certainly my experience of training and talking to lawyers across the globe suggests that to a great extent this is recognized by practitioners. Education and training to tackle this hostility will be most beneficial, as it does challenge some of the conventional and traditional teaching of lawyers. Abrams and Keren explain that law and emotions is 'more epistemologically challenging'[9] than other 'law and disciplines' in respect to conventional legal thinking, perhaps because 'it does not privilege rationality or prioritize the objectivist epistemologies that have become cornerstones of mainstream legal thought'.[10] For a taxonomy of law and emotions, Abrams and Keren outline three dimensions to explore:

(1) *attributes of cognition*: law and emotions scholarship value the affective dimensions of cognition as fully as the classically rational, rather than understanding them as 'other' or as potentially problematic departures from rationality;
(2) *cognate literatures*: law and emotions scholarship may draw on economics, biological science, and more objectivist social sciences, but it also draws on literature, history, philosophy and other humanist disciplines; and

---

[7] Eric Posner, *Law and the Emotions*, John M. Olin Program in Law and Economics Working Paper No. 103, 2000.
[8] https://emotionresearcher.com/what-roles-do-emotions-play-in-the-law/
[9] Abrams and Keren (n 6), p. 2010.
[10] Ibid.

(3) *normative goals*: law and emotions scholarship engage law not simply, or even primarily, to correct the cognitive responses of legal subjects in favour of greater rationality; it aims to modify law more fully to acknowledge the role of specific emotions, or to use law to produce particular emotional effects.[11]

These dimensions can be detected in the workings of the Dialogue Box. A key underpinning of the Dialogue Box, a point also made clear by Abrams and Keren, is that emotions are part of legal behaviour whether legal professionals recognize it or not. Emotion can help improve decision-making and, in the words of these authors, 'Legal decision making is enriched and refined by the operation of emotions because they direct attention to particular dimensions of a case, or shape decisionmakers' ability to understand the perspective of, or the stakes of a decision for, a particular party.'[12] The Dialogue Box is also a decision-making tool, and emotions play a huge part in our decision-making, which needs to be recognized in our dialogue with others. I suggest this is perhaps more obvious in the mediation and negotiation stages of legal dispute, where locating the emotional issues may lead to better decisions that keep cases out of court and avoids more expensive stages of litigation. As noted earlier, emotion is a primary driver in pushing many cases into the legal sector generally and into the courts specifically. There are ample examples, but two cases of people spending vast sums in legal disputes between neighbours easily illustrate the point: one involves homeowners who ran up £70,000 in legal expenses over moving a fence six inches;[13] the second is a dispute between neighbours over who should pay a £4,000 bill to fix a drain, which subsequently racked up legal costs of over £300,000.[14] These disputes – and there are plenty more of them – make little rational sense, and it is only when you look at emotion that you begin to make any sense of it. Without criticism of the lawyers in these two specific cases – who may well have done their best in bad circumstances – I would contend

---

[11] Ibid, p. 1998, fn1. The authors add: 'For a thoughtful article heralding the emergence of the field which defines it in somewhat different terms, see Terry A. Maroney, *Law and Emotion: A Proposed Taxonomy of an Emerging Field*, 30 Law & Hum. Behav. 119 (2006) (arguing that law and emotions scholarship is organized around six approaches: emotion-centered, emotional phenomenon, emotion theory, legal doctrine, theory of law, and legal actor).'

[12] Ibid, p. 1997.

[13] https://www.telegraph.co.uk/news/2020/02/19/millionaire-neighbours-in70000-court-battle-fence-six-inches/

[14] https://www.lawgazette.co.uk/law/dispute-over-4000-repair-bill-racks-up-300000-in-costs/5055447.article

that disputes like these can be better managed by lawyers using emotional management and communication approaches, and the Dialogue Box is a tool that could be usefully deployed.

The work of the Dialogue Box goes hand in hand with work done in the communications field on emotion, along with narrative, but equally goes hand in hand with many of the insights offered by the law and emotions movement. Robin West explains:

> The law and emotions scholars have correctly focused the academy's attention on the emotional root of law's legislative origins and its judicial interpretation, as well as on the emotional and impassioned human being – as opposed to the cost benefit toting calculating subject, or the self-interested egoistic subject, or the politically driven subject hungry for his share of either earth or power – who is at least oftentimes at the center of law's gaze, and certainly at the center of its might.[15]

Emotions in the legal space are products of the law itself, as West notes, and can also be understood as emotions that affect law or the emotions that law affects.[16] It is good to see the emergence of more work in this space, and there is more to be done, as West's criticism of law and emotions scholarship suggests:

> Law and Emotions scholars have looked at emotion's impact on law and on our understanding of justice, and at law's impact on emotional life, and have done so to great effect. What they, or we, haven't much to date investigated, however, are the emotions law produces, or authors, or sires, or births, or fathers – the emotions that law itself generates, rather than the emotions that affect law or the emotions that law affects. To echo William James, we have not generated an understanding of the 'varieties of legal experience.' To echo Foucault, we don't look much at the emotions that both law and legalism produce, rather than the emotions that impact law, or that are censured, denigrated, or regulated by it.[17]

Terry A. Maroney argues that law and emotions scholarship is organized around six approaches: emotion-centred, emotional phenomenon, emotion theory, legal doctrine, theory of law, and legal actor.[18] I don't

---

15 Robin West, *Law's Emotions* (2016), Rich. J.L. & Pub. Int., Vol. 19, pp. 341–2.

16 Ibid, p. 341.

17 Ibid, p. 341.

18 Terry A. Maroney, *Law and Emotion: A Proposed Taxonomy of an Emerging Field* (2006), Law & Hum. Behav., Vol. 30, p. 119.

intend to examine this movement here, though some of its output is certainly helpful, as is its attempt to rebalance the relationship between emotion and rationality. West notes:

> More fundamentally, some law and emotions scholars argue, legal theorists have likely accorded too great a role to rationality, and an insufficient role to emotion, when describing the origin of the rule of law itself, as well as our attachment to it and our ideals for it, as a product of self-interested games, metaphoric contracts, or highly rationalistic bargains. Legalism, they argue, more likely has its origin, as well as its appeal, in the primal fears and tremblings we occasion in each other, in our dread of our collective and individual fates, and at least on occasion, in our hopes for community and our love for each other, borne of our mutual attraction and need.[19]

This primal fear taps into the opening statements of this book, about legal communication as being based on the twin pillars of priesthood and fear. West concludes that the 'law's production of emotions deserves study', which to date has only been sporadic, and concludes:

> Law might reflect emotion, might be influenced by emotion, might regulate emotion, and might precipitate emotional outbursts. But law just can't be the sort of thing that actually produces emotion, so it can hardly be held accountable for doing so in a way that is damaging. This set of assumptions is wrong-headed from top to bottom: Law produces emotions, some of which are destructive. It can also produce emotions, of course, which are essential to human flourishing. But I suggest a critical stance, rather a celebratory mode should motivate this work: right now, we live and work within a legalistic order that worships constitutional authority, celebrates consensual ethics, has settled for equal opportunity, and trumpets the value of individual self sufficiency. Each of these individually, and certainly all jointly, produce toxic legal emotions. They should be in the cross hairs of all of our critical impulses.[20]

The Dialogue Box is a humble contribution to this work; it offers a practical tool for exploration of these themes and for practitioners to turn their gaze towards the emotional needs of clients and the emotional background of their cases. This said, we ought to be careful from the outset in how we examine emotion. There is a danger of giving emotion too much room. I am certainly not advocating in this approach that the law is to pander to unmediated or raw emotion. Lawyers needs to mediate emotion

---

[19]   West (n 15), p. 341.

[20]   Robin West, *Law's Emotions* (2016), Rich. J. L. & Pub. Int., Vol. 19, No. 339, p. 361, https://scholarship .richmond.edu/pilr/vol19/iss4/9

and understand the impact of raw emotion. In mediating emotion, we should examine the different ways in which emotions emerge, how they operate individualistically and in connection to a range of contexts and interests. Some people, and in some respects cultures as well, are more emotional than others. These emotions are developed through experience and education, and they are sometimes inadequately processed by the individual and even a social grouping. We should be aware of these facets, as part of understanding diversity, if emotion is to be understood more holistically and in all its dimensions. There is a perception that emotions are private and internal,[21] but they are also public, because groups can become emotional.

Emotions are also shared experiences. Roberto Unger explored the relation of reason to the 'passions', which he divided into 'good' and 'bad', arguing that 'bad' emotions always threaten to overcome the 'good' ones, which are exceedingly 'fragile'. Unger fashions emotions through the dominant lens of fear of the other, suggesting all the passions arise from longing and jeopardy.[22] He sees paradoxes existing in 'good' emotions, such as love, but less so in 'bad' emotions, such as hatred. Unger draws a further distinction between hatred and envy, and 'justified indignation', the latter apparently being rationally determined. Love, which is the 'cure' for the vices, is undermined by the fear of another because of the threat the other presents: '[L]ove cannot be pure. It must be accompanied by the presentiment of its own fragility and by at least a suggestion of defensive repugnance and inscrutability toward the other.'[23] Envy, greed, hatred and lust feature in many a court case, and play decisive roles in people's behaviour in the events leading up to the point where a situation has become acknowledged as a legal issue. Some of these emotions, like hatred, are tied to acts to become criminalized, like hate speech. Such legislation is as much about the emotional impact of the act as the act itself. Riling up a crowd to incite them to violence is an emotional sequence. Equally, it is emotion that often fuels the desire to see justice done. The satisfaction of seeing justice done is not just to be rationally appeased; rather, the sense or emotion of seeing justice done makes the pursuit of justice itself a holistic quest. Many legal activists, and legal practitioners,

---

[21]   A.R. Hochschild, *The Managed Heart: Commercialization of Human Feeling* (University of California Press, Berkeley, 1983).

[22]   Roberto Unger, *Passion: An Essay on Personality* (The Free Press, New York, 1984), pp. 220–47.

[23]   Ibid, p. 221.

can trace their desire to act or to be lawyers back to an event or situation that made them angry or deeply moved. Emotion is a catalyst for legal work as much as it is for any other aspect of life.[24] It spurs us into action and feeds our ongoing desire to keep acting. Why then, historically, has it been so ignored in the literature as Bandes, West and others have noted?

It need not have evolved this way, but we can return to a more balanced understanding of rationale and emotion. There isn't the space to pursue this point much further here, but we can take a fleeting nod to history. I suggest a look into the Scots and Irish Enlightenment, which explains how emotions were seen as much more central to the liberal enterprise, only to be shut down by Hobbes, English rationalism and the development of capitalism. As I note, there is not space to go into it here, but it is a fascinating history to study. What I do take from this, however, is the Scots and Irish emphasis on the 'sentiments', which is a better term in my view for emotions, but it would be less successful to communicate it this way I suspect in today's way of speaking. Mind you, the term was taken up by Justice Brennan, who once stated that 'it is often the highest calling of a judge to resist the tug of … sentiments.'[25] However, this needs to be unpacked substantially if we are to understand the role of emotion in the process of legal reasoning, and thus see it as a part of legal reasoning rather than an attraction – or distraction – that tugs and pulls away at us contrary to cold legal reasoning. The privileging of rationality over emotion, or the sentiments, came about in the historical and economic process I alluded to above as the triumph of rationality and scientific efficiency in the age of capitalism. As Posner stated, judges discipline themselves to respond to the problems before them with 'careful, linear rationality'.[26] However, in his Cardozo lecture, Justice Brennan said of judging, and being a judge, that legal culture and legal scholars have persistently resisted or overlooked the point that a judge cannot truly approach 'objectivity' until the judge recognizes the subjective, experiential, and emotional 'influences' on his or her reason, adding that 'sensitivity to one's intuitive and passionate responses, and awareness of the range

---

[24] West develops this further: '… most modest claim is that these emotions are the product rather than the subject of law. They emanate from the legal face of our political order, rather than from anything that can be located either in our politics or in our private lives.' West (n 15), p. 344.

[25] Justice Brennan, *Reason, Passion, and 'The Progress of the Law'* (1988), Cardozo L. Rev., Vol. 10, p. 11.

[26] Richard A. Posner, *Emotion Versus Emotionalism in Law*, in S.A. Bandes (ed.), *The Passions of Law* (New York University Press, New York, 1999), p. 311.

of human experience, is ... not only an inevitable but a desirable part of the judicial process, an aspect more to be nurtured than feared.'[27] Many of the legal system's assumptions about emotion are implicit rather than explicit, and perhaps this makes emotion elusive and harder to nurture, requiring as Brennan's statement implies that there is a high degree of self-awareness. The Dialogue Box is structured as a means to creating this self-awareness, providing a framework to examine one's assumptions, biases and emotions.

Cold legal reasoning may also lead us to assume in practice, if not in theory, that there is a normative state of neutrality and impartiality, which tells us what the law is in the given context of a case. We can reason and define the law that applies, and I am not seeking to undermine this important legal principle. However, in doing this in practical terms, I suggest it can be done with both rational and emotional integrity using the Dialogue Box to make the ground of dialogue as neutral as possible, though not necessarily impartial. Because the dialogue includes oneself, impartiality becomes difficult, as we still want something out of the situation. What we can try to create is a neutral picture or narrative of the situation we face, in order to find approaches to dialogue that will be more effective to find a solution to a problem or a resolution of a dispute, because the picture is more recognizable to the other side. To be impartial would be taking a step the participant does not necessarily need – or even want – to take, though it is one the judge seeks to achieve. Learned Hand opined:

> You must have impartiality. What do I mean by impartiality? I mean you mustn't introduce yourself, your own preconceived notions about what is right. You must try, as far as you can, it is impossible to human beings to do so absolutely, but just so far as you can, not to interject your own personal interests, even your own preconceived assumptions and beliefs.[28]

There is a sense in which you are using the Dialogue Box to achieve a level of impartiality, because the process invites you – as far as possible – to remove yourself from the situation to find an objective sense of what is going on. You are trying to stand back from your own emotional investment, or that of the client, to see things objectively, both rationally and

---

[27] William J. Brennan, Jr., *Reason, Passion, and the Progress of Law*, Cardozo Lecture (Association of the Bar of the City of New York, 1987).

[28] I. Dillard (ed.), *The Spirit of Liberty: Papers and Addresses of Learned Hand* (Knopf, New York, 1958), pp. 309–10.

emotionally. This is not the same as acting impartially. You can use your search for impartial insights to pursue dialogue to gain what you need to get out of the dialogue. The obverse of this is commonplace in communication, you end up – to put it crassly – believing in your own bullshit. Emotion can thus be studied by lawyers more productively and harnessed as part of ensuring more effective legal communication. As Harris and Shultz explain: '[W]hen emotions are acknowledged and rigorously examined, they can serve as a guide to deepening intellectual inquiry.'[29] To which we can add legal inquiry.

Hence, when the lawyer is communicating, or participants in the case are communicating, this is done in search of the legal narrative. The Dialogue Box process is one of forming a narrative that describes the emotional landscape and taps into a systemic structure of emotion. The systemic point refers to emotion that runs through the actors, language and apparatus of the case, which has a dialectical relationship. The language of the courtroom is emotional, because it creates fear and intimidation in witnesses, as well as excitement and anticipation, which may then translate into unreliable or distorted testimony. This then affects the interpretation of the evidence and eventually the outcome of the case. We are looking for a narrative understanding that removes, as far as possible, emotion that can hinder the narrative flow and cause the process to be slowed, as participants struggle with the legal language as well as their memory, which is inhibited by the emotion they are experiencing. The language and apparatus of law is also a language of power, and power is also linked to emotion.

9.1   Emotion, judgement and power

Owen Fiss writes that emotion is 'inconsistent with the very norms that govern and legitimate the judicial power'.[30] This view has to be unpacked, because what is taken to be a norm is often power and vested interest. We can ponder whose norms Fiss is suggesting. Bandes suggests the question is not whether emotion can have a role in law, but what kinds of emotion

---

[29] Angela P. Harris and Marjorie M. Shultz, *'A(nother) Critique of Pure Reason': Toward Civic Virtue in Legal Education* (1993), Stan. L. Rev. Vol. 45, p. 1774.

[30] Owen C. Fiss, *Reason in All Its Splendor* (1990), Brooklyn L. Rev., Vol. 56, pp. 789–804. See: https://emotionresearcher.com/what-roles-do-emotions-play-in-the-law/

operate in particular contexts and what sort of a role they play. This is what we can explore in the Emotion Zone.[31] If we say emotion has no place, we are excluding people as well as evidence, because the emotional makeup of any situation is part of the problem. This can also bring in problems of bias. How someone may look at another who belongs to a different ethnic group or gender is a point to raise here. If we have a gender view that says women are emotional – a commonplace assumption in many a court over the ages – and we think emotions are distinct from, and inferior to, the practice of rational interpretation, where does this leave us? We could look at the evidence and say a woman has acted emotionally, thus irrationally, and that will lead to a certain interpretation. Siegel argues that legal actors associate emotion exclusively and restrictively with women, and they address it in that most feminine (or feminized) of domains, namely the decision whether to bear a child.[32] Abrams and Keren write that this approach to women's emotions received its most salient form of support in *Gonzales v. Carhart*, and suggest:

> Emotion – where it has been most forthrightly acknowledged in recent legal argumentation – is a force that besets and infantilizes women; it authorizes a highly paternalistic and restrictive state response.[33]

Even if we accept the courts are more enlightened in these times, I dare say the attitude still persists in many a dispute. It is also an attitude that will hold sway, be persuasive and manipulate outcomes. Law and gender appear as a thread running throughout these points. Such analysis can be applied to a range of biases and assumptions, and these are not just the basis of views someone holds in the belief they are rational; they are also emotionally vested views and have an emotional impact on other parties. Ultimately, they are a source of power, and emotion plays a significant part in how the law operates.

Resnik has argued judges should consider the reality of the 'other' in their decision, which suggests to her:

---

[31] Richard A. Posner, *Emotion Versus Emotionalism in Law*, in S.A. Bandes (ed.), *The Passions of Law* (New York University Press, New York, 1999), p. 311.

[32] Reva B. Siegel, *The New Politics of Abortion: An Equality Analysis of Woman-Protective Abortion Restrictions* (2007), U. Ill. L. Rev., Vol. 1011, p. 999.

[33] Abrams and Keren (n 6).

A modification of the official dogma judging would be required to add the traits of compassion, care, concern, nurturance, identification, and sympathetic attention to the list of aspirations for our judges ... We do not, but we could, demand that those who hold power do so with attentive love, with care, with nurturance, with a responsible sense of one's self as connected to and dependent upon those who are being judged.[34]

This can present us with problems, and Resnik outlines these, but where it leads her to is the observation:

In our current world, in which we do not ask judges to recognize their connectedness to those before them, some judges impose harsh sentences and some more lenient ones; some judges impose obligations upon litigants without much apparent stress while others appear reluctant to sanction. The length of judicial opinions and the energy of some dissents bear testimony to the tugs and pulls of contemporary judging, complete with its claims of dispassion and disinterest.[35]

A last point I want to extract from Resnik's argument is worth exploring as we look at emotion in the court process:

When we recognize the burden and the pain of judging, we might uncover one element of adjudication that exists but is relatively unacknowledged: Much 'adjudication' is not a win/lose proposition but an effort at accommodation, with judges and juries responding to both sides but currently without vocabulary or permission to express empathy with competing claims. Many verdicts allocate victory to both sides, but our tradition is to mask that allocation rather than to endorse the practice of seeing multiple claims of right. Feminism may help bolster our trust in practice and permit us to remove the facades of total victory and defeat.[36]

The Dialogue Box can help lawyers navigate this terrain, and to develop a more appropriate emotional vocabulary to create a more just process. As Henderson explains:

Emotions and empathy should be officially recognized as influences on judges and legal actors. This is not to say that emotions should become dominant – that would be a perpetuation of the either/or. Rather, emotions should be

---

[34] Judith Resnik, *On the Bias: Feminist Reconsiderations of the Aspirations for Our Judges* (1988), S. Cal. L. Rev., Vol. 61, pp. 1922–3.

[35] Ibid, p. 1924.

[36] Josh Blackman, *The Burden of Judging* (November 9, 2014), NYU Journal of Law & Liberty, Vol. 8, No. 1105.

recognized as a valid source of information ... Judges would not be judges, and lawyers would not be lawyers, if they did not acknowledge or consider the laws, doctrines, and principles that are the very nature of their enterprise. But perhaps they can listen to and use the materials more effectively and more humanely, if they do not try to take refuge in the pretension of 'pure reason' alone.[37]

Perhaps this is becoming true as ADR continues to make strides, and parties are encouraged to reach accommodating positions before ending up in the courtroom and before a judge. It makes power less forceful, giving more power to fairness and right over might. The fact people cannot make such accommodations perhaps explains why at the court level it becomes more power, more contested and more male. Resnick's argument suggests we can push more into this territory in making courts less male.[38]

9.2   Lawyers and bullying

There is a range of other emotional issues to be considered in the operation of legal practice. I have already addressed mental health issues elsewhere, but there are other areas to consider, starting with harassment and bullying behaviours in the workplace. Renowned for being a high-pressured environment, the legal sector is typified by long working hours, frequent alcohol consumption and high-stress atmospheres, all of which are often triggers for sexual harassment and other bad behaviours. There is growing pressure, and policies implemented, to eradicate such behaviours in the workplace, but this requires more than policies, procedures and compliance measures. While these approaches are part of the solution, the more productive and deeper process involves behavioural change. The statistics are stark, and we can quantify just how deep and serious the problem is in the profession.

---

[37] Lynne Henderson, *The Dialogue of the Heart and Head* (1988), Scholarly Works, Paper 869: http:// scholars.law.unlv.edu/facpub/869, pp. 147, 148.

[38] More discussion can be found here: https://www.opendemocracy.net/en/transformation/why-shouldn -t-law-ignore-emotion/

Complaints about harassment rose by 70% in 2019, making it a top-three issue, according to findings in the annual report of UK charity LawCare,[39] which runs a helpline, webchat, email and peer support service for legal professionals. In one year, 80 lawyers contacted the charity about bullying compared with 47 in 2018, with 66% complaining of being harassed by a manager or superior. The charity reported an overall increase in the number of legal professionals seeking help of 8% in 2019 – the most common problems cited by the callers were stress (26%) and depression (12%). The majority of callers were women (67%), while 53% were either trainees or had been qualified for less than five years. In May 2019, the International Bar Association (IBA) published the results of a global survey that also found that bullying and sexual harassment were widespread within the legal profession. The survey of almost 7,000 lawyers across 135 countries found that 62% of female respondents and 41% of male respondents reported being bullied in connection with their employment. By comparison, the international averages were 55% and 30% respectively. Sexual harassment in the UK aligns with the global average, with 38% of female and 6% of male respondents reporting abuse, compared with international levels of 37% and 7% respectively. The IBA report also found 'chronic underreporting' of incidents, with 57% of bullying cases and 75% of sexual harassment cases globally not reported. Chief among the reasons is a fear of career repercussions. The IBA report included a number of stories of abuse, including a tribunal case of a junior solicitor alleging she was forced to attend a sex show with a senior partner and had her employment terminated after rebuffing his advances – an allegation denied. Higher levels of sexual harassment and bullying were also recorded in Canada, South Africa, Australia and New Zealand. The report found that younger legal professionals are disproportionately affected by both bullying and sexual harassment.

The problem of gender inequality was flagged as a systemic problem that needs to be set against a relief of the work–life balance issue people face in their career. A survey of the legal profession in Scotland revealed some mixed results that provide useful insights into the problem. According to a Law Society of Scotland *Profile of the Profession*[40] survey, almost 80%

---

[39] https://www.lawcare.org.uk/news/lawcare-2019-figures-more-lawyers-seeking-help-and-calls-about -bullying-continue-to-rise

[40] https://www.lawscot.org.uk/news-and-events/law-society-news/survey-findings-show-improving -gender-equality-in-scottish-legal-profession/

of Scottish solicitors and accredited paralegals believe the profession has improved on gender equality over the past five years and is achieving a better work–life balance. However, in response, the society's president raised concerns over what was a mixed set of results. The survey showed that the gender pay gap within the profession had reduced from 42% in 2013 – when the *Profile of the Profession* research had been previously carried out – to 23% in 2018. In respect of work–life balance, the majority of respondents (73%) felt that they were or mostly were achieving a reasonable work–life balance. At the same time, work–life balance was the most frequently given reason by 54% of respondents who stated they had considered leaving the profession in the past five years. Achieving a work–life balance was the most important career aspiration over the next five years for almost a third of respondents. Promotion and progression were lower down the priorities list, with a quarter stating these issues. A fifth of respondents (20%) had at some stage in their career personally experienced discrimination in the profession, with 16% experiencing bullying over the past five years and 3% reporting having experienced sexual harassment. Also, 37% of respondents with disabilities were either not provided with, or were too apprehensive to request, a reasonable adjustment at work. Alison Atack, president of the Law Society of Scotland, said at the time, 'I have mixed emotions about the survey results. Pleased on the one hand that while there is still more to do, we have made real progress in many areas of equality and diversity but I am also saddened that any member of the legal profession has experienced bullying or discrimination.' The Law Society also published 28 recommendations to address equality and diversity issues within the profession in its report, which can helpfully inform how we put emotion more onto the agenda.[41]

9.3   Emotionally intelligent decision-making

Emotion can illuminate our understanding by giving intensity to our attention towards events and data, and through our having empathy or sympathy for others and situations. Emotion connects us, leading us to explore our understanding more deeply. The obverse can also be true, whereby emotion can cloud our judgement, and distract us or reprioritize our sense of needs or what is important. What makes emotion more dif-

---

[41]   Ibid.

ficult is the unconscious or repressed emotional influence that can come into view when confronted by an emotionally challenging situation. The same can be said of bias as an emotional input. When we act emotionally, we are acting before we think, which is the counterintuitive point in the Dialogue Box. How we put more emotion into the law agenda is a matter of practical and theoretical urgency in a world that is changing and automating rapidly. The Covid-19 pandemic and other critical events in our society can act as catalysts for change, but to be long-lasting and successful takes commitment and action. Bandes and Blumenthal, emphasizing the need for interdisciplinary approaches, offer a very useful agenda for future research on law and emotion,[42] and in some respects this book has offered some input to this agenda, which is reproduced in the box.

FUTURE ISSUES

1. **Underexplored doctrines**: These include First Amendment issues such as the regulation of offensive speech; the emotional dynamics animating the separation of powers doctrine; the role of emotional attachment to property in the measure of just compensation or in adverse possession doctrine; the role of trust in contract law; and assumptions about affective bonds undergirding the law of wills and trusts.

2. **Underexplored legal actors**: Studies of juries should move beyond the focus on individual jurors and take increasing account of the dynamics of the jury as a collective entity. The salutary trend toward studying judicial emotion should be expanded to include studies of how emotion affects decision making by legislators, regulators, attorneys, and other legal actors.

3. **Emotion and persuasion**: Emotion's role in rhetoric and persuasion is often dismissed as a form of manipulation or pandering, yet emotion plays an essential role in effective communication and persuasion. What role does, and should, emotion play in the persuasiveness of various forms of legal argument, including judicial opinions and dissents, the arguments of advocates, and jury deliberation?

---

[42] Susan A. Bandes and Jeremy A. Blumenthal, *Emotion and the Law* (2012), Annu. Rev. Law Soc. Sci., Vol. 8, pp. 161–81.

4. **Emotion and legislation**: In addition to studying legislators, scholars might focus on the relationship between emotion and legislation. For example, what is the appropriate role of emotion in providing an impetus for legislation? What is the role of legislation in acknowledging or giving voice to constituent emotion?

5. **Strategies for educating emotion**: In light of increasing evidence that institutions can be structured to promote a range of values and emotional attributes, debate about the structure and function of legal institutions should encompass the question of which values and attributes are worth promoting in particular contexts and how to do so. For example, institutions can be structured to increase participation, to increase awareness of or empathy for diverse viewpoints, to encourage more thorough and informed deliberation, and to work toward other goals that are consistent with participatory democracy and informed citizenry. Moreover, there is mounting evidence that emotion cannot be cordoned off from ethical and moral judgment without impairing both ethical judgment and well-being; such evidence has broad implications for the teaching and practice of law.

Source: Susan A. Bandes and Jeremy A. Blumenthal, *Emotion and the Law* (2012), Annu. Rev. Law Soc. Sci., Vol. 8, p. 175.

This set of five points should be an agenda that informs debate across the profession, from academia into legal practice and government. We can build this agenda into how everyone does law. Law schools can build this into the curriculum across core subjects, so we find a more holistic understanding of the law. Firms and legal departments can respond by asking these questions in how they operate as individuals and organizations. Governments can reinforce these issues in how they develop policy and create legislation. I have highlighted a tiny portion of the research that looks at emotional issues in the law, and there are vast amounts of data available. However, as with the mental health issues I looked at earlier, there should be more creative and active approaches to the problems, not simply PR or HR campaigns or glib partner statements. The Dialogue Box is a tool that draws on the emotional insights offered in this chapter and provides a framework in which to explore this agenda with your firm or organization. The issues run too deep to be a question of corporate function. It is a transformational issue that goes deep down into the levels of the professional individual, group collaboration and the very soul of law and the lawyer.

9.4 Practical steps: Zone 2 – Emotion

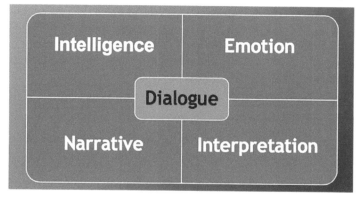

Emotion can easily override intelligence and is the number one culprit when communication goes wrong. Remember how often you have fired off an email in anger or had to hold yourself back from doing so. Recall how emotional you felt about something personal, perhaps your performance or something you'd worked intensely on for a period of time, only to find someone simply ignoring or insulting the product of your hard work. It can be useful here to try an exercise of selecting a very specific event where you clearly felt emotional as events unfolded. Recall the mood you were in before the event and how that changed. What were your instinctive reactions to the people involved? How did you appraise the situation, and how did your emotions change as the event unfolded? Explain the issue and your responses, as well as those of other actors in the event. Now, write down these emotions and how they affected your actions and the outcome. This means understanding the physical and emotional changes you experienced, locating the points at which your priorities were rearranged, what factors and actions of others sparked your emotions, and assessing how you could have handled the situation better. This can be done in a group session as well, so long as you don't mind being open about the subject matter of the problem.

9.4.1   In a nutshell

Emotions are not to be dismissed or avoided, no matter how uncomfortable the situation may feel. It is about recognizing that your audience has a stake in your organization and want to know their place in your intelligence. In good situations we want to raise the emotions, and in bad situations we want to calm the emotions. Internal communication boils down to emotional management; it is something we are trying to do most of the time with our messaging and engaging.

9.4.2   Filling in the zone

Your headline should state neutrally the dominant problematic emotion, having identified the full range of emotions involved in the matter:

- What emotions are people experiencing?
  - negative?
  - positive?
- Who is experiencing what emotion?

Can you state in a single sentence the emotional state of your audience?

9.4.3   Key takeaway

Remember, we want to create an emotional heatmap of our audience, so we list here all the possible emotions amongst our audience, including our own, and we include positive and negative emotions and who may be experiencing these emotions. We can look at the reasons why they have a particular emotion, but this is examined more after we have listed the various interpretations in the next zone, because one emotion may be tied to several interpretations.

10   The Interpretation Zone

Let's start with a puzzling reflection on meaning. One of the more disconcerting opening lines of a novel come from the pen of Franz Kafka: 'Someone must have been telling lies about Joseph K., for without having done anything wrong he was arrested one fine morning.' These words open *The Trial*. In the novel is the story of a guard, called the door-keeper, and a man who waits a number of years for entry through the door of the law. Kafka was a writer *par excellence* on interpretation and meaning, but I will just offer a tiny portion of his work. The story is really a parable told by a priest to K,[1] who has been arrested for reasons he never quite grasps. The parable tells how the man is seeking entry through what is called the door of the law, but despite repeated pleas and questions, he is denied. For many years he seeks entry, all the time asking questions about the door and what lies behind it. The parable concludes:

> Before he dies, all that he has experienced during the whole time of his sojourn condenses in his mind into one question, which he has never yet put to the door-keeper. He beckons the door-keeper, since he can no longer raise his stiffening body. The door-keeper has to bend far down to hear him, for the difference in size between them has increased very much to the man's disadvantage. 'What do you want to know now?' asks the door-keeper, 'you are insatiable.' 'Everyone strives to attain the Law,' answers the man, 'how does it come about, then, that in all these years no one has come seeking admittance but me?' The door-keeper perceives that the man is nearing his end and his hearing is failing, so he bellows in his ear: 'No one but you could gain admittance through this door, since this door was intended only for you. I am now going to shut it.'[2]

The experience of the man in the parable is one many an individual going through the legal system might identify with, and such experience should be taken seriously.

---

[1]   The priest tells K the parable of the law, which draws on biblical material in John 10:1–3.
[2]   Franz Kafka, *The Trial* (Vintage Books, New York, 1969), pp. 247–56.

Earlier, I mentioned the Bar Association of Ireland Chairman's Conference in 2019, which had the title *Laws and Effect*. Two women who had sought justice were invited to give compelling and moving testimony of their experience of the Irish courts. Their experience is one which will resonate with many people in courts around the world. The first was keynote speaker Vicky Phelan, who offered feedback on her experience as a plaintiff in Ireland's CervicalCheck scandal and her €2.5 million case.[3] She encouraged members of the Bar to stop and think about the human impact, which she said 'can sometimes take a back seat' as barristers advocate for their clients in court. Simple things – like being led through the court layout and how events will unfold – can be of immense help, she suggested, while 'some signposting' to demystify the whole court process would also be beneficial. As explained earlier, Vicky did not realize until she was sitting in the courtroom that she would be looking at the back of her solicitor's head, noting:

> I couldn't see the people who I trusted the most. I couldn't see my family or my friends. I couldn't see my solicitors … Until that day I went in to give evidence, I did not know I wouldn't be able to see my solicitor. It threw me.[4]

She had expected to get more comfort in the courtroom – which she found to be 'a terrifying place' – by seeing the person she saw as her key supporter throughout.[5] She said she found it difficult coming to terms with lawyers referring to her terminal diagnosis, which she had still not come to terms with and had just started a new medication at the time. When she tweeted in advance of the conference inviting people to share their insights, so she could include them in her presentation, the responses particularly focused on the lack of 'plain English' and confusion around the physical setting of the court and number of people involved in the process. The second speaker, Leona O'Callaghan, echoed these concerns as she shared her experience of the justice system as a survivor of sexual violence. Explaining how it impacted her, she called on members of the legal profession to play their part in ensuring the fair treatment of victims. She challenged barristers – though accepting they had a job to defend their client – by asking why they had to be so aggressive and ask certain intrusive questions which seemed to her to add more to persuasive

---

3   Discussed in Chapter 2, taken from my notes taken at the conference.
4   Ibid, author's notes.
5   Ibid, author's notes.

rhetoric than to testing the evidence – citing specifically why she had been asked about the colour of her underwear.[6]

There are many such stories and experiences. These are all experiences that impact people's understanding and interpretation of what is happening to them in the legal system. They also affect, as discussed in the previous chapter, their emotional engagement, participation and contribution to the legal process. They also raise an existential question, as Kafka poses it, of the meaning of the law for each one of us. The issues of meaning and interpretation are among the most complex elements in human life and in the life of an organization. They exist not just in the legal system, but co-exist in the various dimensions of life and society. Meaning is subject to emotional, psychological, political, spiritual and philosophical norms, and what we find meaningful is not the same as our neighbour, work colleague or lawyer. We may want to keep things rational, professional or managerial in how we act in an organization or in society, but these experiential stories and Kafka's parable are a reminder that, in the legal process, we are also dealing with, and acting as, individuals and what is meaningful in their – and our – lives. We have explored the role of emotion. And now, having understood how emotion is a response to the facts, and the inherent narrative, we turn to assess how interpretation develops, which I suggest occurs through the emotional lens. The greater the emotion, the broader the range and number of interpretations surrounding a situation. In this zone we can examine how people view evidence, and how emotion can impact and create broad views on the issues arising in a situation. We can also look at how interpretations can include or exclude data to bias a narrative, and how understanding diversity is integral to the process of greater understanding. The Dialogue Box is neutral to diversity, and thus a powerful tool to use in understanding how diversity and different perspectives influence interpretations and impact the situation at hand. Let us look at some areas of law that are a useful focal point to analyse interpretation, starting with agreements, as one of the most common and foundational legal activities.

---

[6] Her horrific ordeal and a 20-year history is reported here: https://www.irishtimes.com/news/crime-and-law/courts/criminal-court/let-me-be-clear-you-did-not-win-leona-o-callaghan-tells-rapist-1.3703153

10.1 Agreement as a matter of interpretation

If we turn to looking specifically at commercial agreements, interpretation of a contract involves looking back at the language used when the parties formed their agreement. In a 2005 Irish case, Justice Clarke explained the travails of converting business arrangements into a legally recognizable form in relation to business expediency:

> ... it is of some importance to emphasise that those engaged in commerce are often critical of what they might see as barriers placed in the way of doing sensible business by lawyers who are concerned with attempting to put arrangements agreed into a legally acceptable form. It must be accepted that there may be times when this can have the effect of slowing down the conduct of business. However, as this and many other cases amply demonstrate, the problem with arrangements not being adequately converted into a legally recognisable form is that significant problems can be encountered if things go wrong. In such circumstances, a court is required to do the best it can with the language used by the parties ...[7]

Language and naming things are important to how we frame meaning, and the key to interpretation is meaning; in other words, we are looking at signs and attempting to determine their meaning and 'give it a name'. On one level, the meaning of a statement may be clear, and often we take things at their face value for convenience or because that is all there is to it. Naming in organizations, in the media and in popular debate can be used as a shorthand way of determining that something will be understood in a particular way. Jargon is used for this purpose, and so is corporate language peculiar to a particular organization. While naming things, by which I also mean jargon and catchphrases, can be good shorthand for describing functions, activities, roles and so on, it can also lead to 'discounting' meaning. By this I mean such naming can lead to lazy thinking or diminished understanding of a complex event, person or situation. In our communications age, an era where we are deluged by communication, we continually face complexity, and as a result there is a drive to name things so that we can readily understand them, because we are too overloaded or lazy to do otherwise. Organizations have their own language, with terms popularized with a particular meaning that may not be readily noticed by those outside the organization. This is how language in a business agreement might distort the process, and the job of

---

[7]   *Stapleyside Company v Carraig Donn Retail Ltd* [2015] IESC 60 at para 6.2.

the lawyer is to test the meaning of words used in the agreement and place that into a text: the contract.

What is happening in a contractual dispute is a change of context, which affects interpretation. At the beginning of a business relationship, an employment contract, a marriage and a host of other agreements, there can be imprecision because people are in a largely positive frame of mind. I suggest that such agreements erode from this point on, and indeed they are on a downward trend where they will never be as optimistic as they were at the formation stage. Perhaps I am being overly cynical, but the point remains that in these early stages we perhaps have a level of confidence or inattention to detail that comes back to haunt us when the context shifts radically enough to cause us to revisit the terms and apply them in this new context. The reason why there is a contested agreement is because some of the variables have changed, either in the context itself or variables in relationship to the context. Hence the agreement is viewed, or tested, in a different light. The more emotional the contextual change, the more there will be a range of interpretations to examine.

In the business context, then, there is an interest to get 'the deal done' and in so doing trying to put precision around the process is seen as a barrier, while the law and legal advisors are seen as more of a hindrance than a help. Justice Clarke returned to the argument in 2011:

> There is often a tension between businessmen and their advisors stemming from the pace at which each might feel that business can safely be progressed. Understandably, businessmen wish to grasp opportunities as soon as they arise. Their advisors often counsel caution and emphasise the need to have legal and accountancy details clarified in advance. There is not necessarily a right or a wrong answer to the question posed by that tension. Often, businessmen press ahead and hope that the necessary details will be put in place in due course. When things work out well, it may transpire that it is possible to allow the legal and accountancy structures to 'catch up' with the actual conduct of business. However, allowing business to get ahead of formalities necessarily involves a risk, most particularly where things go wrong. It is not that there is anything intrinsically inappropriate in business forging ahead of the putting in place of the necessary formalities. Rather, it is that businessmen who make a conscious decision to allow business to progress faster than those formalities, take a risk. Where things go wrong, and it is necessary to define with some

precision the rights and obligations of the respective parties, then the absence of necessary formalities creates an obvious difficulty.[8]

As I previously stated, the seeds of failure are sown at the beginning. Here, as Justice Clarke explains, the court looks at the language used by the parties at the time, and at that time there is often haste, which sidelines formalities, and one might add adequate foresight. The Dialogue Box can be used at the outset of an agreement by assessing all the possible trajectories of the relationship that might flow from the agreement. This can be done in an open and trusting way, rather than seeing it through the lens of suspicion or believing it may undermine the building of a good relationship. The Dialogue Box can also be used to plan against possible difficulties by understanding the full context at the time agreement is made or whilst events are occurring, rather than ignoring or not exploring the full context in which the agreement is being made. Equally, at the stage where things have gone wrong, the Dialogue Box can be used to look back and try to understand the dynamics that led up to the conflict, and then having dialogue around specific areas of concern with more clarity than heated argument when emotions are high and the focus is blurred.

10.2   Interpreting intention

As the old saying observes, the road to hell is paved with good intentions. Agreements are made between people with different and coinciding intentions, holding diverse views and coming from a diversity of backgrounds. These are all differences which can be highly interpretative and deeply contextualized. Diversity is also one of the defining issues of our modern society, with globalization, immigration, travel, gender and sexual identity, inter-marriage and other changes all making our societies more diverse, and traditional categories reinterpreted. Hence, marriage today may imply same-sex marriage, because the definition of marriage has been changed. Understanding gender, race, disability and other needs has led to changing ways of defining and understanding others and attributing rights to all members to society. These changes mean we need to have more sensitivity to diversity than in the past, which is important for reading the text of past cases, legal authorities and other sources. If we were to apply today's values, trained into a computer system, we would

---

[8]   *Simpson v Torpey* [2011] IEHC 342.

find a number of problematic results because biases we define today existed in the past as a matter of course. What we may object to today may have previously been regarded as normative rather than a bias. These are important considerations when we look at legal reasoning, advice and judicial decisions, and there are many difficulties arising from embracing diversity and meaning in legal practice today.

In using the Dialogue Box, we are trying, in some sense, to act as a judge looking above the situation we face and being as objective as we can in assessing all the variables. The judge is an ideal judge, though, because judges can also fail. Lord Steyn humorously stated the judge's problem of interpreting what is placed before them:

> Some might say that to speak of the intractable problem of interpretation of legal texts is an exaggeration. After all, unlike other professionals, a judge usually starts with the comfort that he has a 50 per cent chance of getting the answer to the question right. Moreover, he has the reassurance of Lord Reid's advice to judges that if your average drops significantly below 50 per cent you have a moral duty to spin a coin.[9]

Lord Steyn suggests that ultimately interpretation is an art – a view I wholeheartedly endorse. The Dialogue Box is a way of structuring communication as precisely as possible, and may be the closest we can get to a rational science of communication, but ultimately communication and interpretation are acts of art. As we saw in the last chapter, in understanding the legal reasoning of judges there is an emotional dimension that can impact decisions, which is one of the variables to consider in a range of influences – including bias – in the interpretation of texts and events. Ronald Dworkin posits a Hercules who reaches his opinions rationally by reasoning from texts and principles to the 'best' interpretation, which in turn exempts emotion. How he describes this raises the implicit bias discussed above, because it assumes the judge is male, whereas we have many women judges, and increasingly this is the case. The idea of a woman being Hercules raises questions of whether this is an appropriate description for a woman, along with Justice Clarke's constant reference to businessmen, and we can ask whether there are different ways in which men and women go about the process of legal reasoning. I don't need to tackle this debate here, but it is a fascinating one to pursue. The idea Dworkin was

[9] Johan Steyn, *The Intractable Problem of The Interpretation of Legal Texts* (2003), Sydney Law Review, Vol. 25, No. 1, p. 5, http://classic.austlii.edu.au/au/journals/SydLawRw/2003/1.html

getting at does, however, stand (as does that of Justice Clarke): namely, he is positing the idea of the ideal judge as not someone who interrogates their own attitudes, beliefs, point of view and legal materials to make a decision, but rather as a Hercules, who objectively assesses a range of legal materials and uses reasoning in search of the 'best' interpretation.[10] Professor James Boyd White uses the phrase 'justice as translation', and suggests metaphors can help explain and even justify legal decisions.[11] White discusses how judges impart meaning to authoritative statutes and opinions through a process of translating them into a personal language that makes the legal points more accessible in context.

In reaching this best interpretation, if such a state is possible, like in our example of a business agreement, there are underlying principles in law that will apply, and which the businesspeople, being non-lawyers, in forming the agreement may not fully grasp. What the businessperson intends is treated in specific and sometimes different ways by the law and has done so for centuries. As Brian CJ stated the problem in 1478, 'the intent of a man cannot be tried, for the Devil himself knows not the intent of a man.'[12] The principle is found in *Smith v Hughes*,[13] though less dramatically stated by Blackburn J:

> If, whatever a man's real intention may be, he so conducts himself that a reasonable man would believe that he was assenting to the terms proposed by the other party, and that other party upon that belief enters into the contract with him, the man thus conducting himself would be equally bound as if he had intended to agree to the other party's terms.[14]

Similarly, in *The Hannah Blumenthal*,[15] Lord Diplock stated:

> To create a contract by exchange of promises between two parties ... what is necessary is that the intention of each as it has been communicated to and understood by the other (even though that which has been communicated does not represent the actual state of mind of the communicator) should coin-

[10] R. Dworkin, *Law's Empire* (Hart Publishing, Oxford, 1986), pp. 337–41; also p. 19.
[11] James Boyd White, *Justice as Translation: An Essay in Cultural and Legal Criticism* (University of Chicago Press, Chicago, 1990).
[12] *Anon* (1477) YB 17 Edw 4, fo 1, pl 12.
[13] *Smith v Hughes* (1871) LR 6 QB 597.
[14] *Smith v Hughes* (1871) LR 6 QB 597 at 607.
[15] *Paal Wilson v Blumenthal, The Hannah Blumenthal* [1983] 1 All ER 34.

cide. That is what English lawyers mean when they resort to the Latin phrase consensus ad idem ...[16]

Legal interpretation is set apart from other disciplines, including linguistics and political policymaking, and is driven by pre-existing legal principles and rules guiding us on the use of legal materials. John Finnis explains that the crucial question for legal interpreters isn't 'what do these words mean?' but rather 'what law did this instrument make?' How does it fit into the rest of the *corpus juris*? What do 'the legal sources and authorities, taken all together, establish'?[17] Hence, in law there is a narrower meaning of interpretation, but this still fits within all the legal communication that takes place in the rather less constrained world of law in action. Legal interpretation cannot stand alone; it still has a contextual place and an interpretative stance.

To illustrate by taking the doctrine of mistake in contracts law, and my intent here is not to explain contract law, we have three problems of interpretation to grapple with:

1. *Common mistake*, where the parties share the same mistaken perception. Having reached an agreement, both are in error as they share a common mistake about a significant fact.
2. *Mutual mistake*, where the parties are mistaken but do not share the same mistake and are thus at cross-purposes to the extent one can question whether there has in fact been an agreement.
3. *Unilateral mistake*, where one of the parties is mistaken as to a particular element of the agreement.

Stated in non-legal terms, what we have here is miscommunication. In legal terms, we have a clear set of principles which help to guide us through what constitutes a mistake and how we might ascertain whether there is a valid contract or not. Again, we have a level of precision that is often not in the minds of the parties, which may well explain why they have made a mistake, or miscommunication, in the first place. The role of the lawyer is to preclude making such mistakes, which is not to say mistakes won't still happen. The problem may be exacerbated, certainly for the lay reader trying to understand the law, by any inconsistency in terminology and approach in the courts and legal texts.

---

[16] *Paal Wilson v Blumenthal, The Hannah Blumenthal* [1983] 1 All ER 34 at 48.
[17] John Finnis, *Introduction*, in *Philosophy of Law: Collected Essays* (OUP, Oxford, 2011), p. 18.

10.3   Legislation

What hopefully appears clear now, using the examples from this discussion, is the distance that commonly exists between the law and people going about their business, and how the problem of interpretation is in practice a problem of obfuscation in the eyes of the general public, meaning the 'non-lawyers'. Lord Steyn, writing almost 20 years ago, highlighted how interpretation was a key issue to address:

> the academic profession and universities have not entirely caught up with the reality that statute law is the dominant source of law of our time. The interpretation of legal texts is of supreme importance for a modern lawyer.[18]

To tackle interpretation, we need to look then to legislation and the pressure for clearer language, which continues apace and applies not only in the activities of the general public, businesspeople and others, but also in the formation of legislation and development of regulation in giving these publics the rules of the road. Perhaps it can be easily forgotten sometimes by lawmakers that legislation is made for everyone. If the language is not clear, we have a problem in respect to access to justice and the operation of the rule of law. In the Renton Report on the *Preparation of Legislation* (1975), Lord Simon of Glaisdale wrote:

> It is important to remember why our statutes should be framed in such a way as to be clearly comprehensible to those affected by them. It is an aspect of the Rule of Law. People who live under the Rule of Law are entitled to claim that the law should be intelligible. A society whose regulations are incomprehensible lives with the Rule of Lottery, not the Rule of Law.[19]

In the pursuit of legal integrity and a devotion to accuracy, legislative drafters perhaps go too far, as the Renton Report suggested:

> ... unsatisfactory rules of interpretation may lead the drafters to an over-refinement in drafting at the cost of the general intelligibility of the law.[20]

---

[18]   Ibid: http://classic.austlii.edu.au/au/journals/SydLawRw/2003/1.html

[19]   Lord Simon of Glaisdale, *The Renton Report Ten Years On* (1985), Stat. Law Rev., Vol. 133.

[20]   *The Preparation of Legislation: Report of a Committee Appointed by the Lord President of the Council* (London, 1975), Cmnd. 6053, at para. 19.1.

In respect to legal interpretation, much is made of the ordinary meaning of words. An empirical study of the 2006–2009 United States Supreme Court term found that the majority of Supreme Court Justices 'referenced text/plain meaning and Supreme Court precedent more frequently than any of the other interpretive tools'.[21] The legal significance of ordinary meaning was explained by Oliver Wendell Holmes:

> [In contract interpretation] we ask, not what this man meant, but what those words would mean in the mouth of a normal speaker of English ... In the case of a statute, to turn from contracts to the opposite extreme, it would be possible to say that as we are dealing with the commands of the sovereign the only thing to do is find out what the sovereign wants ... Yet in fact we do not deal differently with a statute from our way of dealing with a contract. We do not inquire what the legislature meant; we ask only what the statute means ... So in the case of a will. It is true that the testator is a despot, within limits, over his property, but he is required by statute to express his commands in writing, and that means that his words must be sufficient for the purpose when taken in the sense in which they would be used by the normal speaker of English.[22]

Courts now pay a great deal more attention to the text and wording of statutory law than before, as is the case in other legal communication. In statutory interpretation, a key feature of the ordinary meaning approach is that it takes a somewhat different approach from that of determining the drafter's intent. Statutory and legal interpretation are growing disciplines within law, given the increasing rate of legislation and regulation. It is not my intention here to rehash learning on these narrower academic and practical concerns, except in passing. My intent is to look at the role of interpretation in the legal process more broadly and highlight the difficulty of negotiating the gap between the law and the people.

10.4   Finding intention in statutory interpretation

Interpretation is important in looking at statutes, and the decision that Hansard is allowed to a limited extent to be used in statutory interpretation to identify the intention of Parliament when a literal reading is unclear – overturning *Beswick v Beswick*[23] – is more than a piece of

---

[21]   Anita S. Krishnakumar, *Statutory Interpretation in the Roberts Court's First Era: An Empirical and Doctrinal Analysis* (2010), Hastings L.J., Vol. 62, p. 251.

[22]   Oliver Wendell Holmes, *The Theory of Legal Interpretation* (1899), Harv. L. Rev., Vol. 12, p. 417.

[23]   [1968] AC 58, 74.

abstruse public law. It represented an admission that interpretation is not a straightforward matter, and when treated so can lead to absurdity:

> My Lords, I have come to the conclusion that, as a matter of law, there are sound reasons for making a limited modification to the existing rule (subject to strict safeguards) unless there are constitutional or practical reasons which outweigh them. In my judgment, subject to the questions of the privileges of the House of Commons, reference to Parliamentary material should be permitted as an aid to the construction of legislation which is ambiguous or obscure or the literal meaning of which leads to an absurdity. Even in such cases references in court to Parliamentary material should only be permitted where such material clearly discloses the mischief aimed at or the legislative intention lying behind the ambiguous or obscure words.[24]

Pepper recognizes the importance of context in the interpretation of statutes but questions the assumption in the case that intention can be attributed to Parliament. Before *Pepper*, the principle used was the exclusionary rule, which came into being in 1769 when the English courts refused to look at parliamentary proceedings for any reason.[25] The reasoning was fourfold. First, a constitutional argument based on the 1689 Bill of Rights, Article 9, 'That the freedom of speech, and debates or proceedings in parliament ought not to be impeached or questioned in any court or place out of parliament.'[26] Second, the possibility of confusion of roles. Third, it affects the role of the courts in interpretation, as the interpretation of a statute is the court's role.[27] Last, at the time there was no reliable reference material for parliamentary proceedings. What the courts were looking at was clear separation of powers and the practical problem of consistent and comprehensive sourcing of what happened in the creation of the statute. Hansard came along to provide such a source and highlights the role of communication in solving the problem, which was a practical one rather than a matter of constitutional law.

However, *Pepper* placed restrictions on interpretation:

(a) there must be an ambiguity, obscurity or absurdity in question

---

[24] *Pepper (Inspector of Taxes) v Hart* [1993] AC 593.
[25] See *Pepper v Hart* [1993] 1 All ER 60–61 (Lord Browne-Wilkinson) citing *Millar v Taylor* (1769) 2 Burr. 2302, 2332 (Willes J) (KB). See also, *McDonnell* (n 85) at [29], 1116–17 (Lord Steyn).
[26] 1 W&M, sess2, c2.
[27] See *Pepper v Hart* [1993] 1 All ER 63–64 (Lord Browne-Wilkinson).

(b) the statements to be relied upon must have authority, such as those be made by the Minister or other promoter of Bill

(c) the statement has to be clear in respect to the specific issue in the legislation.

The decision thus places importance on looking into the context of the formation of texts as a means to interpreting what they mean in a given case, whilst ensuring the normative effects of the legislation are preserved. The principle was more recently stated in *R (Jackson) v Attorney General*:

> ... there are occasions when ministerial statements are useful in practice as an interpretative aid, perhaps especially as a confirmatory aid. I would simply remark myself that it would be wilful blindness for courts to deprive themselves of its assistance in proper cases.[28]

The exchange on *Pepper* between Lord Steyn[29] and Professor Vogenauer's Reply to Lord Steyn[30] is instructive in this regard, and well worth a read. Lord Neuberger recently summarized the courts' procedure in statutory interpretation:

> First, the court's constitutional role in any exercise of statutory interpretation is to give effect to Parliament's intention by deciding what the words of the relevant provision mean in their context. Secondly, it follows that, in so far as any extraneous material can be brought into account, it is only as part of that context. Thirdly, before such material can be considered for the purpose of statutory interpretation, certain requirements have to be satisfied: Fourthly, even where those requirements are satisfied, any court must be wary of being too ready to give effect to what appears to be the parliamentary intention.[31]

This brief excursion into *Pepper* is deserving as it highlights the role of interpretation in law and context. Interpretation is pivotal in the Dialogue Box, as the tool drives the user to delve into the history of interpretations in any given context, much as the learned Lords have seen fit in looking to the meaning of statutes. However, we ought to be careful or we can run the risk of fossilization and keeping to a meaning that belongs in the

---

[28] [2005] 56; [2006] 1 AC 262, 191–2 at para 65. See also *Harding v Wealands* [2006] UKHL 32 [81].

[29] Johan Steyn, *Pepper v Hart: A Re-Examination* (2001), Oxford Journal of Legal Studies, Vol. 21, No. 1, pp. 59–72, www.jstor.org/stable/20468355

[30] Stefan Vogenauer, *A Retreat from* Pepper v Hart? *A Reply to Lord Steyn* (2005), Oxford Journal of Legal Studies, Vol. 25, No. 4, pp. 629–74.

[31] *Williams v Central Bank of Nigeria* [2014] 2 WLR 355, 387 (Lord Neuberger PSC).

past.[32] This process is critical to the operation of law in an era where we have so much on the statute books in search of precision in a context where there is so much postmodern doubt about truth and certainty. Modern communication will keep pressing the issue of clarity in statutes and the writing of laws and regulation, as well as the policy work that precedes this authorship and subsequent interpretation. The advance of technology, and the pace of digital change, will keep this pressure on the legal system, and the coding of rules will take us in some interesting new directions.

10.5   Interpreting 'ordinary meaning'

Theories holding that a legal text must be applied consistently with its ordinary meaning ask how a text would in fact be understood by ordinary people, using empirical methods to inquire into the ordinary meaning of the text, including consulting dictionary definitions or using 'corpus linguistics'. Thus, for instance, the US Supreme Court has examined patterns of word use through newspaper databases. Cass Sunstein and Richard Fallon hold there's nothing about legal interpretation that 'just is', but rather many ways to read a legal text, each making its own claim to authority. In which case, judges – when choosing among competing readings – should engage in case-by-case normative balancing, or selecting, as Fallon puts it, from the 'capacious … range of approaches' and whatever they think, Sunstein says, 'makes the relevant constitutional order better rather than worse'.[33] Ordinary meaning is often taken to mean empirical meanings, and analysis is often associated with textualism, formalism,[34] and a diverse range of theories which endorse the relevance of ordinary

[32] Ibid. Philip Sales, *Pepper v Hart: A Footnote to Professor Vogenauer's Reply to Lord Steyn* (2006), Oxford Journal of Legal Studies, Vol. 26, No. 3, pp. 585–92; M.K. Heatley, *Devolution: A New Breath of Life for* Pepper v Hart? (2017), Liverpool Law Rev., Vol. 38, pp. 287–306, https://doi.org/10.1007/s10991-017-9202-x

[33] Cass R. Sunstein, *There Is Nothing that Interpretation Just Is* (2015), Const. Comment., Vol. 30, p. 193; Richard H. Fallon, Jr., *The Meaning of Legal 'Meaning' and Its Implications for Theories of Legal Interpretation* (2015), U. Chi. L. Rev., Vol. 82, pp. 1235, 1238–9. https://harvardlawreview.org/wp-content/uploads/2017/02/1079-1147_Online.pdf

[34] See Victoria Nourse, *Textualism 3.0: Statutory Interpretation After Justice Scalia* (2019), Ala. L. Rev., Vol. 70, p. 667; Gregory Klass, *Contract Exposition and Formalism* (2017), Georgetown University Law Center Scholarship (discussing interpretive formalism in contract law), https://papers.ssrn.com/sol3/papers.cfm?abstract_id=2913620

meaning in legal interpretation.[35] Yet, what does 'ordinary meaning' mean in a world of diversity? The challenge is to address whether law is no different in that all our communications are contextual, and there is increasing sensitivity to contextual factors.

10.6 Reading interpretatively

We can go further and note that we interpret subjectively and objectively. The subjective involves reading what we understand, or want to understand, into a situation. We interpret from our own viewpoint, assumptions and prejudices. This reading can often be more emotional. When describing an assailant, witnesses may give varying descriptions of the assailant because they are recalling, and reading into, what they see through an emotional state, one of fear or panic. We are not just taking in a description, but also interpreting what we see, such as how threatening or dangerous the assailant looks, which will be in part influenced by the assumptions we have about what threatening or dangerous people look like. The objective is a more rationally based activity, more dispassionate and less emotional. It means we are trying to understand what might be the truth of the matter, giving a fairer viewpoint to all agents in the situation than we might in an emotional state, bearing in mind we may count as one of the agents involved. In certain situations we have vested interests in decisions, changes and strategies, and this influences our interpretation, which can be biased depending on our understanding. We can see two different major categories of interpretation: the talk about something, and explaining the meaning of that thing. They are connected with one another, but in talking about something we are essentially signifying that it means something without defining it. Thus, if I point to a dog and say, 'there is a dog', I am simply pointing out and stating something I see. It is not necessarily signifying anything more than the fact I am naming what

---

[35] See, e.g., William N. Eskridge, Jr. *Interpreting Law: A Primer on How to Read Statutes and the Constitution* (Foundation Press, 2016), p. 35 ('[t]here are excellent reasons for the primacy of the ordinary meaning rule'); Thomas R. Lee and Stephen C. Mouritsen, *Judging Ordinary Meaning* (March 19, 2017), Yale Law Journal, Vol. 127, p. 788, https://ssrn.com/abstract=2937468 or http://dx.doi.org/10 .2139/ssrn.2937468; Lawrence B. Solum, *Surprising Originalism* (2018), ConLawNow, Vol. 9, p. 235; see also Elena Kagan, *The Scalia Lecture: A Dialogue with Justice Kagan on the Reading of Statutes* (November, 17 2015), Harv. L. Today, http://today.law.harvard.edu/in-scalia-lecture-kagan-discusses -statutory-interpretation ('[W]e're all textualists now').

I see. To say what something means, on the other hand, we are offering an interpretation; we are filling the thing with meaning. Hence, when I talk about the dog, I may also be interpreting whether it is a nice dog, a mean dog, a dog on the loose, and so on. These are all descriptions that go beyond the mere statement of the dog before me, and may be contested, for we may have different ideas or knowledge about the dog, such as its tendency to bite postal workers. Lord Steyn argued, 'it is a universal truth that words can only be understood in relation to the circumstances in which they are used, and language can never be understood divorced from its context.'[36] He further noted:

> In the interpretation of legal texts the most frequent source of judicial error is the failure to understand the contextual scene of a legal text. Often judges are not provided with all the contextually relevant raw materials. The essential setting of a text may include in a contract case how a market works, in a breach of statutory duty case competing policy arguments, the structure of a complex statute, the historical development of legislation, and so forth.[37]

The Dialogue Box assists in this grasping of the contextual scene, and can ensure the lawyer gains a holistic insight into the case or client. In *Pepper*, Lord Denning said, 'Why should judges grope about in the dark searching for the meaning of an Act, when they can switch on the light on.'[38] The Dialogue Box provides a methodology for turning on the light.

As implied in the *Pepper* restrictions on interpretation, what makes interpretations challenging is the authority assigned to the interpretations and their sources. However, we have more than texts to deal with; we have real, live, breathing people, even in the courtroom, which influence us. The practical process of interpretation involves us in looking for both verbal and non-verbal signs. When we use words, our speech is mediated by a tone of voice and our physical actions and expressions. We may choose our words carefully, but in the process of using them the tone of voice and body language will ultimately translate a meaning for the audience, which may coincide with what we intended or may appear modified in the audience's perception of what is being said, which is a fuller communication. An obvious example is that we say we are excited for

---

[36] Johan Steyn, Pepper v Hart; *A Re-Examination* (Spring, 2001), Vol. 21, No. 1, pp. 59–72, https://www.jstor.org/stable/20468355?msclkid=469b4194d05011ec8b38f012eaf04e35

[37] http://classic.austlii.edu.au/au/journals/SydLawRw/2003/1.html

[38] *Pepper (Inspector of Taxes) v Hart* [1993] AC 593.

someone, but then our tone of voice and body language actually suggest we are not in the least bit interested, or are jealous, or some other underlying sense of what we are truly thinking. Of course, we can become good actors able to disguise our true self, but even then, the slightest nuance out of step might give the game away. We can also communicate without words. If I look at my watch during a meeting, there may be any number of things I am communicating, and the interpretation will be affected by many things. I may be bored, late for another meeting, impatient, idly curious, keeping track of how the meeting is progressing, all manner of options just with one gesture. We need more than the gesture to fill out the picture, and we look for other signs and subsequent behaviour to judge why the gesture was made; even then the answer may never be clear. We may rely on other information we have about the person and the context of the meeting, in order to interpret the gesture, which may be a simple but telling one. Whether judge or lawyer, in the process of interpreting we are also seeking to divine the truth of statements and signs, and as we make up our mind about how we are interpreting an event there is a process by which the credibility of statements and information gains a stronghold and starts to guide our deliberations. This is important when people are trying to influence us, and plays a critical role when a lawyer, perhaps with the aid of predictive analytics, seeks to persuade the judge, and in some cases a jury.

10.7 Interpreting 'with'

This is not to say we should dumb things down; EF Schumacher said: 'Any intelligent fool can make things bigger, more complex, and more violent. It takes a touch of genius – and a lot of courage – to move in the opposite direction.'[39] This is what I mean here by embracing complexity. Other advocates for this approach to complexity include Ludwig Wittgenstein, who said: 'The aspects of things that are most important to us are hidden because of their simplicity and familiarity,'[40] and Albert Einstein, who said: 'Everything should be made as simple as possible, but not simpler.'[41] The discussion of interpretation in this chapter has emphasized some

---

[39] E.F. Schumacher, *Small is Beautiful* (August, 1973), The Radical Humanist, Vol. 37, No. 5, p. 22.

[40] Ludwig Wittgenstein, *Philosophical Investigations* (Blackwell, London, 1958), p. 50e.

[41] Albert Einstein, *On the Method of Theoretical Physics* (April, 1934), Philosophy of Science, Vol. 1, No. 2, pp. 163–9, https://www.jstor.org/stable/184387?msclkid=83f21a91d05e11ec9a4b9f6da9df522d

nuances of legal interpretation, and they are critical to the way the lawyer interprets as well and works with a client and develops the case. There is always a professional barrier; the lawyer is a support but not a friend of the client. You want to get down and dirty with the client and the details, to see things at their level, but there is need for caution. Doctors have a similar issue. The Scottish psychiatrist RD Laing[42] related an incident in his work, explaining how the hospital he was at in Glasgow had a female patient who sat rocking back and forth in her chair, naked and mumbling incoherently. None of the doctors knew how to reach her. Laing observed the woman for some time before taking off his own clothes, sitting down opposite her and rocking in harmony with her and making similar verbal sounds. The woman started to communicate for the first time since entering the hospital, leaving Laing to ask his colleagues if it ever occurred to them to start from where she was situated, from where she was suffering. Not that I would recommend lawyers strip naked for their clients! The point of the story is that Laing was seeking to understand what level of meaning he had to reach to connect with the woman. On another level, we instinctively do this with children when we crouch down to talk to them at their level, to make eye contact and not to appear as a 'big person'. As Lord Taylor famously stated:

> The principle which runs through ... [the case law] ... is that a man must be able to consult his lawyer in confidence, since otherwise he might hold back half the truth. The client must be sure that what he tells his lawyer in confidence will never be revealed without his consent. Legal professional privilege is thus much more than an ordinary rule of evidence, limited in its application to the facts of a particular case. It is the fundamental condition on which the administration of justice as a whole rests.[43]

Gaining and managing this confidence is a matter of communication and understanding the client. There is a gap between the law and the client, between statutes and the people they apply to, and between law and other disciplines. The unique interpretive work of lawyers, judges and academics is essential to the good working of the law, but in the world in which we live today, this interpretative work cannot be done on an exclusionary basis, and we cannot have hubris in how the law operates or our place within the legal process. Lawyers don't need to get naked, but they do have to be 'with' rather than 'above'.

---

[42] R.D. Laing, *The Divided Self: An Existential Study of Sanity and Madness* (Penguin, London, 1965).

[43] *R v Derby Magistrates' Court, ex parte B* [1995] 3 WLR 681 at 695.

10.8 Practical steps: Zone 3 – Interpretation

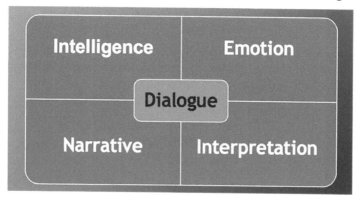

Take a specific event you recall when there was a range of opinion about what happened. Note down the interpretation you had, but also the other interpretations that people told you they had of the event. These do not need to all be radically different; they just need to have a variance with other interpretations. We interpret subjectively and objectively. The technical terms for these two types of interpretation are 'eisegetical' and 'exegetical'. In the former case, we read what we want into the situation; in the latter, we try to understand the situation from a distance. We do this all the time, often changing from one form to the other according to the situation or our emotional state. Can you recall situations where you have looked very subjectively and objectively? How did this turn out? What you are looking for in these various interpretations is how people have looked subjectively at events, depending on their position, personality, relationships, etc. What someone says may reveal or conceal something about themselves or the situation, and when confronted with various interpretations of the same event we have a natural inclination to search for and understand the truth of what is being said, which may come from one person or many.

10.8.1 In a nutshell

You have to look objectively at the situation you are analysing and record as many possible interpretations as possible, even if some may seem very unpleasant or even bizarre to you. Only by entertaining all the possibilities can you get down to distilling the interpretations that are driving the narrative or counter-narrative.

10.8.2 Filling in the zone

Your headline should state neutrally the dominant interpretation, having gathered the full range of opinions expressed irrespective of whether they are: good or bad, right or wrong, apparently sensible or outrageous.

- What views do we hear?
- Is there research or opinion polls on views available?
- What theories are people propounding?
- What are different stakeholders saying?
- What are the positive views?
- What are the negative views?

Can you state in a single sentence what the dominant interpretation is in terms of what your audience is thinking?

10.8.3 Key takeaway

Remember, we want to find out what the pool of views are, which can be done informally or via formal research, and to get a sense of the dominant view or views. We are interested in all views, even if they offend us. We will look at how these views connect to the emotions, and really get to know our audience.

11   The Narrative Zone

Lawyers should be good at this: telling the narrative objectively. However, it has only been in the last 20 years or so that narrative has been taken on board critically. As Peter Brooks noted back in 1996, there is discussion to be had about 'law's dependence on narrative and rhetoric'.[1] Leading on from the work in the previous chapter, given the range of interpretations, it becomes apparent that finding and using objective narrative is a lot harder than it may seem. With the thousands of participants I have trained in workshop groups to use the Dialogue Box, it is this step from the first three zones to the Narrative Zone that is the hardest for participants to make, regardless of their professional discipline or jurisdiction. If this is not done successfully, it becomes even harder to arrive at the kind of dialogue needed. It is in the Narrative Zone that we try to get a bird's eye view of the problem, distancing ourselves and our – or those of the client or other interested party – interests as much as possible. This is so we have a realistic picture of our situation and also of the other dialogue partners. When we can achieve this, we can find an effective dialogue strategy. Later in the chapter we will go through the practicalities of finding the narrative, but to set the scene, there is much work to be done to understand the significance of narrative in the legal space.

As James Boyd White wrote, law is in part story:

> [T]he law always begins in story: usually in the story the client tells, whether he or she comes in off the street for the first time or adds in a phone call another piece of information to a narrative with which the lawyer has been long, perhaps too long, familiar. It ends in story, too, with a decision by a court or jury, or an agreement between the parties, about what happened and what it means.[2]

---

[1]   Peter Brooks and Paul Gewirtz, *Law's Stories: Narrative and Rhetoric in the Law* (Yale University Press, New Haven, CT, 1996), p. 14.

[2]   James Boyd White, *Heracles' Bow: Essays on the Rhetoric and the Poetics of the Law* (University of Wisconsin Press, Madison, WI, 1985), p. 168.

Like in classical journalism and the role of judge, in the Narrative Zone we are looking for the 'real story' of what is going on, with as much subjectivity or manipulation taken out of the picture as possible. Within this there is the legal narrative, the business narrative, the personal narrative and many other narratives that need to be reconciled. This perhaps appears to undermine the notion of there being a 'real story', especially if we accept postmodern ideas and the notion of disconnected narratives. Jean-François Lyotard posited, and doubted the validity of, the term grand narrative or 'master narrative' in his 1979 work *The Postmodern Condition: A Report on Knowledge*.[3] He critiqued institutional and ideological forms of knowledge, of which law is a key component. The postmodern person is said to no longer believe in such grand narratives, which are viewed as oppressive and hegemonic because one grand narrative excludes others. This sense of 'the other' suggests we thus have a problem of defining, prioritizing or privileging one narrative over another, and then who is to judge which narrative is chosen, and has a right to assert their truth over others or 'the other'?

Law has arguably always been based on the assumption of a grand narrative and may indeed be the last discipline to defend it in a robust way. However, whether one accepts the grand narrative or not, the point is there are parties to the dialogue who do not accept it, resist it or do not understand it, and hence we have a disconnect irrespective of acceptance or rejection of any grand narrative. On this basis, the Dialogue Box helps you to discover the contextual narrative and match this to the legal narrative, and then to link this more effectively to the various audiences and needs of specific participants to advance an effective dialogue. Hence, postmodern or not, we can uncover the various competing narratives at work.

Another clarification. This is not about storytelling, which is very popular in the current communications business. Narrative in the Dialogue Box is about seeking to understand the situation faced and how this compares with the inherent narrative of the Intelligence Zone. In dialogue we are attempting to match as closely as possible the narrative of the Intelligence Zone to that of the Narrative Zone, and the reason we need a dialogue is because there is a disconnect or mismatch between two or more nar-

---

[3] Jean-François Lyotard, *The Postmodern Condition: A Report on Knowledge* (Manchester University Press, 1979).

ratives, so we need dialogue to bring us to a better equilibrium and then move on to achieve the outcomes desired or required by the intelligence narrative. To be clear, I am not advocating this approach as a product of the branch of law and/as literature, though there are many useful insights to be discussed here, and there is a deep connection. Communicating legal advice or opinion is inherently a question of persuasion, hence we often read of arguments or opinions being persuasive in the texts. We communicate the law through spoken and written words, as well as by the physical language of persons and the institutions of law.

In some works on legal writing, there is encouragement of legal writers to employ sophisticated literary techniques in their efforts to persuade, as Ruth Anne Robbins writes:

> [b]ecause people respond – instinctively and intuitively – to certain recurring story patterns and character archetypes, lawyers should systematically and deliberately ... subtly portray their ... clients as heroes on a particular life path.[4]

This, she says, allows the lawyer to 'influence the judge at the unconscious level'.[5] The problem with such a storytelling approach is that, while it may be a persuasive form of communication, in the communication planning stage the legal writer runs the risk of privileging the needs of the story over the specifics of the legal issues in play. This is avoided in the use of the Dialogue Box, since we are not constructing a narrative of what we want the story to be, but to find a way of using narrative ideas to understand the situation better. Despite being problematic, the law and literature, or law as literature, approach does have some valid ideas and offers some stimulating as well as provocative input. There is a strongly developing discipline of law and literature, and we can learn much about narrative from this movement. However, I am not arguing here for a law and literature approach.

I mentioned traditional journalism, which for older generations today takes some of us back to the days when in Britain there was the 'man from the BBC' (it was invariably a man in the 1960s) who stood fairly static

---

[4] Ruth Anne Robbins, *Harry Potter, Ruby Slippers and Merlin: Telling the Client's Story Using the Characters and Paradigm of the Archetypal Hero's Journey* (Fall 2006), Seattle University Law Review, Vol. 29, No. 4, p. 767.
[5] Ibid, p. 769.

and suited to give a report on an event. The story he told was assumed to be authoritative, and it had been through an editing and authorizing process. This old style of journalism prided itself on telling the news as factually and neutrally as possible. Today's news is heavily editorialized, rather than simply edited. Referring to this 'New Journalism', Tom Wolfe distinguished the new from the old in the use of four literary techniques in the creation of non-fiction narrative:

(1) scene-by-scene construction as opposed to historical narrative;
(2) large amounts of dialogue in the story;
(3) recording 'status details' or pattern of behavior and possessions; and,
(4) a marked point of view within the story.[6]

It would not be desirable for law, in my view, to go much further than it already has in taking on board such narrative-building, because it starts to loosen its moorings from the law, though this is a contested point we will explore throughout this chapter.

11.1 Narrative and persuasion

The effective use of narrative takes us into an exploration of the persuasive nature of narrative. Robert Burns writes that persuasion 'relies on two strands – one strand of narrative and one of logical argument related to each other like a twisting double helix that forms a lawyer's theory of the case'.[7] Persuasion or rhetoric is a way of organizing discourse and is inherent in all dialogue. In other words, all narrative is interpretive. We provide a narrative of events or tell a story which organizes the facts, people and statements in such a way as to give a specific interpretive version of events to suit our purpose. We can edit our facts, omitting or including information, that may give a positive or negative view of persons or events to suit our purpose. Whether it is the barrister in court, the judge summing up or the solicitor talking to a client, the lawyer is giving a narration. Inherent in this narration is persuasion or rhetoric. The barrister is seeking to persuade the court of the merits of their case.

---

[6]   Tom Wolfe, *The New Journalism* (with an anthology edited by Tom Wolfe and E.W. Johnson) (Harper & Row Publishers, New York, 1973).

[7]   J. Christopher Rideout, *Storytelling, Narrative Rationality, and Legal Persuasion* (2008), Leg. Writing, Vol. 14, p. 53 (citing Robert Burns, *A Theory of the Trial* (Princeton University Press, Princeton, NJ, 1999)), pp. 36–8).

The judge is seeking to navigate a way through the narratives offered by the two sides to the dispute in order to find an objective narrative, and retell the story as persuasively as possible to explain the situation. This needs to be persuasive to both sides to accept the judgment, and to higher courts also to accept the judgment or it may be taken on appeal. Even the Supreme Court, as we saw with Brexit in the UK, needs to offer a persuasive narrative to satisfy the political and public realm – which is never quite achieved. Indeed, the Brexit case reveals just how difficult it is to find a narrative at times.

'All narrative is interpretative' is an insight that has led to a postmodern doubting of authority. If the narrative is interpretive, we can ask who is interpreting, who is maintaining a particular narrative as authoritative or most persuasive, who is being persuaded, and who needs to be persuaded? These are questions up for grabs in this narrative quest for the lawyer, and these are not idle, nor even academic questions. They are practical questions. The Brexit case may highlight the issue, but the issues are quite everyday in the daily activity of offering a persuasive narrative in order to get things done, undone or just left alone. Looking into cases or drafting of legislation, regulations and treaties, and transcripts available to use, we can deconstruct or trace the archaeology of an outcome, and see how the narrative shaped the outcome. We can also look at relationships and deconstruct how audiences have influenced outcomes. In the broader view of law in society, this emphasizes the importance of understanding the context of a narrative. The work done by lawyers and courts has an impact in society. These activities can both reassert norms and influence their change. There will be those in society who oppose the law as it is, and hence we have radical change in society happening in dialogue between the operation of the law and the norms and ideals contested within society. Equally, on the level of daily practice, understanding context has practical implications for lawyers, even if they are not always cognizant of what these implications are. At the social level, then, narrative can challenge the existing legal order, while at a granular level narrative can influence the story of the other. The judge, decision-maker, legal analyst and other arbiters are sifting through competing narratives. The Dialogue Box is a tool to help them in that task, but also help all lawyers to undertake this narrative task.

In common law, the notion of precedent is more than a nod to this point, as the common law is based on the relationship between a set of facts seen in context, rather than simply analysed in respect to legal rules and principles. In developing the narrative understanding, we are seeing movement between the general to the specific, and between the contingent and the timeless. However, telling the story may distort the picture. A persuasive narrative may not in fact be a true narrative. After all, every good conman is a good narrator, and the influence of PR 'spin' testifies to the systemic use of narrative in decision-making. In the media we see how the narrative is pursued, which is driven in part by predestining the interpretation of new facts, as we see in fake news but also in the interpretation of narrative. Some of the facts are shared facts, but they carry different interpretive baggage and thus fit differently into the narrative to become contested facts. There are also sub-stories or narrative fragments to be considered and connected. This question of who controls the narrative is also a question of access to justice. Winston Churchill famously stated, 'History is written by the victors.' Can the same be said of law, or more to the point, is law written by the powerful? If people are scared by the law, fearful of the process, how can their stories be told? If they are told, are they then understood? Again, we can turn to questions of bias to discover how many people did not get access, or were not believed, because of their gender, race or other form of discrimination. Feminist jurists would go further and ask whether, or to what extent, law is written by men and thus male. Not every story is, or can be, told in court, and in stating the narrative there is a process of editing. Many have been excluded, their stories legally edited.

11.2 Enhancing legal narratology

We can also turn to 'legal narratology', which is concerned with the story elements in law and legal scholarship. Paul Gewirtz explains:

> ... treating law as narrative and rhetoric means looking at facts more than rules, forms as much as substance, the language used as much as the idea expressed (indeed, the language used is seen as a large part of the idea expressed). It means examining not simply how law is found but how it is made, not simply what judges command but how the commands are constructed and framed. It understands legal decision making as transactional – as not just a directive but an activity involving audiences as well as sovereign law-givers; indeed, it

emphasizes the ways legal processes involve speakers in exchange with audiences everywhere.[8]

As Gewirtz notes, '... the actual text of the case is typically multiple texts, multiple opinions, which simultaneously present multiple accounts of a single reality'.[9] Where there are multiple opinions, 'there is a debate occurring within the text itself'.[10] Gewirtz then argues, 'The turn to narrative is a clear offshoot of the further loss of faith in the idea of objective truth and the widespread embrace of ideas about the social construction of reality. Narrative, in other words, is seen as the social construction of reality.'[11] This leads to notions that the story need not be true, so long as it has the qualities of coherence, intelligibility, and significance. Stories play a big role in the legal process. Plaintiff and defendant in a trial each tell a story, which is actually a translation of their 'real' story into the narrative and rhetorical forms authorized by law, and the jury chooses the story that it likes better. As Ronald Allen explains, what really happens in a trial is that each side tries to convince the jury that its story is more plausible than the opponent's story.[12]

In 'oppositional scholarship' developed by critical race theorists and by feminists, there is a heavy reliance on stories. Posner questions 'what function they think [they] are serving by swapping stories of oppression with each other'.[13] He suggests that the papers on judicial opinion are concerned with the rhetoric of judicial opinions generally rather than with the narrative techniques used in them. Posner explains:

> Stories often implicitly claim to identify causes. When a defendant in his plea of mercy tells a horrific (and let us assume truthful) story of childhood abuse and neglect, he implicitly asserts a causal relationship between the events narrated and the criminal act for which he is to be sentenced; the story has no relevance otherwise. But to assert and to prove are two different things. The

---

[8]   Paul Gerwitz, *Narrative and Rhetoric in the Law*, in Paul Gewirtz and Peter Brooks (eds), *Law's Stories: Narrative and Rhetoric in the Law* (Yale University Press, New Haven, CT, 1996), p. 3.

[9]   Ibid, p. 11.

[10] Ibid, p. 12.

[11] Ibid, p. 13.

[12] Ronald J. Allen and Michael S. Pardo, *Relative Plausibility and Its Critics* (2019), International Journal of Evidence & Proof, Vol. 23, No. 1–2, pp. 5–59.

[13] Richard A. Posner, *Legal Narratology* (1997), University of Chicago Law Review, Vol. 64, pp. 743–4.

proof is critical, and is not supplied by the story, which may merely be appealing to credulous and sentimental intuitions.[14]

The Dialogue Box addresses this problem by rooting the methodology in the facts, whilst retaining the value of stories by giving them a constructive place in interpreting the narrative. It tackles Posner's concern and another raised by Martha Minow, who noted that '[v]ictim stories risk trivializing pain' and 'adhere to an unspoken norm that prefers narratives of helplessness to stories of responsibility, and tales of victimization to narratives of human agency and capacity'.[15] With the Dialogue Box we are trying to listen to the victim while also understanding the intentions and needs of all parties to a dispute. We need to hear all sides of the story, but as Minow states, there is value in 'disrupt[ing] these rationalizing, generalizing modes of analysis [legal doctrine, economic analysis, and philosophical theory] with a reminder of human beings and their feelings, quirky developments, and textured vitality'.[16] Thus we have to unpack the view from Posner. He argues that 'you need considerable literary skill to write a story that will effectively challenge a reader's preconceptions'. He continues, 'Another risk in legal storytelling, besides atypicality, inattention to causation, preaching to the converted, and lack of analytical content, is emotionality,' and worries 'it would be dangerous to deny the risk that emotionality poses to law'.[17] Posner concludes:

> Evidence is regularly excluded from jury trials on the ground that it would unduly inflame the jury, and jury verdicts are sometimes set aside because the verdict shows that the jury was carried away by passion or prejudice. The legal narratologists know all this and do not, as far as I know, question it. But they have had difficulty specifying the appropriate role of emotion in trials and other legal settings.[18]

This may be true of legal narratologists, but it is possible to specify the emotions, which the Dialogue Box addresses by placing emotion in a clear relationship of discovery between intelligence and interpretation. It is about giving emotion its right place in the legal process, not emotionalizing the legal system. The Dialogue Box highlights that narrative is

---

[14] Ibid, p. 743.
[15] Martha Minow, *Stories in Law*, in Peter Brooks and Paul Gewirtz (eds), *Law's Stories: Narrative and Rhetoric in the Law* (Yale University Press, New Haven, 1996), p. 32.
[16] Ibid, p. 36.
[17] Posner (n 13), p. 744.
[18] Ibid, pp. 744–5.

not about storytelling, which is the point the Posner raises, or telling the stories of law; it is about approaching narrative as a constructive description to find neutral ground. Thus, I would go along with a narratology of the law, described by Brooks, which:

> … might be especially interested in questions of narrative transmission and transaction: that is, stories in the situation of their telling and listening, asking not only how these stories are constructed and told, but also how they are listened to, received, reacted to, how they ask to be acted upon and how they in fact become operative.[19]

He makes a helpful plea:

> I do want to urge that some attention to the 'narrativity' of the law – the narrative transactions performed within the law – could begin to open to thought some of the unthought assumptions, procedures, and language of the law.[20]

He adds that such work can be done better:

> The 'law and literature' movement has been less effective than it might be, I think, because it has, with excessive arrogance or excessive humility (or often some combination of both), proposed a relation to the law ranging from the deconstructive (possible certainly, but largely useless) to the feel good (literature as a cozy humanizing teddy bear for law to curl up with). What it might better do, I believe, is demonstrate to legal studies that it has analytic instruments in its toolkit that might actually be of some use with the legal plumbing.[21]

Again, the Dialogue Box offers just such a practical tool that can help with the 'legal plumbing'. It can also answer a point raised by Jeanne M. Kaiser that the fundamental principle advanced by law and literature scholars is that there is a power in stories that lawyers should harness in their advocacy.[22] In a study by Green et al on the power of the law story, the authors note:

> A power of the law story is that it can translate other stories, including the stories of experts in other fields like psychiatry, paediatrics, criminology. The

---

[19] Peter Brooks, *Narrative in and of the Law*, in James Phelan and Peter J. Rabinowitz (eds), *A Companion to Narrative Theory* (Wiley-Blackwell, Hoboken, NJ, 2005), p. 424.

[20] Ibid.

[21] Ibid.

[22] http://digitalcommons.law.wne.edu/cgi/viewcontent.cgi?article=1080&context=facschol

'law story' may therefore carry more weight than many other stories, not because it is intrinsically more valuable but rather because it has a special power, traditionally seen as the power to command backed by the supreme force of the state. Minow amongst others points out: 'When judges interpret text somebody loses his freedom, his property, his children, even his life.' However, law is not just a power to command. It can also be seen as the power to exclude, for the law sets its own boundaries, establishes what is to lie at the core and what beyond its margins ... Thus law restricts, confines and places into hierarchy those who may speak the discourse, the texts of the discourse and the settings where legal discourse takes place. This power of exclusion may indirectly render invisible individuals and even whole communities, for the law places at its liberal centre the equal, disembodied individual and thereby robs human beings of much of themselves – sex, colour, religion, class, age.[23]

The Dialogue Box provides a methodology to achieve these aims by constructing and understanding the narrative, on the one hand, and showing how to deploy this in the legal space, on the other.

The Dialogue Box keeps the intelligence preserved through its methodology, so we can find ways to develop the narrative that keeps it within the bounds of what we think of as certainty in the law and the notion that the legal system is partly about finding the truth of the situation. The process may sometimes have spectacular failures, but for the most part we can accept that the legal system does work in spite of the many variables, obstacles and human follies involved. We can find truth in the narrative, and the closer we come to defining a neutral narrative for ourselves, the more likely we are to find the right legal process and language to resolve our disputes. And this may mean reaching this point before going to court and having someone else do it for us. Katherine Swiss raises important points about narrative in action, specifically at trial:

> The law is immersed in narrative. This is particularly true within the space of trials, where participants share in the forming of narratives that are then judged by juries. Yet the jury functions in a way no audience of literature ever could: the jury determines what is and is not the 'true' narration of events.[24]

[23] Kate Green, Hilary Lim and Jeremy Roche, *The Indeterminate Province: Storytelling in Legal Theory and Legal Education* (1994), Law Teacher, Vol. 28, pp. 128–37.

[24] Kathryn C. Swiss, *Confined to a Narrative: Approaching Rape Shield Laws Through Legal Narratology* (2014), Wash. U. Jur. Rev., Vol. 6, p. 397, https://openscholarship.wustl.edu/law_jurisprudence/vol6/iss2/6

Swiss explains that legal narratives are thus 'distinguishable from literary fictions because the law presents itself as a self-enclosed system where truth (or at least truth beyond a reasonable doubt) is obtainable'.[25] Swiss elaborates in her footnote to this:

> Much philosophical debate exists over whether the law is, or could ever be, completely 'self-enclosed.' Yet I argue that the law endeavors to control its own language and construct rules that determine specific outcomes because it builds a lexicon of terms and then structures the narrative capacity for story-telling through rules of evidence and procedure. Similarly, the law may not purport to find the absolute 'Truth' outside a legal realm, but it does claim to establish truth—beyond a reasonable doubt—within its own framework.

The wrestling for truth is possible with the right methodology. It is important to establish the narrative, and one that is meaningful to the parties involved. Robert Cover explained in his seminal essay *Nomos and Narrative*, 'no set of legal institutions or prescriptions exists apart from the narratives that locate it and give it meaning.'[26] Hence meaning in the legal space is joined with the narrative frame, as he states:

> The role of story in the law is contested. Humans are wired to digest information in narrative form, but narration can also feign coherence and inevitability when there is none. 'Chekov's gun' is a familiar trope—the axiom that if a weapon is referenced in the first act of a play, then it must be discharged eventually. Literary devices like foreboding create a sense of irony or suspense in our fiction. But selective fact presentation in brief writing or courtroom presentation can craft a teleology of crime where there is mere correlation. Sometimes Chekov's gun is just a gun.[27]

In writing our narrative we ought to be aware that someone has mentioned the gun, to use the Chekhovian analogy, by which I mean the event. We need to record what was said and done by whom in an objective sense, so that we can distinguish whether there is enhanced meaning to a specific event. As Brooks explains, such narratology of an event:

> … distinguishes between events in the world and the ways in which they are presented in narratives. It pays attention to the parts of narrative and how they combine in a plot; to how we understand the initiation and completion

---

[25] Ibid, p. 397.

[26] Robert M. Cover, *Nomos and Narrative* (1983), Harv. L. Rev., Vol. 97, p. 4.

[27] Andrew Jensen Kerr, *Meta-Stories and Missing Facts* (August 2015), California Law Review Circuit, Vol. 6, p. 69, https://scholarship.law.berkeley.edu/cgi/viewcontent.cgi?article=1073&context=clrcircuit

of an action; to standard narrative sequences (stock stories, one might say); and to the movement of a narrative through a state of disequilibrium to a final outcome that reestablishes order. Narratology also studies perspectives of telling: who sees and who tells, the explicit or implicit relation of the teller to what is told, the varying temporal modalities between the told and its telling.[28]

The telling of the stories is highly interpretive, but in the Dialogue Box we are trying to capture a narrative that strips the stories, the evidence, of its interpretation to find a core neutral interpretation, which also explains the emotional drive of the situation being faced. I ponder with Brooks:

> My question, then, is something like this: if the way stories are told, and are judged to be told, makes a difference in the law, why doesn't the law pay more attention to narratives, to narrative analysis and even narrative theory?[29]

I also take his reminder, which takes us back to the Intelligence Zone in the Dialogue Box, that:

> One premise of the legal storytelling movement is that lawyers ignore the story for the sake of emphasis on logic and reason. This is a point well taken. Too often, we forget that our cases involve the flesh and blood, true-life stories of real people.[30]

The point is well taken, because it is at this point that we can find effective dialogue, using a vocabulary that can resonate with our audience comprising real people with a story, which they tell to themselves and to others, which may be illuminated by how their story might fit into another narrative and help them find a meaning that has eluded them to this point. This takes us to the problem of bias in narrative interpretation.

11.3 Narrative bias

Research shows that people unintentionally attribute stereotypical traits to individuals from particular social groups, and that these attributions

---

[28] Peter Brooks, *Narrative Transactions – Does the Law Need a Narratology?* (2006), Yale J.L. & Human., Vol. 18, p. 2, https://digitalcommons.law.yale.edu/yjlh/vol18/iss1/1

[29] Ibid, p. 3.

[30] Jeanne M. Kaiser, *When the Truth and the Story Collide: What Legal Writers Can Learn from the Experience of NonFiction Writers about the Limits of Legal Storytelling* (2010), J. Legal Writing Inst., Vol. 16, p. 182.

affect their decision-making.[31] Take the instance of racial bias. Various studies have revealed widespread unintentional racial biases. In the UK, the Lammy Review[32] put forward evidence of disproportionate treatment and outcomes for BAME (black, Asian and minority ethnic) people by the criminal justice system, when compared with white people. The review stated the jury system is a notable success story, with analysis of nearly 400,000 cases finding that juries were consistent in their decision-making, irrespective of the ethnicity of the defendant.[33] However, in sentencing by judges, BAME offenders were significantly more likely to receive a custodial sentence than white offenders for comparable crimes. BAME women were on average 24% more likely to be found guilty than white women, with the range going from 22% more likely for black women to 43% for Chinese/other women.

In the US, research reveals disparities in criminal sentencing of blacks.[34] Studies reveal that trial judges and death penalty lawyers hold unintentional biases against black people, although it is not clear as to how these biases manifest in practice.[35] Rachlinksi et al conclude:

---

[31] A. Greenwald et al, *Measuring and Using the Implicit Association Test: III. Meta-analysis of Predictive Validity* (2009), Journal of Personality and Social Psychology, Vol. 97, pp. 17–41; B. Payne and B. Gawronski, *A History of Implicit Social Cognition: Where is it Coming from? Where is it Now? Where is it Going?*, in B. Gawronski and B. Payne (eds), *Handbook of Implicit Social Cognition: Measurement, Theory, and Applications* (Guilford Press, New York, 2010), pp. 1–15; A. Hahn et al, *Awareness of Implicit Attitudes* (2013), Journal of Experimental Psychology, Vol. 143, No. 3, pp. 1369–92. In forensic instigation, which is important in looking at the process before court, there are significant signs of bias, see *Unintentional Bias in Forensic Investigation* (2015), https://researchbriefings.parliament.uk/ResearchBriefing/Summary/POST-PB-0015

[32] *The Lammy Review: An independent review into the treatment of, and outcomes for, Black, Asian and Minority Ethnic individuals in the Criminal Justice System*, September, 2017, https://assets.publishing.service.gov.uk/government/uploads/system/uploads/attachment_data/file/643001/lammy-review-final-report.pdf

[33] *R v Lance Percival Smith*, https://www.libertyhumanrights.org.uk/sites/default/files/r-v-lance-percival-smith-court-of-appeal-2001.pdf; Gillian Daly and Rosemary Pattenden, *Racial Bias and the English Criminal Trial Jury* (November, 2015), Cambridge Law Journal, Vol. 64, No. 3, pp. 678–710, https://www.jstor.org/stable/4500840?seq=1; C. Thomas, *Are Juries Fair?* (2010), Ministry of Justice Research Series 1/10, https://www.justice.gov.uk/downloads/publications/research-and-analysis/moj-research/are-juries-fair-research.pdf

[34] *Report to the United Nations on Racial Disparities in the U.S. Criminal Justice System*, April, 19 2018, https://www.sentencingproject.org/publications/un-report-on-racial-disparities/. See also: https://www.ussc.gov/sites/default/files/pdf/research-and-publications/research-projects-and-surveys/miscellaneous/15-year-study/chap4.pdf

[35] Jeffrey J. Rachlinski, Sheri Johnson, Andrew J. Wistrich and Chris Guthrie, *Does Unconscious Racial Bias Affect Trial Judges?* (2009), Cornell Law Faculty Publications, Paper 786, https://scholarship.law

Our study contains both bad news and good news about implicit biases among judges. As expected, we found that judges, like the rest of us, possess implicit biases. We also found that these biases have the potential to influence judgments in criminal cases, at least in those circumstances where judges are not guarding against them. On the other hand, we found that the judges managed, for the most part, to avoid the influence of unconscious biases when they were told of the defendant's race.[36]

The authors offer some useful policy options for altering courtroom practices.[37] We can go a step beyond this by using the Dialogue Box as a means by which we can uncover these unconscious or implicit biases, by leading us to interrogate our own assumptions at an earlier stage in the process, and long before cases go to court. Thus, as has been stated before, the situation is not one of the judge coming down like Moses from the mount to deliver the law. The judge, in coming to a decision, is not emptied of various influences or their own biases. Their decisions are also a product of culture. As we look at precedents, we can detect what today we regard as biases but were regarded as normative for a past era. In areas of gender, race or sexuality, we can quickly uncover the problem if we look, and the Dialogue Box invites us to do this discovery.

11.4 Narrating testimony

While in the United States it is common – and often used in TV dramas – for witnesses to be 'rehearsed' or coached in what they say, it is deemed unacceptable in most other common law jurisdictions. It is often stated in codes of conducts. In Ireland there is the Code of Conduct of the Bar of Ireland, which states at para 5.18, 'Barristers may not coach a witness in regard to the evidence to be given.' The intent in the US context is to manage the trial, ensure everyone has their story straight, and the witness – whether expert or otherwise – will know how to respond to the questions supporting a competing narrative. What is acceptable, and important to undertake, is that prospective expert witnesses should know how to communicate the case in hand. It is common for expert witnesses to attend courses on how to prepare reports or give evidence in relation to court proceedings. These are general in nature and should not be used

---

.cornell.edu/cgi/viewcontent.cgi?article=1691&context=facpub
[36] Ibid.
[37] Ibid, p. 1231.

to prepare a witness for any individual case. They are used to help in preparing the expert in giving evidence, in the hope they will be better able to provide a coherent account of the matter drawing on their expertise.

It is important to help other witnesses to be familiar with the process, including the physical language of the court discussed in an earlier chapter. The duty of the expert is to inform the court and explain technical material based on their expertise, and of other witnesses to explain what they experienced and provide relevant information. That said, in the course of discussion and direction, there remains a danger that an emphasis here or a word there can nudge a witness in a particular direction – not necessarily on purpose but through habitual discussion of the case elsewhere. As Tottenham et al explain:

> While it may be relatively easy to maintain such an 'arm's length' approach in early consultations when considering issues of pleadings and discovery, consultations immediately prior to hearing may be more fraught. When the client is under pressure to decide, for example, whether to accept an offer or to proceed to hearing, expert witnesses are likely to be consulted in relation to some of the relevant issues. It is incumbent on both the legal team and the experts themselves to maintain the appropriate professional distance.[38]

Law is traditionally viewed through the rational lenses of cases, rulings, rules, principles, legislation and regulations. As discussed, movements like law and literature and other interdisciplinary initiatives have given impetus to creating a wider lens for lawyers. In approaching the idea of narrative, there is a lot that can be garnered through these wider lenses, and one useful dimension to explore is that of emotion. All narrative is emotional, and stories connect us emotionally. Hence, the bias discussed above is also an emotional point, as we feel closer to 'people like us'. Rationally we need to disengage from this emotional state if we are to find a neutral narrative, or if we are to have empathy or a better understanding of the other. However, this is not a case of taking emotion out of the equation; rather it is to acknowledge, understand and frame emotion in a more helpful sense. We are sentient beings, and as such we do not just understand or analyse a narrative; we also feel it impact us if there is an impact to be had. In being persuasive, we offer a narrative that can make an emotional appeal. If one thinks about automating the court process,

---

[38] Mark Tottenham, Emma Jane Prendergast, Ciaran Joyce and Hugh Madden, *A Guide to Expert Witness Evidence* (Bloomsbury Ireland, 2019), para 5.07.

aside from the jurisprudential problems involved, we also have a problem of taking emotion out of the process. In many transactions we can perhaps achieve this, though even here anything involving money tends to be somewhat emotional for both parties. The reason why matters end up in court is largely because they have been driven there by emotion, as one side resists the wishes of the other side. It is contentious, and emotion is at the heart of contentious matters. We do not have to dig too deep into a dispute, even among hardnosed businesspeople, to find there is an emotional vein to be mined somewhere.

11.5 Understanding and using the narrative

In the Dialogue Box, the Narrative Zone builds on the previous three zones of Intelligence, Emotion and Interpretation, and acts as a bridge to developing the much-needed dialogue and then deciding on the dialogue word and our vocabulary. In the Dialogue Box Narrative Zone, we are trying to reduce interpretive flaws as best we can in order to tell the story as neutrally as possible so that participants can see their reflection in the story being told. It is also done this way so that we can explain without alienating our dialogue partners. This narrative work helps us to make sense of events, understand what they mean, and place them in a specific framework of time and place. The narrative is contingent, which makes the Dialogue Box specific to the findings discovered in the preceding three zones of the Dialogue Box. We cannot simply transfer one Dialogue Box to another situation, because the variables are all different, and the people and events are different components of a moving narrative. In a legal context, we can see how emphasis on facts is put into a coherent form and then presented in a persuasive way to present a case, which is simply a specific narrative, thus making each case pursued by a party interpretive, and is thus rhetorical or communicative. The law is in there somewhere, but perhaps not as clearly as commonly thought. We have to prise open the narrative in order to get to the law. Inherent in each narrative is a set of biases, as we have discussed, which may be conscious or unconscious.

To create this narrative, there are three parts. First, there is the statement of Intelligence – what is the matter in hand, defined as neutrally as possible? Second, there is what I call the 'but' factor, called so because often it is a 'but', though it can be otherwise. This is where we define what we have discovered in the Emotion and Interpretation Zones. Lastly, we have the 'so what?' factor, where we define what the impact is of the second part of the narrative, and what is of shared importance amongst participants to a possible dialogue. Hence, composing the narrative looks like this:

1. Intelligence stated;
2. Emotion + Interpretation stated;
3. Impact statement.

Once we have formed as objectively or neutrally as possible the narrative, we can start to understand the common ground where dialogue can take place. However, it should be noted that this is also the place where we can find the starting point to manipulate, or – to put it more politely – to persuade our audience into our way of thinking. There is a finer line to be drawn between neutrality and manipulation than perhaps is commonly thought.

11.6 Practical steps: Zone 4 – Narrative

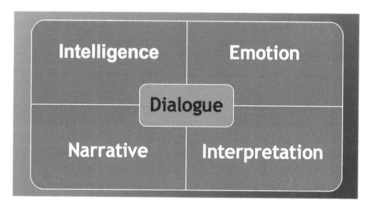

Now we come to understanding what is going on. In the Intelligence Zone we have an implicit narrative. It is what we want people to think of as the rationale or trajectory of our advice, a decision or an event. The narrative we may find emerging from a situation, through the prism of the emotions and various interpretations floating about, may turn out to be quite different. The narrative that emerges may, in fact, turn out to be a strong counter-narrative that challenges the implied narrative in your

Intelligence Zone. In this zone, for instance, you can explore how the stories circulating around your case are used to illuminate a particular event or situation. You can assess what new knowledge emerges out of this narrative: does it tell us something we didn't know before? Is there a narrative that trumps your intelligence, meaning you need a dialogue that will take you back to reconsidering your actions or decisions? Or is this counter-narrative simply a compelling untruth that is trumping your intelligence, requiring you to find a dialogue route that will get your plans back on track? Narrative, in creating knowledge, informs our relationships, and we can look at a situation or event and learn whether new knowledge undermines confidence in the relationship between management and employees, or between colleagues, and so on. In looking at narrative we are receiving an interpretation of events, so the narrative that triumphs can still be untrue or leave room for debate. The stronger a narrative is, however, the less room it gives to other narratives and the more likely it can become dominant.

In presenting your narrative of an event, make sure you include the negative, because only presenting the positive side of things will be less credible. This means being realistic about your narrative when dealing with difficult situations, but it is the 'negative' elements that will be the ones persuading others of a counter-narrative, or they may be the elements that give the receiver of your narrative something to hold on to during the dialogue. The fact you admit to a wrong or a weakness is an invitation to dialogue. Your narrative also has to give scope for the receiver to engage. If the narrative only speaks at the receiver, it will soon be of less interest. Ask the question of how the receiver of your narrative fits into this narrative. As you think through your narrative, remember there are some fixed elements in a narrative, so you can break down your exercise into defining the facts of the situation, assessing the wisdom that is accepted in the company or may arise, who the key characters are, what the situation is you are analysing and the event that everyone expects will happen or has already taken place. You can use this exercise predictively and retrospectively.

11.6.1 In a nutshell

How can we develop a narrative in my Intelligence Zone that is both compelling and engaging, and that allows less room for counter-narrative?

11.6.2 Filling in the zone

The narrative is structured in three steps:

1. The intelligence: What is it we are examining, stated as neutrally as possible?
2. The Emotion + Interpretation: A neutral description of the dominant emotion and interpretation – what I call the 'but…' factor, because it is a departure from the intelligence narrative.
3. The outcome: What is the implication of the first two stages – what I call the 'so what…?' factor, because we need an objective understanding of the outcome, and then we can decide if we want to live with that outcome or have a dialogue to bring our intelligence and the Dialogue Box narrative into a closer alignment.

You can check:

- Have I stated the intelligence neutrally?
- Have I located the emotional source of the problem?
- Do I know what dominant views exist?
- Have I truly defined an objective narrative?

Can you state the narrative in the three-step process, objectively, as defined?

11.6.3 Key takeaway

Remember we want to establish a neutral narrative, so that we have an understanding of the emotion that will allow us in the Dialogue Zone to acknowledge that emotion. If we don't, we won't get past the emotional blockage. The narrative is a report of the situation, not what we think it should be nor what we want it to be.

12   Ready to dialogue?

In the 1739 publication, with a title almost the length of the average tweet today, *The Law Unmasked: Or, a Dialogue in English, Between a Lawyer and a Country Justice of the Peace (whether the Laws of the Country Ought to be in the Language of that Country where They Govern)*, the justice asks the lawyer his opinion concerning debates he hears in the coffee houses of the laws being in English. The lawyer replies it is:

> The most absurd thing in the world; for then the People would understand them as well as the Lawyers, which, in my opinion, is very unreasonable, for that would tend to the spoiling our Trade.[1]

I have already discussed in earlier chapters the problems of language and naming as forms of obfuscation, so I won't rehearse the arguments here.[2] Suffice to say, there is a problem in legal dialogue, and to an extent we might want to ask the same kind of question today about legal language as the 18th-century justice. Language can protect the guild, just as unions protect the labour, and legal language may appear to the outsider to be the language of polite demarcation disputes for the more well-to-do. This goes back to the opening statement of this book, the priestly notion of being a lawyer. Plain language may well spoil the trade, along with the help of technology and commodification of the law. However, I am rather more optimistic that we need not have such a defensive view of the law and practising law, because effective dialogue and communication will enhance the law and sustain lawyers for generations ahead. That said, there are a great number of concerns for lawyers to address, as Pearce and Wald summarize in rather bleak terms:

---

[1] *The Law Unmasked: Or, a Dialogue in English, Between a Lawyer and a Country Justice of the Peace (whether the Laws of the Country Ought to be in the Language of that Country where They Govern)* [1736].

[2] For some general reading on dialogue and language, I suggest D. Bohm and L. Nichol, *On Dialogue* (Routledge, London, New York, 1996); Laurie Bauer and Peter Trudgill, *Language Myths* (Penguin, London, 1998); David Crystal, *How Language Works* (Penguin, London, 2006).

... surveys indicate that the public has lost respect for lawyers and that lawyers exhibit lower levels of job satisfaction and higher levels of substance abuse and anxiety related mental illness than the general public. Even the notion that legal work shares a common core of responsibilities has come under challenge from critics who argued that professional responsibilities were better promoted through fragmented and specialized roles, or that professionalism was nothing more than a self-serving myth.[3]

The individual lawyer – as well as law firms and legal departments – is undergoing radical change with many pressures. Effective dialogue will help the individual and organizations to navigate their way through this paradigm shift, and the Dialogue Box will be effective in holding such dialogue, which is the central zone of the Dialogue Box. In the first part of this chapter I will discuss some aspects of Dialogue Box that are specifically about dialogue and have as yet not been covered. The remainder of the chapter will take you step by step practically through using the Dialogue Box.

In the Dialogue Zone, we will have used the Dialogue Box to find out the narrative of the situation we face described as objectively as we can. We now need to have the dialogue that will help us address the gap, or the disconnect, between the inherent narrative of our own situation, advice or decision and that of the narrative we have formed in the Narrative Zone. We are looking for the language that will help us to have dialogue in a neutral or persuasive space, so that we may encourage participation and create collaboration. This disconnect has been analysed by looking into the emotions and interpretations involved in the situation or event being analysed. Using the Dialogue Box, the communicating lawyer can encourage opening a neutral space through dialogue because we have reached an understanding of the situation that accounts for our audience and the context as fully as possible. In the Dialogue Zone we bring the other four zones together in order to understand how the communicating lawyer manages the emotions and interpretations that are a barrier to overcoming the disconnect between the parties, and bridge the gap between the inherent narrative of the Intelligence Zone and the outcome of the Narrative Zone. The Narrative Zone is where the real difficulties arise in using the Dialogue Box, but the better this is understood, the more successfully the reader will be able to engage in effective dialogue, because

---

[3]   Russell G. Pearce and Eli Wald, *Being Good Lawyers: A Relational Approach to Law Practice* (2016), Geo. J. Legal Ethics, Vol. 29, p. 601.

we can develop the language and messages that will resonate with our audience. We have been through successive chapters on each of the zones, but this is the step process we can following practically, and I will return to this in the latter part of this chapter.

There has been in recent years the application of design thinking in law, which can play a pivotal role in how law and the legal system develop in our new electronic age and inform the disruption occurring now in the legal profession. Part of this design thinking involves looking at how dialogue works within the legal system generally and the courts specifically. This goes back to two points made in this book: miscommunication and poor communication create problems; and the seeds of failure are sown at the beginning of design. In the legal and court system we cannot revisit the origins and change things, obviously, but we can ensure that we improve our understanding and communication as we implement the necessary changes using good design principles and in addressing the design faults that already exist. To take one critical example: in designing systems, privacy is a major area where people interact with law and do so without knowledge or dialogue. Even lawyers are in the habit of clicking their agreements when downloading apps and accessing websites without reading what they have agreed to in fact, hence the introduction of GDPR. We can look at design and communication to improve how we protect rights and enjoy the user experience at the same time. Some product and service providers have made more efforts than others to simplify the process, but it is still a challenge. Equally, looking at remote and online court services, communication can improve the experience. In this respect, addressing many of the communication issues raised in this book would go a long way to alleviating stress on the court system before designing new processes, as I have mentioned previously. One area of concern in using such courts is the lack of physical communication and the emotional issues that may arise in not physically interacting with the legal system. The courts have always been a physical place for dialogue, but what sort of dialogue do we have if we cannot have, as such, our day in court?

12.1   A word about dialogue

Literary critic George Steiner, in *Grammars of Creation*, a book based on the Gifford Lectures he delivered at the University of Glasgow in 1990, said:

> … [it] is my astonishment, naïve as it seems to people, that you can use human speech both to love, to build, to forgive, and also to torture, to hate, to destroy and to annihilate.[4]

To have dialogue is to find a shared space in which to participate in the dialogue, and to share meaning and understand whether what is being said, in context, is a sentiment of love or hate, forgiveness or destruction. When we have respect for another, we create a shared space for creating and finding understanding. We can meet each other in an appropriate way, which in some cases means meeting halfway, and in other cases may mean having to go to the other person's level and meet them eye to eye. Society, and therefore law, has a problem with dialogue. Today we worry much about the impact of social media – and such concern is merited – but this is not the cause of the hatred or even love we might find in the public social media space. Rather, it has created a platform and channel for people and has given access to a public voice that can go from the extremes of individual insight or trolling to mindless mob-like or popular generosity. In the past people formed in social groups, rioting or protesting in the streets. Efforts like crowdfunding and whistleblowing can have a very good effect or equally cause problems as mobbing or bullying takes hold. It is paradoxical that a single person, with some ingenuity or creativity, can start a great public project or cause problems while remaining anonymous. And their significance is created by being a number in a crowd, with the significance being the size and behaviour of the crowd or mob. Social media can promote democracy and wider participation, as each individual has a voice and a platform to participate. Yet, we see how the reaction has often led to restriction on free speech or influential hate speech. This raises questions about democracy, because technology has made democratic access much more achievable, but it has the problems that political scientists, philosophers and jurists have struggled with since Plato. This is another fascinating topic beyond the scope of this book, but we do seem to have a problem of how to have public dialogue.

---

[4]   https://www.giffordlectures.org/lectures/grammars-creation

One of the things we are trying to achieve in a dialogue is to persuade others to agree with us or to be convinced we should agree with the other. Like access to democracy, persuasion has a long intellectual history, going back to the rhetoric of the classical age. Aristotle explained:

> Rhetoric is useful because things that are true and things that are just have a natural tendency to prevail over their opposites … [W]e must be able to employ persuasion, just as deduction can be employed, on opposite sides of a question, not in order that we may in practice employ it both ways (for we must not make people believe what is wrong), but in order that we may see clearly what the facts are, and that, if another man argues unfairly, we on our part may be able to confute him. No other of the arts draws opposite conclusions: dialectic and rhetoric alone do this.[5]

Persuasion is an attempt to bring people with us, to be on our side or at least accept our side of an issue. The lawyer in court seeks to persuade for their client, and may well have ended up in court because the client could not be persuaded to do otherwise. A step on from persuasion is the use of power. Our rhetoric may be powerful enough to persuade, but we can communicate in other powerful ways. History is littered with stories of powerful orators and the manipulation of power through dialogue. George Orwell's novels *Animal Farm* and *1984* are among the best parables of power and communication one can find. Power in dialogue is when we try to assert our view over the other, creating a status dialogue that puts the other person in their place. This can often work, in the sense that if we have power we can coerce. However, it is more effective to inspire in order to lead. Having someone do what we want them to do because they want to do it is often a more productive exercise. Following orders is not the same thing, though sometimes essential. In certain types of relationships and activities, it is best that orders are followed. This is not the same as coercion; rather, it is to follow an established line of communication based on a shared understanding of the need for these rules. A soldier obeys the officer because it is proven to be an effective rules-based approach of communication. An office worker follows a fire drill because it can save lives. There are exceptions to the rule, but we

---

[5] Aristotle, Rhetoric I.1.1355a22–35, in Jonathan Barnes (ed.), *The Complete Works of Aristotle: The Revised Oxford Translation* (Princeton University Press, 1984). See also, Stanley Fish, *Rhetoric*, in Frank Lentricchia and Thomas Mclaughlin (eds), *Critical Terms for Literary Study* (2nd edn, University of Chicago Press, 1995), p. 203.

know it is an exception because we know what the rule is and understand that sometimes the rules don't work. This is a case-by-case issue.

The issue is also tied up with authority. In earlier times, people accepted the authority of the media. It was both authorized and authorizing. People believed the media because it was a process of authorizing. Recording and commenting on events went through a process of editing, an authorization process, that ensured the information reported had been verified. In the earlier decades of television, when the man (and it was always a man) from the BBC stood still in front of a camera, he was reporting the story as tested facts, and we the audience believed him. We watched the news at set times of the day, and today's newspapers were not so quickly out of date because of the television. Today's social media space is quite different, and mainstream news outlets have changed dramatically. It is good that women as well as men are telling the story, but the still reporter has been replaced with exaggerated gesticulation and head nodding (please stop!), because the reporter is now a persuader much more than someone giving us the tested facts. Underlying this physical change in reporting is a recognition, rightly or wrongly, that what the reporter is reporting is contested, and may even be untested or doubtful. This is further highlighted by 'fake news'. The change is also bound up with notions of time. In the 24/7 news cycle, we are all journalists and editors, and we are always scrambling for the story or to participate in the story. The trail soon goes cold, and people want to jump in while the story is hot. The reporting often drives the narrative.

This short discourse on rhetoric, power and modern media is important to note, because it represents changes in society and how we communicate in society, and these problems are also the problem of the legal system and lawyers. The dynamics of persuasion and concerns over authority have become as much a part of the legal landscape as they are of the media landscape, and like other sectors and professions, lawyers have to have a platform and presence in the media and social media space. What is authoritative in the law? How do we manage the legal process in real time, 24/7? To explore dialogue further, we can look at different levels of dialogue that lawyers are involved in and highlight ways in which we might look at their communication aspects. I have selected three areas:

1. lawyer–client dialogue;
2. assaultive speech;
3. constitutional dialogue.

Naturally, there are many more areas we could look at, but in the interest of space I have chosen three that belong to three levels of communication: client relations, public debate and legal debate. These examples cannot be gone into in depth; they are simply illustrative and there is much nuance to the issues raised, but the footnotes provide material for further reading should you wish to delve deeper, and each is certainly worthy of deep reflection and study.

12.2 The lawyer–client dialogue

Lawyers perhaps differ from journalists in that they have a more structured professional ethics regime. The world of media today is more of a Wild West, whereas lawyers abide by the domestic Bar Council and Law Society codes of conduct, which define what is and is not acceptable. The search for precision and legal integrity in the advice or opinions given is another differentiator. Client communication has set rules on attorney–client relationship, which are not quite as priestly as clients and popular conception might think. Confidentiality is the bedrock of the lawyer–client relationship. It is also part of the trust and clear communication that should underpin the relationship,[6] and arguably should be the hallmark of legal communication. However, Wald takes up the issue that the relationship is set up in lawyers' interest, 'while often leaving clients in the dark', suggesting:

> … the asymmetric distribution of information in the attorney-client relationship is not in clients' best interests but rather grounded in lawyers' self-interest and in a paternalistic approach that fails to take communications, and therefore clients, seriously. Finally, taking communications, and thus clients, seri-

---

[6]   See https://ir.lawnet.fordham.edu/cgi/viewcontent.cgi?article=1358&context=faculty_scholarship

ously requires adopting a new communications regime that would mandate disclosure of all material information to clients.[7]

Wald's essay proposes a materiality-based communications regime and explores its application in several contexts. It is worthy of examination, though space does not permit doing so here. Zacharias takes us further into the attorney–client relationship:

> [C]lient 'dignity' is respected most when clients are treated as individuals who can understand moral limitations on attorney conduct and are informed of those limitations. Informing clients of potential limits on zealous representation, so that clients can make their own decisions regarding how to act within the attorney client relationship, enhances client autonomy. Lawyers with the deepest respect for client autonomy should be the most forthcoming in identifying regulatory and moral constraints on their behavior for the clients.[8]

Zacharias added that respect for the dignity of clients requires that 'clients must understand the rules that will be applied to them'.[9]

Klinka and Pearce offer the following rubric for a good communications relationship with clients, which provides a statement lawyers can make to their clients that serves as the basis of the ongoing relationship and good communication:

> I want you to know that I have an ethical obligation to maintain the confidentiality of information you share with me. I will not disclose this information unless you give me authorization or the law authorizes disclosure. The law authorizes disclosure in very few circumstances – to prevent serious bodily or financial harm to others, to prevent fraud on the court, and to protect my interests in very rare instances, such as if you were to sue me for malpractice or I were to sue you to collect fees. Even then, I could only disclose the information to the extent necessary. Do you have any questions about my obligation to keep your information confidential? If you have any questions about confidentiality at any point during our relationship, please let me know. We can talk about this again at any time. You should also know that if I feel we need

7 Eli Wald, *Taking Attorney-Client Communications (and therefore Clients) Seriously* (2008), University of San Francisco Law Review (U.S.F.L.), Vol. 42, p. 747, U Denver Legal Studies Research Paper No. 08–19, https://www.ssrn.com/abstract=1180655
8 Fred C. Zacharias, *Rethinking Confidentiality* (1989), Iowa L. Rev., Vol. 74, pp. 386–88.
9 Ibid.

to discuss these issues again, I will let you know. I want our relationship to be a two-way street.[10]

This approach, they suggest, is direct and honest, and explains 'the confidentiality exceptions in a framework that encourages dialogue and demonstrates the lawyer's honesty and commitment to a mutual relationship'.[11] As I have noted earlier in the chapter, the seeds of failure are sown at the beginning. The suggestion by Klinka and Pearce is to have a rubric for setting the relationship off on the right foot, and is a statement of reference should issues arise.

12.2.1 Using the Dialogue Box practically

This is a form of dialogue which is essential to the daily work of a lawyer, and the Dialogue Box can be used to manage these relationships. As a reiterative tool, it can be constantly updated to deal with the changing dynamics of the case and the relationship, as well as ensure the code of practice is retained. As I stated, the Intelligence does not need to change. To keep the code, perhaps starting with the use of the kind of rubric noted above, you can have a dialogue around any ethical issues, and then, as events unfold, you can maintain the code in dialogue with changing events and client concerns.

12.3 Assaultive speech

One of the biggest concerns arising out of social media and our current political landscape is the prevalence of assaultive speech, popularized as hate speech. It has become hugely problematic in identity politics and how we change in society as diversity in our societies increases. Kaplin and Lee suggested over two decades ago that:

Hate speech is an imprecise term that generally includes verbal and written words and symbolic acts that convey a grossly negative assessment of particu-

---

[10] Elisia M. Klinka and Russell G. Pearce, *Confidentiality Explained: The Dialogue Approach to Discussing Confidentiality with Clients* (2011), San Diego L. Rev., Vol. 48, p. 157.

[11] Ibid.

lar persons or groups based on their race, gender, ethnicity, religion, sexual orientation, or disability.[12]

Dialogue is essential to negotiate these changes and the array of identities that are being recognized. These identities change meaning and are perceived as threatening by some people and as a cause of great pain by others. How we understand sexual identities is changing radically as the binary designation of male and female is contested. On race issues, it seems there is not a minute that goes by without someone accusing someone else of being 'racist'. Matsuda[13] offers three characteristics of racist speech:

1. The message suggests racial inferiority.
2. It is directed against a historically oppressed group.
3. The message is hateful, degrading, and persecutory in nature.

Though Matsuda is discussing racist speech, her criteria may be applied more broadly to all types of hate speech. Speech directed against people identifying with different notions of gender could be understood to constitute a historically oppressed group or people, and thus becomes a dialogue of power, and dominance.

Free speech issues have been rumbling on campuses across America and elsewhere. Lawrence documents a number of incidents back in the 1980s, so the issues have been around a lot longer than the current atmosphere of 'no-platforming' and 'snowflakes'. Lawrence wrote in 1990:

> In recent years, American campuses have seen a resurgence of racial violence and a corresponding rise in the incidence of verbal and symbolic assault and harassment to which blacks and other traditionally subjugated groups are subjected.[14]

Lawyers have a fundamental role to play in society in helping a society that is struggling to have dialogue in a period of radical change. These are deep-rooted, and in using the Dialogue Box to address issues like hate speech, we have to look at the context – and this includes the history.

[12] W. Kaplan and B. Lee, *The Law of Higher Education* (3rd edn, Jossey-Bass Publishers, San Francisco, CA, 1995), p. 509.
[13] Mari J. Matsuda, *Public Response to Racist Speech: Considering the Victim's Story* (August 1989), Michigan Law Review, Vol. 87, No. 8, Legal Storytelling, pp. 2320–81.
[14] https://scholarship.law.duke.edu/cgi/viewcontent.cgi?article=3115&context=dlj

This is why I chose a 1990 statement, because what Lawrence wrote then could be written today. Has nothing changed, and if yes, then why can what someone wrote in a law journal 30 years ago sound so much like something the journal might publish today?

Lawrence argues that:

> We must eschew abstractions of first amendment theory that proceed without attention to the dysfunction in the marketplace of ideas created by the racism and unequal access to that market. We must think hard about how best to launch legal attacks against the most indefensible forms of hate speech. Good lawyers can create exceptions and narrow interpretations limiting the harm of hate speech without opening the floodgates of censorship. We must weigh carefully and critically the competing constitutional values expressed in the first and fourteenth amendments.[15]

How we are named or described affects us. It can cause a physical reaction, and it can also build up over time. If we are constantly named by our racial, gender or other identity, it does have a psychological and physical effect. Even our name, if someone makes fun of it or twists it, can be problematic. How we are named is important to us, indeed it is something that is given to us at birth and can be decided before we even make an appearance. There are some who choose to change their name because they don't like the name their parents chose for them, while traditionally women have changed their name to their husband's name, which is indicative of prevailing views and sexual politics – many women now eschew this change.

12.3.1 Using the Dialogue Box practically

This is a form of dialogue that is part of creating your platform and having a voice outside of the daily work, for reasons that may range from building your professional reputation through to communication surrounding a particular case. You may have a client where diversity issues are present, and your awareness of such dynamics is important to managing not just your dialogue with the client but the dialogue with a range of stakeholders and through public channels. Responding to assaultive speech requires attempting to forge a dialogue with those issuing the messages and – even if this is doomed to failure – doing so indirectly by your communica-

---

[15] Ibid.

tion with various stakeholders and channels that may reach their ears, however tin those ears may be. How, when and why to respond are crucial questions in such communication, and the Dialogue Box will help you to understand your audiences and to answer these questions.

12.4 Constitutional dialogue

In constitutional theory in the past two decades, it has become 'commonplace for legislative–judicial engagement on contested constitutional questions to be described as a dialogue'.[16] This has created a dialogue about dialogue theories. Bateup succinctly describes the landscape:

> Dialogue theories emphasize that the judiciary does not (as an empirical matter) nor should not (as a normative matter) have a monopoly on constitutional interpretation. Rather, when exercising the power of judicial review, judges engage in an interactive, interconnected and dialectical conversation about constitutional meaning. In short, constitutional judgments are, or ideally should be, produced through a process of shared elaboration between the judiciary and other constitutional actors.[17]

Kent discusses a number of areas for dialogue scholarship, with a further 'fertile area' being to:

> …study how various reforms to the electoral and legislative process may affect dialogue between courts and legislatures. Dialogue theory can be seen as part of the new legal process movement in legal scholarship that paid increased scholarly attention to the legislature. Political scientists who have contributed significantly to the debate about dialogue were by definition always concerned with the legislature, but there is a need for all students of dialogue to reflect on the way changes in electoral and legislative structures may affect dialogue between courts and legislatures.[18]

---

[16] C. Bateup, *The Dialogic Promise – Assessing the Normative Potential of Theories of Constitutional Dialogue* (2006), Brook L Rev, Vol. 71, p. 1109; P. Hogg and A. Bushell, *The Charter Dialogue Between Courts and Legislatures (or Perhaps the Charter of Rights Isn't Such a Bad Thing After All)*, (1997) Osgoode Hall L J, Vol. 35, No. 1, p. 75; K. Roach, *The Supreme Court on Trial: Judicial Activism or Democratic Dialogue?* (Irwin Law, Toronto, 2001); E. Carolan, *Dialogue Isn't Working: The Case for Collaboration as a Model of Legislative–Judicial Relations* (2016), Legal Studies, Vol. 36, No. 2, pp. 209–29, doi:10.1111/lest.12099.
[17] Bateup (n 16), p. 1109.
[18] https://digitalcommons.osgoode.yorku.ca/cgi/viewcontent.cgi?article=1260&context=ohlj; See also, https://www.law.ox.ac.uk/sites/files/oxlaw/j_king_dialogue_finality_and_legality.pd

Carolan describes the difficulties with dialogue theories, and suggests:

> despite the existence of many different versions, these theories share certain constitutionally problematic characteristics. Dialogue theories promote a view of government that is unrealistic, susceptible to normative bias and that overlooks the critical importance of disagreement and institutional differences to a system of democratic government based on the rule of law.[19]

Carolan argues that an idea from Christopher Ansell of 'collaboration-as-fruitful-conflict' provides 'a more descriptively and normatively appropriate account of the relationship between the legal and political branches of government'.[20] Ansell explains 'a new form of governance has emerged to replace adversarial and managerial modes of policy making and implementation'.[21]

12.4.1 Using the Dialogue Box practically

This is a form of dialogue that raises a discussion of whether dialogue gives too much room to non-legal influences, such as dialogue theories. My intent throughout this book has been to look at various communication and dialogue ideas and practices and to see how they may serve the lawyer in effective communication. I have also attempted to keep the law and the lawyer's tasks as the primary function, and not to make it subservient to other disciplines. Interdisciplinary discussion does not entail creating a mélange; it is about learning and absorbing lessons from other disciplines and creating communication that makes one's own discipline understandable to others and thus more engaging, inclusive and participatory. The law should be participatory and inclusive, and the Dialogue Box is a methodology for achieving this and maintaining the legal integrity. In this constitutional debate, the focus is on a legal debate, and hence disciplinary language and principles are central to the dialogue, but this does not mean we cannot make use of dialogue theories to inform the debate, simply that they are not the decisive theories in the end. As Bateup concludes, there are dual-track approaches, which she describes

---

[19] E. Carolan, *Dialogue Isn't Working: The Case for Collaboration as a Model of Legislative–Judicial Relations* (2016), Legal Studies, Vol. 36, No. 2, pp. 209–29, doi:10.1111/lest.12099.

[20] Ibid.

[21] Chris Ansell and Alison Gash, *Collaborative Governance in Theory and Practice* (October 2008), Journal of Public Administration Research and Theory, Vol. 18, No. 4, p. 543.

in detail, that can be synthesized and she stresses that 'dialogue should ideally incorporate both society-wide and institutional aspects'.[22]

Ansell describes collaboration well, to which I add that this process works across all levels of dialogue. His description fits in well with how the Dialogue Box works and why it was created. Ansell identifies various factors crucial within the collaborative process itself:

> These factors include face-to-face dialogue, trust building, and the development of commitment and shared understanding. We found that a virtuous cycle of collaboration tends to develop when collaborative forums focus on 'small wins' that deepen trust, commitment, and shared understanding.[23]

Having looked at how the Dialogue Box can be helpful on different levels of analysis, we can conclude with some practical steps to make use of the Dialogue Box.

12.5   Practical steps: Zone 5 – Dialogue

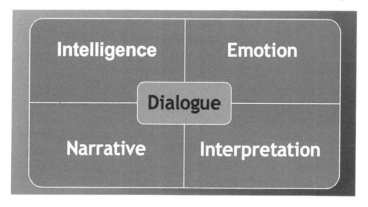

This is the zone you are trying to get to, finding the single word that will guide you through the dialogue you need to have with your audience. You

---

[22] Bateup (n 16).

[23] Chris Ansell and Alison Gash, *Collaborative Governance in Theory and Practice* (October 2008), Journal of Public Administration Research and Theory, Vol. 18, No. 4, pp. 543–71.

are looking for a word that will anchor your conversations, a word that you can keep at the forefront of your mind to keep your conversation anchored in calmness. It is also a word that is a compass to guide your dialogue and to help you through to the endpoint. When you communicate empathetically, you use an approach that shows you understand, which need not mean that you agree with others. It is a first dialogue step, to move your position towards them or draw them towards you. It also involves recognizing what the other person thinks or feels, which will tend to open them up a little, some more quickly than others. You can communicate to connect and disconnect with people. However, it is easy to resort to language and actions that throw up the barriers and stop dialogue, which may have their place but not usually when you are trying to foster dialogue.

Dialogue is best achieved in person. Being together, we can more easily see the impact our words and actions are having on another person, and we can react to verbal and body language signals as cues to either push forward or back off. This is rarely achieved in email, which more often results in miscommunication and electronic warfare. Dialogue is also a creative process that allows us to learn more about a situation, ourselves and others. It leads us into deeper knowledge and improves our work in the Intelligence Zone. There is also something inherently empathetic about dialogue. While sometimes we need 'tough talking', mostly we are trying to find a point of connection in a fractured situation. As the Leonard Cohen song says: 'There is a crack in everything, that's how the light gets in.' We are standing in that light, trying to illuminate our spirit and points of connection or agreement. This allows us to explore a situation together rather than remain in conflict or silence. We can also check our own feelings when faced with someone in dialogue. Imagine if the person we are about to fire off an angry email to was standing in front of us. Would we do it? No. We behave differently when in contact with people, though admittedly sometimes someone can have the ability to really annoy us in person.

12.5.1 In a nutshell

You are looking here for the single word can you put in the Dialogue Zone that will guide you through your engagement with your audience, and act as both your conversational anchor and as a negotiating compass. One last, but important thing: we are looking for a single description for each zone to define the situation, and to arrive at a single word that can go into the Dialogue Zone. This is the discipline you are asked to exercise in full. It takes one word to offend, so we want to use this final step as a way to interrogate all the intelligence and data we have gathered in the Dialogue Box. As we look at our findings and see what words work, we also find what words might not work, are wasteful, offensive or counterproductive. Write these words out and score out the ones that don't work, and in due course you can arrive at a vocabulary for this client in this case, with a clear context. There will be one word that can act as your north star, and in searching for that you will be able to analyse at a very deep level the language of your case.

12.5.2 Filling in the zone

Based on your narrative, list words that come to mind:

- Do the words we choose have focus and clarity?
- Do they capture the essence of the emotional problem?
- Do they resonate in tone and connect emotionally?
- Do they have impact?
- What works better, a positive or a negative word?
- Do they fit with the context?
- Can you test your word in a sentence? Does it work?

Can you come up with a vocabulary of words that will resonate with your audience? Can you identify a single word that captures the essence of your narrative so that if your audience heard this word, they would feel their position has been acknowledged?

12.5.3 Key takeaway

Remember, we want words that acknowledge the emotion, speak to the context and arguments that people have, and can be used to build connections rather than to alienate the audience. They are not your words; they are the words of your audience, and if they use them, it may be an indication you have established a connection between you, the audience and the problem.

The Dialogue Box can help create 'small wins' that incrementally move the dialogue on, which in turn can then bring parties together in a reiterative process. As the Dialogue Zone starts to impact the narrative, the narrative changes, and so we need to change the dialogue incrementally – and yes, perhaps in 'small wins' – in order to win over our dialogue partner, and even ourselves.

Index

practical steps 211–13
testimony 208–10
understanding and using
    narrative 210–11
natural language processing (NLP) 75
natural law 130
negotiation 13, 45, 52, 59, 110–15, 159
    checklist 112
    Dialogue Box 113–14, 159
neighbours: boundary and other
    disputes 159–60
networks
    integrated 60, 72, 74
    women-only 77
Neuberger, Lord 35
neutrality 134–5, 177, 204, 206, 209,
    210, 211
New Zealand 169
nudge theory 22

Obama, B. 143
obsolescence 28
O'Callaghan, L. 176–7
O'Callaghan, P. 4–5
Omar, I. 41
open communication 57–8
open-ended questions 113
'ordinary meaning' 185, 188–9
organizational communication 29
Orwell, G. 218
overload, communication 69

Pardo, M.S. 138–9
paternalism 166, 220
pay gap
    disability 79
    gender 77, 82, 170
Pearce, R.G. 214–15, 221–2
persuasion 218, 219
    narrative and 198–200
Phelan, V. 36, 176
Pink Floyd (*Nobody Home*) 19
plain language 176, 214
    movement 132, 133
Posner, E. 157–8
Posner, R.A. 156, 163, 201–2, 203
posters 50, 56, 93–4

postmodernity 32, 131, 140, 188, 196,
    199
power in dialogue 218
power relations 32, 87, 133, 149
PowerPoint 99–101
practising law 9–12
precedent 199–200
precision 39
    and words in communication
        16–18
predictive analytics (PA) 5
prepared mind 60, 72, 74
privacy 27, 67–8, 216
Probert, W. 46
process, communication 46–7
    how we communicate 49–50
    knowing the what 48
    knowing the when 49
    listening for the why 47–8
public opinion 123
public relations 122

Quine, W.V.O. 141

race 82, 200
    critical race theory 201
    racial bias 207–8
    racism 49, 65, 223, 224
Rachlinksi, J.J. 207–8
Ramsey, F.P. 129
rational decision-making 146–9
rationalism, English 163
Reagan, Ronald 143
relational lawyering 64–7
repetition 56
reputation 116, 123, 124
Resnik, J. 166–7, 168
rhetoric 218
risk aversion 22, 53
Roach, K. 225
roadshows 101–2
Robbins, R.A. 197
roles for lawyers, new 72–3
Rubinstein, H.J. 122
rule of law 20, 21, 161, 184, 226
Rumsfeld, D. 144–5

This is a highly useful, clear and interesting read. David Cowan guides us through why great communication is such a vital skill for legal professionals but then, most importantly, he gives the tools which enable us to do this ourselves – impactfully and simply. An excellent contribution.
Christina Blacklaws, entrepreneur and innovator, Chair of LawTech UK and former President of the Law Society of England and Wales

If communication, as David suggests, is better understood as the activity of sharing, then I think we are all fortunate that he has shared with us his insights into effective communication in this invaluable book. As a practising lawyer, I would rank effective communication as the most valuable skill a lawyer can possess; one that we must continually develop. The Dialogue Box is an excellent practical tool which aids that development for everyone from the first year law student to the most seasoned practitioner.
Tara Doyle, Matheson, Dublin, Ireland

This book does much more than it says on the tin. As well as being a first-rate practical guide, it offers a deeply informed analysis of the changing nature of legal communications in a digital society. Wide-ranging, well-researched, and ambitious, it should be mandatory reading across the world of law.
Richard Susskind, President, Society for Computers and Law